THE CHANGING FACE OF
WESTERN COMMUNISM

The Changing Face of Western Communism

EDITED BY DAVID CHILDS

ST. MARTIN'S PRESS   NEW YORK

ISBN 0-312-12951-3

Library of Congress Cataloging in Publication Data
  Main entry under title·

The Changing face of Western communism.

    Includes bibliographical references and index.
    1. Communism—Europe—Addresses, essays, lectures.
  2. Communist parties—Europe—Addresses, essays, lec-
  tures. I. Childs, David.
  HX238.5.C53 1980   335.43′094   79-25754
  ISBN 0-312-12951-3

Printed and bound in Great Britain

CONTENTS

1. The Changing Face of Western Communism   7
   David Childs

2. Eurocommunism: their Word or Ours?   37
   Philip Elliott and Philip Schlesinger

3. The PCE in Spanish Politics   74
   Eusebio Mujal-Leon

4. The Italian Communist Party: between Leninism
   and Social Democracy?   112
   Martin Clark and David Hine

5. The French Communist Party and Eurocommunism   147
   Peter Morris

6. The Finnish Communist Party: Two Parties in One   172
   Seija Spring and D. W. Spring

7. Communism in the Nordic Countries: Denmark,
   Norway, Sweden and Iceland   205
   Trond Gilberg

8. Austria: from Orthodoxy to 'Normalisation'   260
   Karl Stadler

Appendix: The Electoral Strength of Communism in
Western Europe   276

Notes on Contributors   277

Index   279

1 THE CHANGING FACE OF WESTERN COMMUNISM

David Childs

The tendency known as Eurocommunism was already in existence when the term was coined in the 1970s. How the term has been used and abused is discussed in the next chapter by Elliot and Schlesinger. Here we are concerned with the tendency which has deep roots in the history of the international Communist movement. To a certain extent the tendency reflects the tensions which have always existed in working-class movements between reformists and revolutionaries, between those who hope they can transform their societies in socialistic directions by peaceful and democratic means and those who believe the propertied classes will eventually force them to use violence. Of necessity, a discussion of Eurocommunism must involve some discussion of the origins and development of Communism itself, and especially of the development of the relations between the Communist Party of the Soviet Union (CPSU) and the other Communist parties.

Socialist movements were developing across the continent of Europe, and indeed beyond, before the First World War. Some, like the German SPD, were Marxist, others, like the British Labour Party, were not. All regarded themselves as part of a crusade. They had won considerable democratic and trade union rights for the workers and forced the development of a rudimentary welfare state. Though they inspired their followers with the rhetoric of social revolution, their practice was aimed at getting a parliamentary majority through the ballot box. But there were always those who questioned the assumptions of this tactic. The outbreak of the First World War seemed to vindicate these critics. After decades of formal opposition to militarism, the majority of European socialists were swept along by the tidal wave of nationalism and came out in favour of 'defence of the fatherland'. Long before the final shots were fired, the anti-war minorities broke away, or were expelled from, the parties of the old Second International. Lenin offered such minorities an alternative as the leader of the only successful, self-styled,

socialist revolution. The towering figures of European Marxism –
Kautsky, Luxemburg and Plekhanov – had little time for Lenin's
ideas. They preferred the Marx of 1872 to the Marx of the
Manifesto. Lenin's converts tended to be those less well schooled
in Marxism, and the young with little previous experience of
working-class politics.[1]

The parties of Lenin's Third International, established in 1919,
were required to subordinate their policies to those formulated in
Moscow. Under Stalin in the 1930s and 1940s, they became
largely tools of Soviet foreign policy. The outsider has the
greatest of difficulty in understanding how this could happen,
how national parties, including those of considerable size like the
French and Germans, could allow themselves to be dominated by
an outside power. To understand this one must remember that
these were not ordinary parties. Their founders were impressed
by the fact that Lenin, and Lenin only, appeared to have fulfilled
the prophecy of Marx. He alone claimed to have wrested power
from the bourgeoisie and to have set up a workers' state. His
achievement appeared more impressive because the Tsarist
regime had been perhaps the most hated in pre-war Europe. In
Western Europe the social democratic parties held office briefly
without shaking the capitalist system. Moreover, in Europe and
America, in the aftermath of the First World War, nervous
governments used violence and repression against radical
minorities. In this situation Lenin became recognised as the true
interpreter of the spirit of Marxism. The 'peacefully if we may'
Marx of 1872 and the 'legal methods' Engels of 1895 seemed
outmoded in the age of the iron heel of imperialism.[2] Lenin's
pronouncements were soon welded together with suitable ones
from Marx to produce the new doctrine of Marxism-Leninism
which, for devotees, combined the precision of natural science
with the certainties of Islam or Catholicism.[3] The ideological
schooling of cadres, given high priority in Communist
movements, greatly strengthened this religious-style devotion to
Moscow world-wide. As Koestler has explained, 'My Party
education had equipped my mind with such elaborate
shock-absorbing buffers and elastic defences that everything seen
and heard became automatically transformed to fit the
preconceived pattern.'[4] Indoctrination produced what Carrillo
has admitted was a 'mythical and almost religious element in our
attitude towards the Communist Party of the Soviet Union'.[5] Tito

later recalled his attitude to the Soviet Union when, in the 1930s, he was a prisoner in his own country:

> through dismal nights and endless interrogation and maltreatment, during days of killing solitude in cells and close confinement, we were always sustained by the hope that all these agonies were not in vain, that there was a strong and mighty country, however far away, in which all the dreams for which we were fighting had been fulfilled. For us it was the homeland of the workers, in which labour was honoured, in which love, comradeship, and sincerity prevailed. With what joy I had felt the strength of that country as, emerging from prison in 1934, I listened in the dead of each night to Radio Moscow and heard the clock of the Kremlin tower striking the hours, and the stirring strains of the 'International'![6]

Moscow's ideological hegemony was reinforced by the financial dependency of the other parties on the CPSU. It was not unknown for rich social democratic parties, like the SPD for instance, to help the poorer ones before 1914, so weak Communist parties did not find it odious to be assisted by the Russians after 1917. The difference was that the Soviet party headed a powerful dictatorship and its policies could not be challenged within the frontiers of the USSR. In addition, many of the inter-war Communist parties were small and often illegal in their own countries. This was true of most of those in Eastern and central Europe, of the Italians after 1922, and the Germans after 1933. Many of their leaders lived as guests of the Soviet party. As for the small parties in the democracies, often a few weeks of luxurious living in the USSR, with pomp, ceremony and flattery added, served to reassure the doubting cadres from abroad of the correctness of Moscow's analysis.[7] One other key factor which helped to make the non-ruling parties subservient to Moscow in the 1930s was the fight against Fascism. Of course there were those who became disillusioned and left the party. As early as 1921 the Kronstadt mutiny resulted in resignations.[8] The upheavals associated with the downfall of Trotsky later in the 1920s produced some more. The dramatic change in the Comintern line in 1934 also caused some to turn in their party cards. Most devastating of all, the Hitler-Stalin Pact of August 1939 led to mass resignations. For many, doubts about the use of the secret police, forced labour and the death penalty in the Soviet Union could always be resolved by reference to the historical backwardness of Russia and the fierceness of the onslaughts of the class enemy. And in the end, the prestige of the USSR as the first workers' state and the apparent failure of social democracy always meant that enough cadres remained and new crises – the General Strike in Britain (1926), the Wall Street crash (1929), civil war in Vienna (1934) and in Spain (1936) – brought in new recruits.[9]

The 'popular front' line of the second half of the 1930s led the Communists into a patriotic and democratic posture. At the Seventh Congress of the Comintern, the Bulgarian Communist leader, Georgi Dimitrov, proclaimed the new policy, which called on Communists to cherish bourgeois democracy and co-operate with social and bourgeois democrats to preserve it from Fascism. In Spain the Communist Party was moving to this position as a result of the logic of its own situation. In France too voices were raised in favour of a popular front line. However, the French comrades advocating this new policy were expelled and it was only adopted by the PCF on instructions from Moscow.[10] In the USSR itself a new constitution was adopted in 1936, a constitution designed in part to win over socialist and liberal opinion in the Western democracies.[11] This provided for, among other things, elections based on universal adult suffrage and secret ballot. The Western Communists now presented themselves as the true patriots displaying their national flags, where previously they had only displayed the red flag, and singing their national hymns at rallies. In the USA, for instance, the party's meetings in Madison Square Garden now opened with the singing of the 'Star Spangled Banner', 'somewhat self-consciously, to be sure'.[12] In 1939 the American party even took the step of disaffiliating from the Comintern to emphasise its independent, native American posture.[13] It did so with the apparent approval of Moscow. No other party went so far. With their emphasis on preserving bourgeois democracy, the Communists resembled the Eurocommunists of today. Many were sincere in their belief in the new line. However, for most of the trained cadres, 'It was a temporary retreat, but justifiable in the light of Marxist thinking. The new tactic was to soft-pedal in public whilst sticking to everything as before in private.'[14] The popular front, let's-all-be-friends line did not stop the Nazis or the Fascists, but it did help the Communists world-wide to recruit members and extend their influence through the various front organisations they controlled, such as the Left Book Club in Britain and the American League against War and Fascism in the United States.

The Communist parties again showed their fidelity to Moscow by nimbly switching their line in September 1939 in conformity with the needs of the Hitler-Stalin Pact signed the month before. They lost a good deal of goodwill in the process and many members. Naturally their policy provoked bans and proscriptions as with increasing militancy they opposed the war efforts of their respective countries. When much of Europe was occupied by the Nazis their relations with the occupying power were, to say the least, ambiguous.

The forced entry of the USSR into the war in June 1941 could have led to the freeing of the Communist parties from dependence on Moscow. The abolition of the Comintern in 1943 provided hope that this would happen. In fact, wherever it could, the Soviet party retained its dominance over the fraternal parties. In the case of the CPUSA, ten months after the Comintern's dissolution, confidential party documents were despatched to Moscow so that Dimitrov could adjudicate between the rival factions in the American party.[16] The war gave the Communists exceptional opportunities to extend their influence. In the occupied states many members of the political and economic elites collaborated with the Germans either out of sympathy for Nazism, or because they had little choice, or because they felt they could minimise the effects of German policies in this way. The military and political elites were often criticised for not having protected their states against Nazi aggression. There was a widespread feeling that new leaders with new policies were needed. The massive contribution of the Red Army to the victory over Germany made it easier to convince people that perhaps Communism, albeit in a modified form, offered a progressive alternative to the old ways. Obviously, the attractiveness of Communism differed greatly from country to country. Where the old regimes had clearly been deeply compromised, as in France and Italy, the Communist appeal was so much greater. Communist efforts in the resistance movements were also of decisive importance in winning them mass support in both countries.[17] In a country like Holland, on the other hand, the

Communists made only limited progress. There too they were active in the resistance. The pre-war order was not, however, discredited. Both the monarch and government had gone into exile in Britain, thus avoiding any ambiguity about their position. The Dutch Communists increased their vote in 1945 but were not included in the national coalition government. Nor were they in government in the six neutral countries. Yet even in Sweden and Switzerland they registered increased support. Of the European belligerents only in Greece and Britain did the Communists not succeed in gaining office in the immediate post-war period. In Greece the regime was weak and compromised. However, it was saved by British military might from being overturned by the pro-Communist resistance forces.

In Britain the Communists failed to make significant gains because of their own mistakes. It is true that the Conservative-Labour-Liberal coalition headed by Churchill had made concessions to the increasing demands for social reforms. Nevertheless, by-election victories by left-wingers, such as Common Wealth, during the war were an indication of growing dissatisfaction. The Communists failed to exploit this. Because of Moscow's instructions, they did not oppose the by-election candidates of the three main parties after June 1941, and they opposed militancy in the trade unions. The Communists fought the battle for higher production rather than the battle for higher wages and better conditions. Strikers were denounced as little better than Nazis. Yet strikes took place. Once the tide of war had turned against the Nazis, rank-and-file workers started to want more. The only major issue which led the Communists to verbally clash with the Establishment was over the second front. Echoing Stalin's plea to Churchill, they demanded an early Allied invasion of Western Europe to take the pressure off the Red Army. In 1945 the British Communists made another mistake, again at the instigation of Moscow, by arguing for the continuation of the three-party coalition. This policy was anathema to the ordinary members of the labour movement. In the election of 1945 the CPGB put up a mere 20 candidates with a programme which was not more noticeably socialist than that of Labour. In these circumstances it was easy for Labour to dismiss the CPGB as an irrelevance. Only two Communists were elected. This was a doubling of Communist representation! One was William Gallacher, who was returned by the electors of West Fife, a constituency he had represented since 1935. The other was Phil Piratin, a Jew elected in the small London constituency of Mile End, where many electors were of Eastern European Jewish descent. Altogether the Communist candidates received 102,780 votes, up to 1979 the highest total for CP candidates in Britain. The programmatically more left-wing Common Wealth Party, with a weaker organisation and less publicity, polled 110,634 votes and elected one MP. The CPGB increased its membership from 12,000 in June 1941 to 56,000 in September 1942. Its influence was much greater than these figures suggest because its members had gained positions of authority in several unions, and because its front organisations were prospering. It is unlikely, though, that it could ever have been a real challenge to the Labour Party. Labour was backed by the bulk of the trade unions which were directly affiliated to it. Moreover, Labour could claim it had not yet had a chance to put into operation its own brand of socialism. It could further claim to have been more consistently anti-Nazi than the Moscow-directed Communists. Yet had the Communists, like some of the Labour left, been more militant on some issues, and more thoughtful on others, whilst consistently supporting the war, it is likely they would have increased their support somewhat more. While the wartime party truce limited Labour's room for manoeuvre, it need not have limited the opportunities of the Communists quite so much.

On the whole the American Communists too had a good war. Party membership, which had been only 7,000 in 1930, reached between 80,000 and 100,000 by the end of the war.[18] In New York two Communist councilmen were elected. After campaigning under the slogan 'The Yanks Are Not Coming' before June 1941, they became the exemplars of patriotism after that date. 'They soft-pedaled the Negro issue, called for speedup in the factories, and mobilized their entire propaganda apparatus to exert pressure for a second front in Europe.'[19] The American Communists had become so cautious and fanatically moderate in the interests of the anti-Hitler coalition that they backed Harry Truman, in preference to the more left-wing Henry Wallace, for the Vice-Presidential nomination of 1944.[20] They missed their opportunities amongst the workers. In both 1943 and 1944 the number of individuals involved in work stoppages was higher than the comparable figures for all other years after 1916 except 1941.[21] The Communists opposed such stoppages, seeing in them

the sinister hand of Trotskyism. They fell out with Walter
Reuther, the radical leader of the United Auto Workers Union,
because he was more inclined to sympathise with rank-and-file
discontent. One novel aspect of the American situation was the
decision, taken by the Communists in 1944, to dissolve their
party and replace it with the American Communist Political
Association. This was supposed to be an educational body rather
than a party. The main protagonist of this strategy was party
General Secretary Earl Browder. His reasoning was that the
Tehran accord of Roosevelt, Stalin and Churchill made continued
co-operation between the superpowers after the war likely. Thus
American and British capitalism had a way of solving their
economic problems by assisting the reconstruction of the Soviet
Union, the Allied states and the colonial territories. In this
non-revolutionary situation American Communists could best
extend their influence through joining existing political parties,
trade unions and front organisations rather than through their
own sectarian Communist Party. This move was apparently taken
with the blessing of the Kremlin.[22] It is impossible to know why
Stalin agreed to the change. Was it seen as a necessary temporary
concession to American public opinion? Later, as we shall see, it
was denounced as a notorious deviation.

As the war ended the Communists had increased their strength
everywhere. In Europe they were in coalition governments in
Austria, Belgium, Denmark, Finland, France, Iceland, Italy,
Luxembourg, Norway and throughout Eastern Europe. They were
also given positions of responsibility in all the occupation zones
of Germany. How did they see the future? What factors went
into their evaluation of the situation? With one exception, the
Yugoslavs, the European Communists still looked to Moscow for
guidance. Indeed, the war had resulted in the Soviet myth taking
on a new lease of life. Many Communists who had remained loyal
to their respective parties had had their doubts about Soviet
policies at various times between 1935 and 1941. Soviet
successes in the war seemed to indicate that 'Uncle Joe' knew
best after all. All the harsh measures adopted before the war by
Stalin had been merely a necessary preparation for the inevitable
war to come. At the end of the war it was easy to swallow the line
of argument put by one British friend of the USSR in 1942, 'We
who have known the sabotage of the Nazis and Fifth Columnists
nearer home may reconsider the scepticism with which we

received the reports of sabotage from Russia in 1933.'[23] The second factor which influenced Communists was their actual experience of the war, in most cases of occupation and resistance. This experience varied from one country to another, but everywhere there had been rivalries. In Yugoslavia, Greece, Italy and France civil war conditions had prevailed. Even in the concentration camps some old political rivals remained deeply hostile to each other.[24] On the other hand, the resistance did bring about co-operation between Catholic and Communist, socialist and conservative. Many of these rivals believed that continued co-operation after the war would not only be desirable but essential to the survival of their countries. In Europe, at a minimum Communists expected widespread reforms carried through by broadly based anti-Fascist governments, reforms which would represent a real break with the past, and the possibility of a gradual advance to socialism in the future. This was not unrealistic. Many who had stood right of centre regarded the old order as dead. This was the logic of such new political groupings as Christian democracy and Gaullism. Of course there were Communists who sought more, who thought their 'October days' were at hand. This was especially true of the Albanians, Greeks and Yugoslavs, who were unaware of the deal between Churchill and Stalin on spheres of influence. In successfully resisting the call of Stalin and Churchill to establish a coalition with the exiled government of King Peter, the Yugoslav Communists, though they did not fully appreciate it at the time, were freeing themselves from intellectual and spiritual dependence on the Soviet Union. It was a far more important milestone on the road to Eurocommunism than the abolition of the Comintern. Elsewhere the Communists behaved themselves according to Stalin's ideas, which, for the most part, coincided with their own. In most countries, despite their progress, they were far too weak to contemplate any take-over. In France and Italy, where this could have been a possibility, the presence of the Anglo-US forces made this impossible. The policy of broad coalitions was the most sensible in the circumstances. We shall never know whether Stalin expected the broad coalitions of Western Europe to be turned, at a later date, into Communist dictatorships as happened in Eastern Europe. Naturally the French and Italian Communists thought in terms of violence. They had been fighting a bitter irregular war against domestic Quislings as well as foreign occupation forces. How deeply they would have been committed to maintaining genuine broad alliances had their countries been free of outside, that is, Allied, interference, it is impossible to say.

After 1945 the peoples' democratic road became the model for Western Communists rather than the Soviet model. To some extent this had already been tried out in Spain before the second World War. At the time of the outbreak of the Civil War in Spain in 1936 the Communist Party was quite weak. In the crucial elections of that year they gained 17 seats in the Cortes, as against 99 for the socialists and 278 for the parties of the popular front as a whole. In all, the Cortes had a membership of 473.[24] Communist influence increased as the Civil War progressed because the Republic was largely dependent on Moscow for its supply of arms. Though the Communists never got complete control of the Republic, they demonstrated how it was possible for a relatively small number of individuals to wield enormous power by holding key offices, and backed by a disciplined party. It is interesting that Santiago Carrillo, General Secretary of the Spanish Communist Party, quotes this period as proof of the democratic intentions of Spain's Eurocommunists![25] In fact, thousands of left-wing rivals of the Communists were executed in the purges in the Spanish Republic, so Carrillo's evidence is not very convincing. He does not deny that individuals and groups were 'unjustly accused', but blames the wartime situation and the youthful inexperience of the Communist leadership.[26]

One aspect of the pre-war Spanish situation was the attempt by the Communists to secure a merger with the much stronger Socialist Party. This was a tactic adopted throughout Europe after the second World War. In Britain the Communists, once again, applied to be affiliated to the Labour Party and in 1945 came closer than ever before to that objective. Like their comrades in pre-war Spain, the Labour Party did, however, reject the Communist application for affiliation. The social democrats of Eastern Europe after 1945 were not really given any choice. This merging of the working-class parties in Eastern Europe was a key aspect of the development towards 'people's democracies'. The folly of the earlier fratricidal struggle was emphasised, the co-operation in the underground, the fact that both social democrats and Communists claimed to be the heirs of Marx, the Communist acceptance of the parliamentary road, and, finally, the fact that, because the Comintern had been abolished, national

Communist parties were free to pursue their own policies. Pressures of all kinds were used, including violence and blackmail, to bring about the mergers, and there were ideological concessions. The chief ideological concessions were the proclamation of the theory of different national roads to socialism, and the playing down of Leninism. It was Anton Ackermann, the East German Communist, who became most closely associated with this thesis. In January 1946 he published his authoritative contribution in the East German party journal, *Einheit*. It was back to the Marx of 1872! The justification for Ackermann's view was that, since the capitalist class in Germany was no longer in control of the military-bureaucratic machinery of state, socialism could therefore develop in a relatively peaceful way. Gomulka in Poland, Dimitrov in Bulgaria, Thorez in France and Togliatti in Italy were all saying the same thing at this time.[27] In Britain the same line was evident with the British Communists supporting the new Labour government – even against its own left wing! This happened over the American loan proposals in 1946. The Communist and fellow traveller group all voted for the loan, in the spirit of wartime Allied co-operation, while the genuine independent left in the Commons were among those who voted against it.[28] There was no Cominform at this time, yet all roads still seemed to lead to Moscow. One puzzling aspect of this period was the attack made on the American Communists by Jacques Duclos, a leading member of the French Communist Party. Duclos attacked the Americans for changing the name of their organisation, claiming that it heralded 'a notorious revision of Marxism . . . a revision which is expressed in the concept of a long-term class peace in the United States'.[29] The attack was made in April 1945 and 'is one of the crucial and most mystifying milestones of wartime and postwar Communist policy'.[30] The intervention by Duclos was in contradiction to what the various Communist parties were advocating at the time. With his militant line, 'Duclos was denying the prospect of peaceful co-existence as a new stage in the struggle between two systems. He was denying the validity of seeking to avoid civil war'.[31] Yet Duclos prospered and the Americans took his criticism as having the authority of Moscow behind it. Earl Browder was expelled by his comrades and the American Communist Political Association was disbanded and the party restored. At the very time then when the Communists were trying to impress the world that each party was completely independent, and was seeking evolution towards socialism rather than through dictatorship and violence, Moscow, through Duclos, was indicating its reservations, cautioning about going too far, and even beginning a revision of this moderate policy.

The setting up of the Socialist Unity Party of Germany (SED) in the Soviet Zone of Germany in April 1946 was also at variance with the policy of genuine coalitions in Western-style parliamentary institutions. It is perfectly true that many social democrats and Communists favoured a united party after the war. They believed their rivalry before 1933 had paved the way for Hitler. By the end of 1945, however, the policies of the Soviet occupation authorities had destroyed much of the goodwill which had existed. In the end the unity move was pushed through against the doubts and opposition of many social democrats.[32] As mentioned above, this tactic was repeated throughout Eastern Europe and by late 1947 or early 1948 the period of genuine alliances was over throughout the area. Czechoslovakia, where the Communists had gained a relative majority by democratic means, was the last state to take the road to 'people's democracy' after the Communist *coup* of February 1948. In the same year Yugoslavia, which regarded itself as having gone further along the socialist road than its neighbours, and which was often seen as Moscow's most consistent follower, was expelled from the new Communist Information Bureau (Cominform) on Stalin's orders.[33] Individual Communists in the West were shocked but the Western CPs found no difficulty in condemning Tito just as thoroughly as they had lavished praise on him before the split.[34] Reviled as a Trotskyite Fascist and hangman of the Yugoslav people, he managed to withstand the Soviet blockade of his country. Later, many of those who had helped to build the 'new democracies' or 'people's democracies' – Kostov in Bulgaria, Rajk in Hungary, Slansky in Czechoslovakia among them – were consumed by the flames of the Stalinist hell they had created. As for the Western comrades of these unfortunates, they joined in the chorus of condemnation and continued to extol the virtues of the Eastern Europe regimes, except, that is, for Yugoslavia. The workers of the West were given to understand that their road to socialism would be like that built in Eastern Europe. In Eastern Europe the Ackermann thesis of separate roads was dead and this obviously caused some difficulty for Western parties.   The

British party was apparently given a special dispensation to go ahead with its programme, *The British Road to Socialism*, which was adopted by its executive committee in January 1951.[35] This programme was relatively moderate by the standards of the time, but it too pointed in the direction of the East European model:

> The enemies of Communism accuse the Communist Party of aiming to introduce Soviet Power in Britain and abolish Parliament. This is a slanderous misrepresentation of our policy. Experience has shown that in present conditions the advance to Socialism can be made just as well by a different road. For example, through People's Democracy, without establishing Soviet Power, as in the People's Democracies of Eastern Europe.
>
> Britain will reach Socialism by her own road. Just as the Russian people realised political power by the Soviet road which was dictated by their historical conditions and background of Tsarist rule, and the working people in the People's Democracies and China won political power in their own way in their historical conditions, so British Communists declare that the people of Britain can transform capitalist democracy into a real People's Democracy, transforming Parliament, the product of Britain's historic struggle for democracy, into the democratic instrument of the will of the vast majority of her people.[36]

Another British Communist pamphlet emphasised that the 'new popular democracies' were 'higher forms of democracy than bourgeois democracy' as existed in Britain.[37] As for what would happen when the Communists got power, John Gollan, later CPGB Secretary, explained in another publication that 'All the experiences of the People's Democracies in Eastern Europe prove this; the class struggle will sharpen in every way.'[38] This policy was later denounced as one of Stalin's mistakes.

The British Road to Socialism did nothing to halt the exodus of members from the CPGB in the first half of the 1950s. It was, like the other CPs of Western Europe, facing stagnation of membership and loss of electoral support.[39] The post-war recovery of the economies of Western Europe of course played a part in this in that it weakened the case for socialism. The entrenched position of social democracy, including the success of the British Labour government (1945–51), was another. But undoubtedly the close association of these parties with the USSR was also of key significance. What is remarkable is that there was not more open conflict in these parties about the causes of their decline. This contrasted sharply with the position in the social democratic and Labour parties. The reason for this lack of discussion was, of course, the democratic centralist nature of the organisation of the Communist parties. In the case of the British party, virtually all the members of the Political Committee were full-time officials of the party dependent on it for their livelihoods. This must have been a powerful factor promoting unity. Second, the Executive Committee, a broader-based body nominally superior to the Political Committee, was elected by congress delegates on the basis of a list drawn up, officially, by a Panels Commission. The members of the Panels Commission were the nominees of the existing leadership. Thus delegates at the national congress were presented with a list, recommended by the leadership, which they could either accept or reject. In the immediate post-war period there was a secret ballot to decide the fate of the list, but in 1952 open voting was reintroduced.[40] As for national congresses, after 1947 they were held, once again, every two years, instead of annually, as they had been before 1943. These congresses were highly orchestrated, 'the cheers, handclaps and speeches are as individual and spontaneous as the movements of a drill-squad.'[41] They were made up of a relatively large number of full-time officials on the one hand, and a large number of inexperienced delegates on the other. At the lower levels of the CPGB the same kind of organisational pattern repeated itself. Bob Darke, formerly a Communist borough councillor in Hackney and a London bus conductor by profession, has given us a detailed picture of party branch organisation at this time. In the period under discussion, the London, Hackney, branch of the CP was the strongest and most successful branch.[42] It was divided into North and South and controlled by a single Borough Secretariat. The 14 members of the Secretariat were carefully chosen so that, as far as possible, all industries, professions, social and minority groups were represented on it. As for election to the Secretariat, 'Each year the existing Secretariat draws up its own panel of names for the new Secretariat. It does this after it has consulted with the London District Committee.'[43] Election then followed at the annual members' meeting of the branch. The election was more or less a formality for rejection of the list 'would indicate a lack of faith in the wisdom of the branch and district leadership. It would smack of "fractionising", a heresy punishable by expulsion.' The Secretariat held weekly meetings. Members' meetings were held once a month. It must be admitted that all democratic organisations end up by being run by minorities. It must also be admitted that all large political parties have their problems in ensuring a free and continuous dialogue between leaders and ordinary members, but the structure of Marxist–Leninist parties, and the mentality of their trained cadres, make a difficult problem much worse. The writer will agree that, in the case of the CPGB, there appears to have been some improvement in the 1970s. The other factor making discussion more difficult in the Communist Party was the mentality of many of the members. The quasi-religious faith of the 1930s reached new heights with the deification of Stalin during and after the war. Stalin was revered by Communists in the way that Hitler and Mussolini had been by their followers, that is, almost as a god. No doubt the deification of the Fascist leaders made the 'cult of personality' more acceptable, though it was profoundly anti-Marxist. In a chaotic world, in which the supreme evil was represented by one man, Hitler, it seemed desirable, even necessary, to represent the supreme good incarnate in one man, Stalin.[44] The kindly, clever, modest, shrewd 'Uncle Joe' of the 1930s had given way to the brilliant supremo of the 1940s, wise, decisive, even ruthless, in the cause of peace and socialism. He had dominated international Communism since at least 1929 and it was almost impossible to envisage the movement without him. Party members had seen him as he liked to present himself, as the brilliant architect of victory, in Soviet films such as the 'Fall of Berlin' and 'Meeting on the Elbe'. Such films were shown not only in Warsaw, East Berlin and Paris, but also in London, Manchester and Glasgow, where they were given special showings put on by the British-Soviet Friendship Society or the Society for Cultural Relations with the USSR or similar bodies. Translations of Soviet novels and Soviet English-language magazines did the same job for Stalin.

The Nineteenth Congress of the Soviet Communist Party, the first held since March 1939, gave fresh impetus to the Stalin cult. Held in October 1952, it was attended by the British Communist leaders Harry Pollitt and William Gallacher. A big campaign was launched to popularise and explain the proceedings and decisions of the Congress by the CPGB and the other parties. Stalin's latest work, *Economic Problems of Socialism in the USSR*, was the subject of considerable activity to popularise it. Stalin's *On the Problems of Leninism on the Roots of Leninism* and the Stalin-inspired *Short History of the CPSU (B)* were also regarded as key literature in the fight for socialism. With so much emotional and ideological capital invested in Stalin, his death in March 1953 led many individual Communists in Britain and elsewhere to experience gloom, fear and even despair. Some felt the Americans would exploit the situation and strike at the Soviet Union. Others feared that their secret doubts would be realised, and that a struggle for power would break out among the Soviet leaders, in the way the hated Western experts on the Soviet Union had forecast. Referring to such experts, R.P. Dutt, the theorist of British Communism, wrote in the April (1953) edition of the Communist magazine *Labour Monthly*:

> The jackals and wild asses sought to dance on the grave of the dead lion . . . The pigmies of Transport House, conscious of their own abject failure to achieve socialism . . . assiduously scribbled to 'debunk' the 'myth' of Stalin and expose his 'colossal blunders'. Would that we could enjoy a few such 'blunders' here.

What intellectual difficulties and ideological tangles and plain political embarrassments Communists can get into is shown by Dutt's quotation, at the beginning of his article, from Mao Tse-tung, 'Our task is to transform sorrow into strength.' Soon, he would not feel free to quote either lion of world Communism. It was Harry Pollitt's job to find adequate words to convey the CPGB's loss to *Daily Worker* readers. He tried hard to do so:

> Stalin – who has written golden pages in world history, whose lustre time can never efface . . . Never the dictator, never one to lay down the law, always eager and willing to listen, to understand another's point of view . . . No words, no monuments, no tributes can ever do justice to the revolution in people's minds and actions, in changing world history, in freeing millions from darkness, oppression, poverty and misery that

have been brought about by the work of Comrade Stalin . . .
Eternal glory to the memory of Joseph Stalin.

It was all a beautiful dream. The grim reality was to be revealed
just under three years later, a reality which many Communists
could not face.

Looking back today at the events surrounding the Twentieth
Congress of the CPSU, what stands out as remarkable is not the
anti-Stalin campaign which followed, but the fact that so little
changed within the USSR and in the relations between the CPSU
and the other Communist parties. There are a number of reasons
for this. First, given the organisational structure outlined above,
the leaders could, for the most part, hold the line against the tide
of criticism which did take place. Many critics simply left, or were
expelled from, the Western parties at this time. In the case of the
CPGB, membership slumped from 33,095 in 1956 to 26,742 in
1957. In 1958 it declined further to 24,900.[45] It was at this time
that the 'New Left' was born in Britain, often on the initiative of
ex-CP members, around the magazines *New Reasoner* and *Universities And New Left Review*. The Italian party is said to have
lost some 250,000 members at this time.[46] There were splits
among the Communists in Scandinavia, as Trond Gilberg
explains below, and in Denmark the new People's Socialist Party
quickly eclipsed the official CP. A second reason why there was
not more change was that the Soviet leadership offered enough in
the way of reforms to stabilise the situation. Further improve-
ments in living standards were announced to the long-suffering
Soviet people. More importantly, an end was promised to the
brutal and arbitrary methods of the secret police. Thousands of
Soviet citizens had by that time been released from the camps, and
thousands of others had their names cleared posthumously, which
was important for their relatives. Today, with the labour camps
still in existence and the treatment of dissidents still a controversial issue, it is difficult to remember just how much worse conditions were under Stalin. Khrushchev also attacked the income
disparities in the Soviet Union and called for greater equality
among its citizens. Reviewing the world situation, he recognised
the possibility of peaceful change, urged Communists to co-
operate with social democrats and admitted that in certain countries socialism would be achieved without Communists playing a
leading role. The rehabilitation of Tito announced when Khrush-

chev and Bulganin visited Yugoslavia in 1955 was confirmed. All this suited the Soviet leadership at a time of nuclear stalemate, military blocks, economic progress in the West, and the desire of the USSR to raise its own standard of living with the help of Western technology. The third reason for the relatively modest change after the Twentieth Congress was that the CPSU's new line offered the Western parties a more dignified position as independent national parties. At the same time, the Soviet Union improved its image enough for them to retain it as a basic model. Their whole *raison d'être* was based on the 'correctness' of Lenin's revolution, on the belief that a fundamentally new society had been built in the USSR by the creative application of Marxism–Leninism. Most of their demands for solutions to the problems which afflicted their societies were based on the assumption that the Soviet Union had solved such problems or was well on the way to doing so. This myth could continue to circulate successfully in the second half of the 1950s because of unexpected Soviet achievements in space, Soviet progress in higher education and the growth of the Soviet economy. Soviet firsts in space started in 1957 with the world's first artificial earth satellite, continued with the first rocket to hit the moon in 1959, and became even more spectacular when Yuri Gagarin was successfully launched into orbit in 1961, followed, in 1963, by the first woman cosmonaut, Valentina Tereshkova. These achievements surprised Western experts, which made it easier for Communists to claim that they were due to the superiority of the Soviet system because the Americans too were striving hard in this area. To some extent, Soviet space exploits forced the West to treat Soviet progress in higher education more seriously. Certainly the Soviet system of higher education was one of those investigated by the Robbins Commission when planning the expansion of higher education in Britain in the early 1960s. Claims by the Soviet Union about the performance of its economy were also taken seriously:

> the other aspect of production is the hard fact that for many years now the rate of growth of output in the Soviet countries has regularly exceeded that of the average Western state, and particularly of Britain and the U.S. This is the point which should be worrying us.

So wrote one of the most quoted British 'bourgeois' economists, Michael Shanks, in 1961.[47] And he also commented about the Communist states, 'Whatever else it lacks, this society contains within itself a sense of purpose. This, *vis-à-vis* the West, is its great strength.' The reality of the Soviet Union and its allies was far more complex, and far less flattering, than so many well intended, non-Communist writers, journalists and politicians, who wanted to improve their own societies, supposed. As for Western Communists, they believed that if even bourgeois writers 'admitted' some of the USSR's achievements, how much better must the Soviet homeland really be! One other aspect of Soviet reality was the man at the top. Khrushchev was, on occasion, as friendly, informal, charming and homely as any publicity-seeking, office-hungry American politician. It must also be remembered too that, although 'Mr K's' taste in the arts was rather simple, he gave Solzhenitsyn and some others like him their chance. The 'socialist camp' as a whole looked more prosperous, more civilised and even more colourful under Khrushchev than it had under the Generalissimo. China appeared united and made considerable economic progress with Soviet aid. Poland was enjoying a liberal interlude, and even Hungary, the invasion of which in 1956 had caused so much heart-searching among Western Communists, was becoming a little more relaxed. Fidel Castro added a touch of badly needed romance and colour to the 'socialist camp'.

The meeting of Communist parties in Moscow in November 1960 was the most representative of its kind. It was, in fact, the last time to date that so many Communist parties were assembled at one time. In the long-winded compromise declaration of the conference, the Soviet Union was acknowledged as the 'universally recognized vanguard'. This to some extent disguised what had happened since the Twentieth Congress and indeed since the meeting of Communist parties in 1957. There had been the proclamation of polycentrism by the Italian Communist leader Palmiro Togliatti:

> there are countries in which they wish to find the way to socialism without the Communist Party being in the lead. In still other countries, the advance towards socialism is an objective for which there is a concentration of forces from different movements . . . The whole system is becoming polycentric, and

even in the Communist movement we cannot speak of a single guide; but rather of progress which is made by following ways which are often different.[48]

In the same article Togliatti criticised the CPSU for not offering a Marxist analysis of Stalinism. Clearly, with the Soviet leaders having admitted that all had not been well under Stalin, and with other models, recognised models, of socialism developing in Yugoslavia, China and Cuba, the Soviet party had to compromise over its claims to lead the world movement.

The new decade brought many more problems for the 'socialist camp'. The Berlin Wall went up in August 1961 – a grievous blow to Communist prestige. In December 1962 came the open split between Moscow and Peking when one of the Italian Communist leaders, Giancarlo Pajetta, denounced, no doubt with Soviet approval, the Chinese comrades. Hitherto Sino-Soviet differences had been thinly disguised by reference to the Albanians and the Yugoslavs. The Moscow–Peking dispute was something the Communists had always denied could happen, but Western Kremlin-watchers had predicted was inevitable. In 1964 Khrushchev fell after a palace *coup* rather than through the workings of inner party democracy. Overnight he became an unperson. This was indeed difficult for Western Communists to swallow and was criticised by several parties, including the CPGB. In the same year the Rumanian party leadership felt strong enough to issue a so-called Declaration of Independence emphasising their country's national independence, sovereignty and so on. The development of Rumania's national Communism began in 1952 with the removal from the party leadership of Anna Pauker and her group, who represented 'the crudest kind of subservience to Moscow'.[49] It is still not quite clear how this was managed, as Stalin was still alive. Possibly the fact that Pauker was Jewish helped. The Russians, in keeping with the new course throughout Eastern Europe after Stalin's death, somewhat relaxed their hold on Rumania's economy in 1954. In 1958 they withdrew their troops from the country, convinced of the Rumanian party's loyalty and its ability to handle the situation. After 1960 the Rumanians increasingly went their own way in the economy, in cultural affairs and especially in foreign affairs. But they always took care not to go too far and Rumania's internal regime always remained repressive enough for Soviet taste. The situation was therefore

quite different from that which developed in Czechoslovakia
under Alexander Dubcek, where the emphasis was on re-
establishing internal democracy without antagonising the Soviets
over foreign policy. The invasion of Czechoslovakia in August
1968 by the Warsaw Pact forces exposed once again Moscow's
view of fraternal relations. It also revealed the deep-seated fears
of the Soviet leadership of anything approaching democracy.[50]
The invasion was condemned by the Chinese, Yugoslav, Rumanian and Albanian Communists, as well as the Italians and
French, the Scandinavians and British, and most of the others.
Only the totally insignificant West German Communist Party,
SEW of West Berlin, illegal Greek and Portuguese parties, and
the parties of Cyprus and Luxembourg supported the invasion,
together with Castro's party and the North Vietnamese. Certainly
the discussion which followed the invasion was an important
milestone on the road to what we now call 'Eurocommunism',
but the amount of criticism of the Soviet model should not be
exaggerated. After all, critics such as Ernst Fischer, leading theorist of the Austrian party, and Roger Garaudy, theorist of the
French Communists, were expelled for going too far. One other
factor which emerged strongly in the 1960s as a cause of friction
between Western and Eastern Communist parties was the question of the treatment of Jews in the Soviet bloc. From Marx on,
the Jews have made an important contribution to Communism
in both Eastern and Western Europe, and in the 1960s Jews
were over-represented in the Communist movement relative to
their numbers in the populations of the various states. The Jews
had been treated with suspicion, in some cases purged, by Stalin
after 1948, and then quietly rehabilitated by his successors. But
the Soviet Union's courtship of the Arabs brought difficulties for
them, especially after the Middle East war of 1967. In 1968
many Jews, including many old Communists, were purged from
public life in Poland and forced to leave the country. As increasing numbers of Soviet Jews, many of them with valuable skills,
sought permission to emigrate to Israel, the Soviet authorities
turned to repressive measures to curb the flow of applicants. This
in turn brought protests from groups in the West which the Western European CPs could not ignore. Some attempts were made to
defend the Soviet position. In Britain the old Jewish Stalinist
Andrew Rothstein could find nothing but praise for the USSR's
record on the issue.[51] In the long run, however, the major parties

felt compelled to break ranks and criticise their comrades in the Kremlin. There were electoral considerations to think of, and the likelihood of serious tensions within the parties concerned had they not done so. They also had to consider the growth of the New Left.

In the first half of the 1970s a number of events took place which led most of the Western Communist parties along the 'Eurocommunist' road. After pondering the fate of Allende in Chile, PCI leader Berlinguer proposed to his party the 'historic compromise' with the Christian democrats. He had come to the conclusion that socialism could not be built in Italy on a mere 51 per cent of the popular vote. Compromise was therefore necessary. All Communists were pondering the significance of the end of Fascism in Iberia. The French Communists were left to ponder the Soviet ambassador's well publicised support for Giscard in the French presidential campaign of 1974. It was the same Soviet ambassador who had been accredited to Prague in 1968.[52] Many French Communists felt they ought to rethink their position on the USSR. The Helsinki Conference on Security and Co-operation focused the attention of the whole of Europe once again on the human rights issue. Furthermore, with the collapse of the detested right-wing dictatorships in Portugal, Greece and, in effect, Spain too, there seemed even less excuse for malpractices in Eastern Europe, and Western liberals now had more energy left to devote to that area. The Communists were also given food for thought by the various changes in leadership around the world. In West Germany the Christian democrats left office quietly in 1969 after 20 years to give way to the universally admired Willy Brandt. In every way save perhaps one, Brandt was more than a match for his Communist counterparts anywhere East of the Elbe. His only weakness seemed to be that he was too trusting. His resignation because of the East German spy in his entourage was no credit to the Communists. There were changes too in Eastern Europe. Gomulka was forced out of office by workers' strikes in Poland in 1970, and Ulbricht went after a peaceful political *coup* in the SED in 1971. Though he was no friend of the Eurocommunists, they could not help questioning in private the shabby way he was treated. For a time he too became virtually an unperson in the German Democratic Republic. The victories of social democracy in such highly prosperous countries as West Germany and Austria put strong pressure on the

Western Communists to ask themselves what they were really after, what they had really got to offer. This point was underlined by the revival of socialism in France and the growth of the socialist parties in Spain and Portugal. Even the fall of President Nixon in 1974 could be interpreted as showing the strength of American democracy rather than, or as well as, the corruption of American politics. It could be thought that most of the members of the Politburo of the CPSU wished they had a similar method of replacing their own ailing, ageing, decaying General Secretary. In these circumstances it is not surprising that Western Communists should not keep up their criticisms of the Soviet Union.

The easiest criticisms to make are obviously those concerned with particular cases regarding civil rights. An instance of this was the denunciation by the PCF of the banishment of Alexander Solzhenitsyn from the USSR. *L'Unità* (24 May 1978) published an attack on the 'severe penalties' passed on Yuri Orlov and other Soviet dissidents. The author of the article believed the case 'confirms the general impression that it is not a question of isolated episodes but a determined and precise conception of the relationship between authority and the citizens'.[53] In a similar vein the British Communist Party journal *Comment* (25 November 1978) criticised the law under which Alexander Ginzburg and Viktoras Pyatkus had been tried for anti-Soviet propaganda. It found the law 'is of such an all-embracing character that it lays the way open to infringements in practice, of the people's right to criticise and express their views'. *Comment* urged the Soviet authorities 'to rescind the recent sentences and release those charged in these trials'.

Undoubtedly the most thorough examination of what Eurocommunism means, both in relation to domestic politics and in relation to the USSR, is that of Santiago Carrillo, *'Eurocommunism' and the State*. Carrillo, General Secretary of the Spanish CP, wrote the book in 1976 when his party was still technically illegal. He sums up the Eurocommunist position as follows:

> The parties included in the 'Eurocommunist' trend are agreed on the need to advance to socialism with democracy, a multi-party system, parliaments and representative institutions, sovereignty of the people regularly exercised through universal

suffrage, trade unions independent of the State and of the parties, freedom for the opposition, human rights, religious freedom, freedom for cultural, scientific and artistic forms of popular participation at all levels and in all branches of social activity.[54]

Even at the level of rhetoric this goes beyond the formulations of the pre-war popular front era and the early post-war anti-Fascist period. As mentioned above, it is true that Carrillo harks back to the earlier periods as evidence to prove the sincerity of the Eurocommunist position. He even seeks to justify Lenin's position in 1917, but he then goes on:

It must be recognised, however, that the approach to the problem of the State in the following pages involves a difference from Lenin's theses of 1917 and 1918. These were applicable to Russia and theoretically to the rest of the world at that time. They are not applicable today because they have been overtaken in the circumstances of the developed capitalist countries of western Europe.[55]

As for the Soviet Union itself, 'The October Revolution has produced a State which is evidently not a bourgeois State, but neither is it as yet the proletariat organised as the ruling class, or a genuine workers' democracy.'[56] Carrillo admitted he was unable to give a precise definition of what the Soviet Union actually represents[57] but goes on:

the bureaucratic stratum, at its various levels, wields excessive and almost uncontrolled political power. It takes decisions and settles questions over the heads of the working class, and even of the party, which, taken as a whole, finds itself subjected to that bureaucratic stratum.[58]

Although this sort of thing had been said many times by Trotskyists and some Yugoslavs, Carrillo's critique of the Soviet Union is the most sophisticated, and honest, to date by a Communist party leader. Soviet attacks on Carrillo were only to be expected. Sam Aaronovitch, a theorist of the CPGB, correctly analysed the Soviet party's attitude and fears:

Not surprisingly, Carrillo's book has been reviewed with great hostility in the Soviet press, though no Russian edition has been published there which would enable the people of the Soviet Union to evaluate Carrillo's arguments. There seems to me to be substance in Claudín's view that the Soviet Party's hostility to Carrillo partly stems from its fear that if this view became widespread among communist parties, it would represent a withdrawal from the CPSU of its 'legitimacy' in the eyes of Soviet communists and sympathisers and have powerful internal repercussions.[59]

As the various authors below indicate, by the time Carrillo's book was published, Eurocommunist tendencies were evident in most of the parties of Western Europe. There had been the famous meetings of the leaders of the Italian and Spanish parties in July 1975, and of the French and Italian CP leaders in November of the same year. The French party's Twenty-Second conference in February 1976 decided to drop its traditional commitment to the dictatorship of the proletariat. The CPGB, not covered below, was increasingly addicted to vino rather than vodka. Under the leadership of John Gollan, Secretary from 1956 to 1975, and later Gordon McLennan, it took its place amongst the parties seeking alternatives to the Soviet model. In its revised programme adopted in October 1968 it erased the name of Lenin, retaining only a commitment to Marxism.[60] As part of its conception of socialist democracy it declared, 'Democratically organised political parties, including those hostile to socialism, would have the right to maintain their organisation, publications and propaganda, and to contest elections.'[61] It had also dropped its previous reference to 'democratic centralism' as a positive feature of the Communist Party. In most respects its programme was that of the Labour left. Its increasing 'moderation' did it no good at the polls. In October 1974 its 29 candidates gained only 0.1 per cent of the vote, and in 1979 none of its candidates got anywhere near winning a seat. The CPGB's programme was revised once more in 1977, strengthening its commitment to Western democratic norms still further by announcing that a socialist government would be prepared to retire from office peacefully if it were turned out by the electors. Except for the issue of Czechoslovakia, the CPGB's foreign policy has remained more nearly orientated to that of the Soviet Union than some other parties. Roughly 25,000 strong, the British Communist Party has suffered its internal tensions over the revision of its programme. In June 1977 a breakaway group led by Sid French, Chairman of the Surrey party organisation, formed the pro-Moscow New Communist Party. The new party did not appear to have much of a following and suffered a significant blow with the sudden death of Mr French early in 1979.

The setting up of the New Communist Party is an indication of just one of the problems of the Eurocommunists. Inevitably all these parties have their pro-Moscow factions. If and when the CPSU feels it could gain from establishing new pro-Moscow mini-parties, it has the resources to do so. Many of the Western parties are still involved with the USSR financially. The British party, for instance, exports a considerable number of its publications to Eastern Europe and it is doubtful whether many of them would survive without such external support, which includes advertising in them as well. This must be a consideration for a party which is in financial difficulties. As Clarke and Hine point out below, it is still a consideration for the powerful PCI. The holiday visits to the Soviet bloc are also still part of Communist party life. Just how effective these visits are in boosting pro-Soviet sentiment it is difficult to say. But the author has found that normally reasonable individuals suspend criticism of manifestations in the 'socialist camp' which they would strongly condemn in their own countries. There are those too who find the more 'Spartan'. less developed, societies of Eastern Europe more appealing than the more varied consumer societies of the West. The effects of such visits are, however, by no means uniform. Another factor which to some extent helps the Soviet Union is the relatively high turnover of membership of the Western CPs. Very many of these short-term members have no idea of Communism's past. Their knowledge of the history of the Soviet Union is less than sketchy. They have only a romantic notion of the October Revolution and their own perception of the reality of their own society, a society in which there is unemployment, inequality, racism, selfishness and politicians who fail to keep their promises. If the reactionaries, so they argue, go on about the danger of Communism and the Soviet Union, this must be an indication that there is something positive about the USSR. These are some of the limiting factors in Eurocommunism. This is in no way to suggest that this tendency exists only on Soviet terms and is somehow phoney.[62] The Stalin–Tito split and the Moscow–Peking dispute were originally regarded with great scepticism by many in the West. Yet they have provoked lasting changes. The fact is Eurocommunism is a genuine development which is a response to political experience, the challenge of the 'affluent' society, the challenge of the 'permissive' society, and equally the challenge of the left-wing rivals of Communism. Eurocommunism represents one of the serious challenges facing the Eastern European Communist leaders in the 1980s.[63] They fear the effect on their own people of Eurocommunists denouncing them as a 'bureaucratic stratum'. The Italian Communists have encouraged such self-styled Eurocommunists as the East Germans Havemann and Bahro, they have intervened on behalf of Soviet Jews, Polish workers, Czech reform Communists and Catholic priests. As for the role of the Eurocommunists in the West, the writer finds it difficult to believe that if a few Communists become members of a coalition government this would represent a serious threat to freedom in Italy.[64] It is often forgotten that Communists have already been in and out of office in Finland, Iceland and, a special case, Portugal, in recent years. The Italian Communists have only reached, so to speak, the Ministerial antechambers and appear to have paid a penalty for this in electoral terms. Given Italy's probable condition in the 1980s, are they not likely to pay at least as large a penalty if they actually hold office? At the present time the Western Communist parties, be they Eurocommunist or not, do not seem to represent a strong challenge to 'democratic socialism'. In those countries where they were likely contenders for the left-wing vote – Spain, Portugal and France – the democratic socialist parties have successfully met the challenge.[65]

One final question remains – could the Eurocommunist parties revert to more orthodox, pro-Moscow policies accepting 'Marxism–Leninism', the 'dictatorship of the proletariat' and 'proletarian internationalism'? This possibility cannot be ignored. The possibilities for continued Soviet influence have been outlined above and are indicated by other contributors to this study. The other critical factors are, first, what the rivals of the Communists are doing. Second, it will depend on developments in the advanced industrial societies of the West. Will 'bourgeois democracy' survive – or will it, in the troubled times ahead, give way to right-wing authoritarianism? Will the welfare state, built up in prosperous times to a significant extent on cheap imported fuel, be maintained? The face of Western Communism will depend too on what is happening to the millions of unemployed forecast by Western economists for the 1980s. Finally, it will depend on what is happening in the Soviet camp itself.

Notes

1. Albert S. Lindemann, *The 'Red Years': European Socialism Versus Bolshevism 1919–1921* (Berkeley, 1974), p. 296.

2. Robert Conquest, *Lenin* (Glasgow, 1972) gives a short clear account of Lenin's ideas.

3. Bertrand Russell, *The Practice and Theory of Bolshevism* (London, 1920) called Bolshevism a religion and described 'This habit, of militant certainty about objectively doubtful matters' (p. 9).

4. Arthur Koestler in Richard Crossman (ed.), *The God That Failed* (London, 1950), p. 68.

5. Santiago Carrillo, *'Eurocommunism' and the State* (London, 1977), p. 112.

6. Vladimir Dedijer, *Tito Speaks* (London, 1953), pp. 95–6.

7. Fred Copeman, *Reason in Revolt* (London, 1948) gives an illuminating account of a British Communist delegation to Russia in 1939. Wal Hannington, *Never on our Knees* (London, 1967) gives a more sympathetic account (pp. 163–8).

8. P. Avrich, *Kronstadt 1921* (Princeton, 1970) gives an account of the revolt.

9. Crossman, *The God That Failed*, tells why various individuals joined.

10. G.F. Hudson, *Fifty Years of Communism* (London, 1971), p. 137.

11. Leonard Schapiro, *The Communist Party of the Soviet Union* (London, 1963), p. 411.

12. Joseph T. Starobin, *American Communism in Crisis, 1943–1957* (Cambridge, Mass., 1972), p. 45.

13. Ibid., p. 45.

14. Douglas Hyde, *I Believed* (London, 1950), p. 56. Hyde was a leading British Communist.

15. For the CPGB see David Childs, 'The British Communist Party and the War, 1939–41: Old Slogans Revived', *Journal of Contemporary History* (April 1977).

16. Starobin, *American Communism*, pp. 74–5.

17. Henri Michel, *The Shadow War Resistance in Europe 1939–1945* (London, 1972); M.R.D. Foot, *Resistance: an Analysis of European Resistance to Nazism 1940–1945* (London, 1976); Stephen Hawes and Ralph White (eds.), *Resistance in Europe: 1939–45* (London, 1975); all three give some exposure of the part played by the Communists.

18. Starobin, *American Communism*, p. 21, puts the figure at nearly 100,000; David A. Shannon, *The Decline of American Communism* (London, 1959), p. 96, puts the figure at 70,000–80,000.

19. Daniel Bell, *Marxian Socialism in the United States* (Princeton, 1976), p. 184.

20. Starobin, *American Communism*, p. 72.

21. Joshua Freeman, 'Delivering the Goods: Industrial Unionism During World War II', *Labour History*, vol. 19, no. 4 (Fall 1978), p. 583.

22. Starobin, *American Communism*, p. 75.

23. Maurice Edelman, *How Russia Prepared* (London, 1942) p. 22. Edelman was a Labour MP after 1945.

24. Hugh Thomas, *The Spanish Civil War* (London, 1965), p. 133.

25. Carrillo, *'Eurocommunism' and the State*, p. 120.

26. Ibid., p. 117.

27. Wolfgang Leonhard, *Eurocommunism Herausforderung für Ost und West* (Munich, 1978), pp. 54–5.

28. See details in David Childs, *Britain Since 1945* (London, 1979).

29. Starobin, *American Communism*, p. 79.

30. Ibid., p. 78.

31. Ibid., p. 81.

32. Henry Krisch, *German Politics under Soviet Occupation* (New York, 1974) gives much detail on this period; Wolfgang Leonhard, *Die Revolution Entlässt Ihre Kinder* (Cologne, 1955) remains a classic. Leonhard was then a German Communist.

33. A. Ross Johnson, *The Transformation of Communist Ideology: the Yugoslav Case 1945–1953* (Cambridge, Mass., 1972) for the details.

34. James Klugman, *From Trotsky to Tito* (London, 1951). This book ranks as one of the lowest attacks on Tito by a British Communist who had previously praised him.

35. Starobin, *American Communism*, p. 216.

36. CPGB, *The British Road to Socialism* (January 1951), p. 14.

37. CPGB, *The Transition to Socialism: a 3-Lesson Syllabus* (London, December 1948).

38. CPGB, John Gollan, *People's Democracy for Britain* (London, April 1952), p. 21.

39. The Italian party was an exception, but even it lost some membership.

40. Henry Pelling, *The British Communist Party* (London, 1958), pp. 133–4.

41. Bob Darke, *The Communist Technique in Britain* (London, 1953), p. 19.

42. Ibid., p. 20.

43. Ibid., p. 23.

44. This was the kind of argument advanced by Sidney and Beatrice Webb in their *Soviet Communism: a New Civilization* (London, 1936).

45. Peter Shipley, *Revolutionaries in Modern Britain* (London, 1976), p. 219.

46. Fernando Claudin, *Eurocommunism and Socialism* (London, 1978), p. 38.

47. Michael Shanks, *The Stagnant Society* (London, 1961), p. 24 and p. 15.

48. From the *Nuovi Argomenti* interview of June 1956, as published in full in the British Communist journal *World News*.

49. David Floyd, *Rumania: Russia's Dissident Ally* (London, 1965), p. 53. For a recent sceptical look at Rumania see Ion Ratiu, *Contemporary Romania* (London, 1975).

50. Claudin, *Eurocommunism and Socialism*, p. 42, comes to this conclusion.

51. *Labour Monthly*.

52. James O. Goldsborough, 'Eurocommunism after Madrid', *Foreign Affairs* (July 1977), p. 802.

53. Guiliano Procacci, 'Orlov and Detente', *Marxism Today* (July 1978), p. 235.

54. Carrillo, *'Eurocommunism' and the State*, p. 110.

55. Ibid, pp. 9–10.

56. Ibid., p. 157.

57. Ibid., p. 160.

58. Ibid., p. 164.

59. Sam Aaronovitch, 'Eurocommunism: a discussion of Carrillo's "Eurocommunism and the State"', *Marxism Today* (July 1978), p. 227.

60. CPGB, *The British Road To Socialism* (London, October 1968), p. 22.

61. Ibid., p. 52.

62. Among the many sceptical views on Eurocommunism are Hugh Thomas, 'Eurocommunism the Sunset, Not the Dawn', *Daily Telegraph*, 6 March 1978; Michael Stewart, 'Western Communists – in New Dress?' *Socialist Commentary* (May 1978); Roy Godson and Stephen Haseler, *'Eurocommunism': Implications for East and West* (London, 1978) are also among the sceptics.

63. There are other ideological challenges facing the Eastern Communist leaders. As the Pope's visit to Poland indicated, the Catholic Church remains a serious challenge there. In East Germany the SPD remains a challenge, and in parts of the USSR perhaps Islam. Jiri Valenta, 'Eurocommunism and Eastern Europe', *Problems of Communism* (March–April 1978) analyses the impact of Eurocommunism on the Soviet bloc. More briefly Leonard Schapiro, 'Soviet Reactions to "Eurocommunism" ', *Socialist Commentary* (April 1978).

64. This is a view shared by Milovan Djilas, jailed for his democratic socialist views by the Tito government. See Manfred Steinkühler, *Eurokommunismus im Widerspruch* (Cologne, 1977), pp. 383–8.

65. See the Trotskyist analysis of Eurocommunism by Ernest Mandel, *From Stalinism to Eurocommunism* (London, 1978).

2 EUROCOMMUNISM: THEIR WORD OR OURS?[1]

Philip Elliott and Philip Schlesinger

1 Introduction

The term 'Eurocommunism' is an ideological construct. Our object in this paper is to chart its origins, development and elaborations in current ideological struggles. It is no small irony that a concept coined by anti-Communists should have largely set the terms of reference for Marxist and bourgeois theorists alike. This irony is twofold: first, the adoption of the term by Communists; and second, the tendency for the term to 'take off', to run away from the purely anti-Communist meaning intended by its creators. This latter development has produced its own fair share of ideological repair work. The sociological significance of such developments lies in the way in which it illustrates how the ideological initiative may be taken by crucial elites, how they may, to a certain extent, lose it and then once more regain it.

'Eurocommunism' provides a useful case to investigate the division of labour which exists between different ideological elites. There is a distinction to be drawn between those who report events and provide information for political and economic elites, those who analyse such information and assess its implications for policy and those who interpret events directly or indirectly for popular consumption. We shall have occasion below to elaborate these distinctions and suggest in a preliminary way how they relate to different institutional positions, different types of journal and different communication media. In our view there is no simple process of dissemination or popularisation working downwards through these strata. The construct of 'Eurocommunism' itself has only achieved limited distribution in English language media. Accounts of related phenomena in truly popular media in Britain have largely been managed in pre-Eurocommunist, that is Cold War, terms. Our analysis of the system through which knowledge and meaning is produced and distributed leads us to expect that this will continue to be the case.

Ideological elites in the West – here consisting of politicians, journalists and academics – generally build up a considerable investment in established patterns of thought. Occasionally, particularly in moments of crisis, they have to engage in ideological retooling. So far as Communism is concerned, such a process of retooling has been necessitated by the change in international relations from Cold War to *détente* and by the emergence, particularly since 1956, and latterly 1968, of a number of significant developments in major Western European Communist parties. These developments have had to be located and interpreted, and have posed problems for the dominant, static, ideological framework, which is based on assumptions of Communist totalitarianism and the unquestioned writ of Soviet orthodoxy in the international Communist movement. Western political elites have faced the problem of explaining the gap between the traditional Cold War view of Communism and the current professions of, in particular, the Italian, French and Spanish Communist parties (the PCI, PCF and PCE). This problem was forced on to the agenda as these parties approached political power in their respective countries. Our contention is that the coining of the term 'Eurocommunism' and the development of the subsequent debate have reflected the need to make major ideological adjustments at a time of *détente*. This has given rise to a number of differing non-Marxist views, which are explored below.

We should say, at the outset, that we do not take the view that a 'Eurocommunist' phenomenon as such exists. That there are convergent analyses and programmes amongst some Western Communist parties cannot be doubted. That these have been produced by similar structural developments in capitalism's present crisis, that they have been actuated by a rejection of Stalinism and the Soviet model as the sole road to socialism, and that they reflect a new appraisal of the prospects of revolution in Western Europe, can also not be doubted. But such considerations do not, in our view, add up to a homogeneous phenomenon – as is implied by the term 'Eurocommunism'. Nor does the somewhat *ad hoc* set of links between major Western Communist parties and some socialists as yet constitute a coherent movement about to change the face of Europe. Potentially, of course, it might herald a *rapprochement* between elements of the Third and Second Internationals. But in our view, an assessment of the political prospects in Western Europe needs to pay more attention to *national* realities, rather than to over-emphasise convergence.

2 The Origins of the Term

It is hardly surprising with a term which has had such considerable ideological reverberations that there are three separate claims to have coined it.[2]

Alfons Dalma, an Austrian journalist of Croatian origins, based in Rome, and contributor to a right-wing book entitled *Euro-Kommunismus*, asserts that the Catholic philosopher Augusto Del Noce first thought up the label (Dalma, 1977). Given the greater strength and the more detailed support for the other two claims, our conclusion is that Del Noce is not the most significant of the originators.

The second claimant is Arrigo Levi, editor of the liberal Turin newspaper *La Stampa*, and columnist on Italy for *Newsweek*. In December 1976 in *Newsweek*, Levi speculated on whether he himself was the originator of the term in an earlier *Newsweek* column in December 1975. In that first column he had set out in a remarkably prescient passage why 'Eurocommunism' was on the world agenda:

> The evolution of 'Eurocommunism' – which has also been called 'white communism' or 'neo-communism' – may become a decisive factor for European history and East–West relations. It challenges the traditional political balances in the West but it also threatens the rigidity of Soviet power in the East. In the end, who will be more affected? To some extent this is a consequence of detente, a diplomatic strategy of movement that demands much greater inventiveness than the old 'trench warfare' of the Cold War (*Newsweek*, 15 December 1975).

The passage was buried in a discussion of developments among the European Communist parties associated with another postponement of the pan-European conference. The lack of prominence and the range of alternatives offered suggested that the choice of a single ideological figure had yet to be made and the choice was moving from one which alerted Italians to a new danger in their midst to one which had wider potential on the international scene.[3]

However, the most precise and best documented claim has

been made on behalf of Frane Barbieri, a Croatian who was formerly editor-in-chief of the Belgrade weekly *Nin*, and who in 1974 joined the editorial staff of the anti-Communist Milanese daily, *Il Giornale Nuovo*. This newspaper was expressly set up in that year in order to combat the growing strength of the Italian left by a number of prominent journalists from *Corriere della Sera* who dissented from the *Corriere's* leftish line. According to one of *Il Giornale Nuovo's* editors, Enzo Bettiza (who is also a Liberal senator for Milan), the term was first used by Frane Barbieri 'writing an editorial on "Brezhnev's expectations"' (*Giornale Nuovo*, 26 June 1975). He continues:

> It was not exactly intended to be a pro-communist formulation; and indeed one leading Spanish Marxist (Ramón Tamames) classified it in the Western vocabulary next to Winston Churchill's 'Iron Curtain' and Walter Lippmann's 'Cold War'. *Is it then, our word or their word*? (Bettiza, 1978, pp. 21–3; emphasis added)

This question is a crucial one. It makes central and explicit the issue of how ideological constructs are to be controlled. Bettiza's observations were made in *Encounter*, to which he is a regular contributor, and which, as will be seen, has figured importantly in the ideological activity focused on 'Eurocommunism'.

The 'archaeology' of the term is revealed in greater detail in an interview with Barbieri conducted by Dr Manfred Steinkühler, a West German diplomat (Steinkühler, 1977a). This interview presents Barbieri's assumptions and intentions when he coined the neologism 'Eurocommunism'. He says that he was particularly influenced by the formulations of two of the leaders of the Spanish Communist Party, Santiago Carrillo and Manuel Azcárate, concerning a 'genuine European alternative' to Soviet-style socialism in the context of developed Western capitalist societies. Barbieri makes the point that in originating the term 'Eurocommunism' he was specifically intending a contrast with Arrigo Levi's 'neo-Communism' which he felt went 'too far'. In an elaborate account, which deserves to be fully quoted, he explains his intentions further:

> I decided to use the expression 'Eurocommunism' because I considered it to be geographically precise, but considered it

ideologically imprecise. By contrast, the expression 'Neo-communism' is a much more defined, self-contained concept. 'Eurocommunism' is an ideologically fluid, imprecise phenomenon, which I would not completely deny has a new ideological component. However, I would not acknowledge it to be a self-contained ideology. This does not mean that 'Eurocommunism' has no social basis whatsoever. It does, but of an instrumental manner, insofar as it makes use of existing social arrangements. Precisely because of this, since it is not clear what 'Eurocommunism' actually is, I ask myself whether an EEC ruled by the Eurocommunists would remain an EEC in the same way it was created. Today, the European Community is bringing West European traditions to fulfilment. The Eurocommunists say that they want to remain independent from both the USA and the USSR. If you were to follow the Spanish Manifesto-Programme you could infer that their intention was also a step-by-step Europeanisation of the Soviet system. But that is an illusion. A Eurocommunist Europe would definitely mean the Sovietisation of Europe (Steinkühler, 1977, pp. 348–9).

For Barbieri, the Eurocommunists have a developed conception of the stages to the seizure of power, but none of how they should actually exercise it; they lack a fully developed critique of the Soviet system; they have not specified how democracy is to be guaranteed; and finally, unlike the Yugoslav Communists, they are *dirigiste* and state-centred rather than decentralist. In sum, Barbieri formulated his conception in the framework of a set of theoretical assumptions about recent developments in Western Communism, presenting them in a newspaper which is part of the anti-Communist crusade of the Italian right.

In its origins, therefore, the concept of 'Eurocommunism' was intended to indicate opposition to and scepticism about current trends in some of the major Western Communist parties. But in the next stage of the elaboration of 'Eurocommunism' what was involved was less outright opposition than containment.

2.1 Containment Theorists

In an article written in January 1976, first published in *Foreign Policy* in spring, and then republished in another elite journal *Across the Board* in July, with a title now including the term itself

– 'Eurocommunism: the Italian experience so far' – Arrigo Levi outlined three positions on the subject (Levi, 1977a and 1977b). It was rejected by the right on the essentialist ground that all Communism was the same under the skin. It was rejected by some on the left on the opposite ground that all revisionism was a form of social democracy. But in between there were those who were prepared to take it seriously, though not without necessary caution. Levi outlined two reasons for adopting this third view: one, internal to Italy, that the PCI had shown considerable restraint in avoiding moves which would split the Christian democrats and make parliamentary government in Italy impossible; the second, the foreign policy point that there were good reasons for taking the PCI's protestations of independence from Moscow seriously. In the *Newsweek* column in which he had first used the term, Levi had gone some way towards accounting for the difference between sceptical opposition as against cautious acceptance by citing its geographical basis, pointing to opposition in Britain and America as against more open discussion in Italy and France (Levi, 1975).

This distinction between open-minded Europeans and closed-minded Anglo-Saxons has its attractions, but it is impossible to sustain. For one, there were numerous American advocates of containment, and for another several prominent Europeans among the professional anti-Communist backlash (of which more below). American advocates of containment apparently included the American Secretary of State, Cyrus Vance, at least a section of the State Department and US diplomatic service, and most of the contributors to influential American foreign policy journals in 1976 and 1977. Articles on Europe in *Foreign Policy* were almost exclusively of this type, including papers by Levi (1977a), two American political scientists, Peter Lange (1976) and Robert Lieber (1977), and an ex-US ambassador turned academic, Laurence Silberman (1977). Similarly, *Foreign Affairs* published papers taking a containment position by Guido Carli (1976) ex-Governor of the Bank of Italy and currently Chairman of the Italian Association of Manufacturers (Confindustria), Peter Nichols (1976), Italian correspondent of the (London) *Times*, Charles Gati (1977), another academic, James O. Goldsborough (1977), chief European correspondent of the *International Herald Tribune* and *Newsweek* correspondent, and Ugo La Malfa (1978), leader of the Italian Republican Party and Prime Minister designate in February 1979. There were also articles by prominent CP spokesmen (Segre, 1976, Kanapa, 1977 and Napolitano, 1978), setting out their case in terms calculated to be appealing to Westerners who were influential in business and politics. Interestingly, European Communism slipped off the agenda in *Foreign Policy* in 1978 and *Foreign Affairs* published two essentialist, anti-Communist papers in that year (Revel, 1978, and Chirac, 1978).

Both these journals are closely linked to elite groups active in American foreign-policy-making. *Foreign Policy*, with a circulation of approximately 18,000, is published by National Affairs Inc. with the support of the Carnegie Endowment for International Peace. Its editorial board includes prominent journalists such as David Halberstam, as well as foreign policy academics and government officials such as Zbigniew Brzesinski and Elliot L. Richardson. *Foreign Affairs*, published by the Council on Foreign Relations, New York, has a much wider circulation of 72,000. It was founded in 1921, and, as Domhoff has pointed out, is an important 'link in the specific mechanisms by which the corporate rich formulate and transfer their wishes into government policy'. Its major sources of finance are 'leading corporations and major foundations', and the CFR has, until recently, had a great measure of success in placing its members in the USA's defence and foreign affairs policy-making apparatuses (Domhoff, 1969, pp. 28–30). Like the Royal Institute for International Affairs (RIIA) in London, and the Society for Foreign Policy in Bonn, the Council on Foreign Relations (CFR) holds off-the-record briefings for its membership by government officials.

The comparable British journal, the *World Today*, associated with the RIIA, also published articles taking a containment position in 1976 and 1977 (Stehle, 1976 and 1977, Timmermann, 1976 and Popov, 1976). So did the bi-monthly of the United States Information Service, *Problems of Communism*. The sophistication and wide-ranging nature of the analyses to be found in this journal certainly defeat any crude conspiracy theorists who would expect a government publication simply to be a propaganda mouthpiece. Rather, its commitment to a balanced appraisal of the options supports our theory of ideological retooling. Policy-makers need answers, not disinformation, and such a journal therefore has an important place in the ideological division of labour. This place is occasionally made quite explicit by contributors. Ronald Tiersky (1976), for example, concluded his account of the possibility of 'non-dictatorial socialism' in France if the PCF achieved a share of power with the warning that those anxious 'Atlantic political elites' likely to read *Problems of Communism* needed to be well informed and not take refuge in reductionist analysis.

Needless to say, there are noteworthy differences between the analyses provided by those whom we have labelled containment theorists. Nevertheless the similarities are more striking, as all have investigated current developments in ways which balance the reasons for acceptance against continuing reasons for distrust. All move to the conclusion that either Communism can be socially integrated into bourgeois democracies or that at the very least it can be contained. A number of themes and arguments recur which are summarised below.

(1) The argument that the inevitable must be accepted if not welcomed. Thus, for example, Lieber set out the basic pragmatic case that 'in the relatively open, free and pluralistic systems of the West it is extremely difficult to *prevent* change,' and so 'American toleration of reformist or even radical European domestic politics including – if and when it is unavoidable – a role for indigenous Communist parties (e.g. Italy) may be a realistic course of action' (Lieber, 1977, pp. 47–8). Similarly Goldsborough (1977) argued that the policy of quarantining the CPs had not worked and their 'systematic exclusion from government has contributed to the crises of the countries of Latin Europe'.

(2) The argument from incorporation contends that if one of the CPs were to approach political power this could only be exercised within the existing constitutional framework. Ronald Tiersky (1976, p. 46), for example, a political scientist and author of an authoritative study of French Communism (1974), stated this case for France and the PCF with great clarity. 'Given a viable Socialist Party, strong opposition parties, a strong bureaucracy and military, and the historical memory of public opinion, it is extremely doubtful that the PCF leadership could manoeuvre with enough skill to make *its* revolution.' Others (e.g. Lieber, 1977) have emphasised the role of the national and

international economic infrastructure with which any Western government has to deal – including one which included Communists.

(3) The containment theorists accept that the CPs in question have genuinely changed their policies and strategy. Tiersky (1976, p. 46) was convinced that 'Stalinism is becoming a dying ember in French communism.' Kevin Devlin (1977, p. 19), political analyst for Radio Free Europe, argued that 'Eurocommunism' derives from the convergent interests of the major Western CPs which 'might be described as the tendency . . . to give priority to their own political interests in the course of adaptation to their sociopolitical environments'.

(4) From the standpoint of international relations Eurocommunism appears to pose a challenge to the Soviet Union as the Communist parties distanced themselves from its leadership and advocated positions attractive to dissidents in the East. Neither Devlin (1977) nor Heinz Timmermann (1977), a member of the Bundes Institut für Ostwissenschaftliche und Internationale Studien, Cologne, who considered this view, were inclined to give it much weight beside the evidence of continuing contact between the 'Eurocommunists' and the Communist Party of the Soviet Union (CPSU) and their general support for Soviet foreign policies. Nevertheless Timmermann stressed that *détente* was a key condition for the survival of the new developments, and that these would be imperilled if, for example, the PCF pulled out of NATO or if Eurocommunist ideas began to destabilise the Eastern bloc. Timmermann noted Soviet attacks on recent developments, particularly on the PCE leader Santiago Carrillo's book, *'Eurocommunism' and the State*, which showed Soviet fears about Eastern Europe's internal stability. His conclusion, however, was that the USSR would not break with the Western CPs, since they were assisting its foreign policy objectives. More likely was an attempt to split the parties, and to 'Finlandise' them.

(5) There is an economic argument for the potential value of the Western Communist parties in stabilising capitalism which is rarely openly stated.[4] However, articles by John Earle, the Rome correspondent of the *Times Business News*, in *World Today*, and by Guido Carli, of Italy's Confindustria, in *Foreign Affairs*, in 1976, have explicitly made this case. 'Thirty years of Christian democratic hegemony have resulted in a wasteful, inefficient and

irrational economy,' wrote Earle (p. 218). Carli too argued that the PCI was particularly well placed to restructure the economy fundamentally in ways the dominant political forces could never achieve – to make the bureaucracy more efficient, renew state control of public enterprises, modernise industry and introduce an effective incomes policy. Thus, he concluded, what is needed is 'a broader political consensus. To believe otherwise is to engage in fantasy politics' (p. 718).

These arguments, with the exception of the international relations one, were repeated by the Communist leaders in the articles published by *Foreign Affairs*. Sergio Segre, Head of the PCI's Foreign Section, Jean Kanapa, Head of the PCF's Foreign Affairs Section, and Giorgio Napolitano, the PCI's economics spokesman, all addressed US policy-makers in a way calculated to be reassuring. All took a similar line stressing their parties' commitment to democracy, the break with the Leninist conception of the dictatorship of the proletariat, their independence from Moscow and their acceptance of such Western institutions as NATO and the EEC, their honesty, efficiency and technocratic bias. They called on the US not to intervene, particularly when in the Italian case the PCI could make a real contribution to the rehabilitation of the Italian economy and had shown it was not intending to disrupt the political scene.

A commentator who straddles the boundary between those whom we have labelled containment theorists and those who take a fundamental, anti-Communist line is Neil McInnes, author of several authoritative studies of Western Communism and European correspondent of *Barrons Weekly*, a New York financial magazine produced by Dow Jones. McInnes follows the methodology of many containment theorists in his study of 'Eurocommunism' published in 1976. He evaluates the CPs' claims to have changed, country by country, and topic by topic. But the method leads him to different conclusions. In spite of his financial connections, he gives the economic argument short shrift, claiming that vague policies and good intentions amounted to no more than a form of nationalist, economic populism. The central flaw he identifies in the Eurocommunists' case is their continued addiction to democratic centralism as a mode of internal party organisation, a mode which 'enables the boss to catapult his cronies into top jobs' and which threatens that the economic and political management of any society in which they come to power will be carried on by a party bureaucracy of the familiar (Eastern) type. McInnes argues that in the final analysis we are dealing with CPs which

> have abandoned the dictatorship of the proletariat, made numerous compromises with the social-democrat and bourgeois parties, relaxed their defence of the Soviet Union, and defined international authority in the communist movement – but they still seek to maintain the discipline, the tactical suppleness, and the centralisation of the original Leninist party (1976, p. 48).

2.2 Fundamental Anti-Communists

Few fundamental anti-Communists have been prepared to concede as many points as McInnes. Their arguments are constructed using their own distinctive methodology. Instead of discussing changes in the Communist parties point by point and balancing the alternatives for current policy, fundamental anti-Communists set about identifying those characteristics which still link the Eurocommunist parties to their Stalinist past and so enable them to fit this type of Communism into the familiar framework of totalitarian theory (see Elliott and Schlesinger, 1979). Often the argument is an explicit attack on those in the West who have been duped or seduced into accepting Communist protestations at face value. Walter Laqueur, for example, who entered the field early to counter the political and economic attractions of 'Eurocommunism' (in *Commentary* in August 1976), argued that West European or 'Eurocommunism as it is coming to be called' was the equivalent of pre-war Fascism. It offered the promises of economic salvation at the price of freedom. Many contemporary American journalists and intellectuals had been seduced in just the same way as their predecessors had at first been seduced by Mussolini. The equation between Communism and Fascism has been one of the central tenets of totalitarianism theory, the theory which underpins the anti-Communist attack.

Laqueur is typical of the academic polymaths who take a fundamentalist position. He is Director of the Institute of Contemporary History in London, has other appointments in the United States and an interest in contemporary history that includes Weimar, the Middle East, terrorism and guerrilla warfare. He is also a contributing editor to *Commentary*[5] and editor of the Sage series of policy papers, the *Washington Papers*, in which McInnes's study of 'Eurocommunism' appeared. A comparable – and more widely known – figure is Raymond Aron, who is accepted as a global thinker of international standing and whose writing on a wide range of subjects is internationalised through translation.

In 1977 two extracts from Aron's latest book castigating those seduced by Marxism appeared in *Encounter*. In 1955 Aron had published a similar attack entitled *The Opium of the Intellectuals*. In 1977 the attack was titled *Plaidoyer pour l'europe décadente* (*My Defence of Our Decadent Europe*). In this book Aron plays the whole hand of anti-Communist arguments dealt by totalitarianism theory. Of primary significance is 'the Weimar syndrome', defined as 'a situation where the electoral structure of a democracy can only offer a choice between two forms of suicide: either by giving power to those who will destroy it, or by violating its own principle of legitimacy' (Aron, 1977b, p. 8). 'Eurocommunists' are not to be trusted because while they 'may be distancing themselves from the Red capital . . . they remain linked to it by a common faith' (ibid., p. 10). As evidence of this, Aron also pointed to the continuation of democratic centralism:

> They profess essentially the same doctrines as the Soviets, interpreted in the same manner for years: they have not renounced democratic centralism: and their concept of the regime to come is still identical with the Soviet concept, although they maintain that they will avoid its totalitarian implications. Whether the Eurocommunists are concealing their aims or not is less important than the consequences, probable or inevitable, of their methods and their ideas (ibid., p. 18).

The same point has been made by Jean-François Revel, author of *La Tentation Totalitaire*, a book in which he castigates the US 'academic and liberal press establishment' for its gullibility in swallowing 'the myth of Eurocommunism'.[6] In 1978 *Foreign Affairs*, which hitherto had appeared to be an organ of that establishment, published an article by Revel in which he argued that the critical test of de-Stalinisation was the purely 'technical' issue of democratic centralism – 'all the rest is literature and impressionistic gossip.' 'Eurocommunism can be logical and coherent only if it results in the disappearance of communism' (Revel, 1978, pp. 297 and 305).

Encounter's coverage provides a useful illustration of our general thesis that by 1977 the process of ideological retooling associated with 'Eurocommunism' had slipped out of the hands of the anti-Communists into those of the containment theorists. The magazine was engaged in an attempt to regain the initiative by questioning the protestations of the CPs now calling themselves 'Eurocommunist' in a series of articles and interviews. George Urban, described as 'a writer on contemporary history', conducted two major interviews, one with Lucio Lombardo Radice, a number of the Central Committee of the PCI, and the second with Altiero Spinelli, preceded by an editorial gloss as follows: 'Europeans were appalled. Altiero Spinelli, one of the founding fathers of Common Market Unity and for many years Italy's High Commissioner in Brussels . . . became a leading spokesman for "Eurocommunism" ' (Urban, 1978a, p. 7). Urban's questions emphasise the same grounds for distrusting the PCI and its strategy as Aron had rehearsed earlier. In 1978 these two interviews, together with others Urban had conducted on Radio Free Europe, were collected in book form with an editorial introduction which repeats the essentialist argument:

> The Eurocommunists are attempting to unbutton the Marxist–Leninist–Stalinist straitjacket in reverse order. . . . Whether or not these moves have been merely tactical, their political implications are significant. They reveal a geological fault running through the base of the Eurocommunist initiative. . . . Eurocommunism is a freak which must either end in Social Democracy or revert to some form of Leninism. In the first case it will cease to be Communist, in the second it will no longer be Euro (Urban, 1978b, p. 8).

Essentialists have a penchant for aphorisms of this type. Revel's version has already been quoted above, and Aron has also made his contribution: 'Eurocommunism is like the Euro dollar: it remains Communism even when it is preceded by the word "Euro" ' (quoted in *Newsweek*, 2 January 1978).

It would be misleading to give the impression that *Encounter*'s treatment of 'Eurocommunism' simply contained one set of views. Leszek Kolakowski, an ex-Marxist Polish philosopher and author of a recent authoritative history of Marxism (1978), accepted the social-democratisation thesis as a possibility:

> So far, we lack empirical proofs that a democratic communism is at all possible, and all the existing proofs are to the contrary. Still, we cannot exclude that a new variant of regenerated Social Democracy could ultimately emerge out of the Communist schism (1977, p. 19).

The same point was made in an earlier *Encounter* article by Richard Löwenthal, Emeritus Professor of International Relations at Berlin, who argues the explicitly essentialist case that if the necessary changes occurred then 'Eurocommunism' would 'cease to be communism as we have known it'. However, such nods in the direction of *Encounter*'s more leftish readers have been coupled with fundamentalist anti-Communist assumptions. These included, in Kolakowski's case, an insistence that Eastern European states are still totalitarian, that the 'Eurocommunists' may be sincere, but do they realise the incoherence of their ideas? (cf. Aron and Urban); that 'Eurocommunism may emerge, but so far it has not' (cf. the French anti-Communist authority Annie Kriegel); that Eurocommunists must 'prove that they really distrust and detest despotism' by breaking with the Soviet Union and international Communism, and getting rid of the Leninist party (loyalty tests also proposed by Neil McInnes, Raymond Aron, George Urban and David Owen, the former British Foreign Secretary).

Georgetown University has provided a base for a number of other ideological initiatives in addition to those already discussed. The Director of the University's International Labor Program, Roy Godson, and Stephen Haseler, known in Britain for his attacks on the alleged growth of Marxist influence in the Labour Party, collaborated there on a book entitled *'Eurocommunism': Implications for East and West* (1978). The authors set out to reject both the view that a new political phenomenon has come into existence and that a new pan-European movement is in the process of formation. The argument is partly strategic: any advances made by the Western Communists will favour the strategic interests of the Soviet Union. It also rests on the persistence of democratic centralism and is grounded in an unreconstructed essentialism:

> while there have indeed been variations in doctrine and in attitudes towards Soviet hegemony of the international Communist movement, such subtle departures from orthodoxy cannot as yet, in our view, lead to their being dignified as a wholly new category, indigenous to Western Europe, unlinked to the Communist past and experience in the Soviet sphere (1978, p. 4).

The authors' refusal to give the term credence is a position shared by David Owen and Walter Laqueur. Their affinity with Owen's views is even more marked when they suggest, as he does, that social democrats should try to split the CPs and detach 'reformist' voters.

Apart from being backed by the International Labor Program, the Godson-Haseler book was also funded by the National Strategy Information Center, a body which exists 'to encourage an understanding of strategy and defence issues on the grounds [*sic*] that, in democracies, informed public opinion is necessary to ensure a viable Western defence system' (1978, p. 125). Haseler's research while at Georgetown was also backed by the Heritage Foundation, which publishes the right-wing *Policy Review*. Haseler is a member of this journal's editorial board.[7] Clearly, therefore, several sources of funding were specifically combined to make available the means for the continuing ideological counter-offensive based at Georgetown. Haseler and Godson were backed up by a panel of six experts on various national Communisms who all contributed background papers for the principal authors – a rather uncharacteristic procedure in academic circles. In addition, some seven assistants are credited.

In 1978 another essentialist voice appeared on the scene in the shape of the *Washington Review of Strategic and International Studies*. But while the voice was new, some old faces were associated with it. The *Washington Review* is published at the Centre for Strategic and International Studies, Georgetown University, home of the *Washington Papers*. One of the new journal's editors is Walter Laqueur, and its executive editor is Michael Ledeen, who has also contributed to *Commentary* on European issues. Some contributors to the review, like Rosario Romeo, a professor of history at Rome University (interviewed by the ubiquitous George Urban) and Daniel P. Moynihan, US senator and ex-UN ambassador, have been content simply to fit Eurocommunism into the totalitarian equation. Others have provided more specific political scenarios as, for example, Xavier Marchetti, a former aide of President Pompidou, who took the view that a victory of the left in the March 1978 French parliamentary elections would be dangerous for both the economy and the state's security. His argument was premised upon an internal domino theory: Mitterand would be the captive of the socialists' left wing, 'who in turn might turn out to be a hostage of the Communists' (p. 47). Helmut Sonnenfeldt, who had been one of Kissinger's associates in the State Department,[8] provided a broad international perspective in an interview with Michael Ledeen. Should the West encourage Eurocommunism as a force which would destabilise the Soviet bloc? Sonnenfeldt was cautious, suggesting that it had probably had 'effects in Eastern Europe that add to already existing tendencies toward greater diversity'. But

> the ultimate question for us is whether these effects, whatever their possible benefits, are not offset by the very deleterious consequences that these parties, were they in power, would undoubtedly have on our own Western institutions, Western security, and the relationship among Western European nations and between Western European nations and the United States (p. 50).

These scenarios were set out in the context of broader discussions. However, the credibility of 'Eurocommunism' was the central focus of David Owen's speech which was reprinted in the April issue of the *Washington Review*. Owen's position is by no means a simple-minded essentialism. Indeed he takes a rather sophisticated line on the historical development of Communism, arguing that its 'natural condition' had 'never been one of monolithic unity; and there is no inherent reason why such unity should prevail today, still less under the direction of Moscow' (p. 7). However, Owen's main interest lay in stressing the need to maintain strong boundaries between social democrats and Communists. Fraternisation across the lines was undesirable. Owen's explicit refusal to use the term 'Eurocommunism', and his reason for doing so – 'the battle is for people's minds' – places him on the same ideological ground as that occupied by *Encounter* and *Commentary*. He is remarkably candid:

> It is deliberate that I have not once mentioned the term Eurocommunism. I am deeply sceptical that any such unified phenomenon exists. It is a dangerous term. It confers a coherence and a respectability on an ill-defined, disparate and as yet unidentifiable phenomenon. It is very interesting that Western communist leaders are now using the term Eurocommunism. They recognise it has an appealing quality. It is a convenient portmanteau term. It tends to make people suspend their critical faculties, avoid analysing the phenomenon seriously, country by country, and instead take refuge in generalities. 'Eurocommunism' is becoming respectable. It is a term which socialists should eschew. We should give it no currency (p. 14).

Walter Laqueur, in an editorial statement commending Owen's views, also showed an awareness of the advantages the term had come to have for the Communists.

> There are great differences between the structures and policies of the Italian and French parties ... and the term Eurocommunism tends to blur their differences. A good case could be made for declaring a moratorium on its use, but unfortunately this is unlikely to be accepted by all parties (1978).

One can understand such anxieties. The term has become part of the conventional political discourse of elite journals and newspapers. In July 1978 an editorial note in *Problems of Communism* referred to 'trends loosely termed "Eurocommunism"'. The *Daily Telegraph*, no friend of Communism of any variety, accepts it as a way of referring to the PCI and the PCE. In February 1979, *The Economist*, in an article discussing European Communist attitudes to events in South-East Asia, pointed to the different positions taken by the PCI, PCF and PCE as evidence of 'a split' in the Eurocommunist ranks – an 'occurrence' which only the use of the term has made possible. While the meaning and the merits of the term remain subjects of controversy, its use does tend to give the parties a positive gloss. They have a distinct position whose basic features are clear. They claim a preference for parliamentary over violent means of achieving power, a respect for political and civil rights, a tempering of the more extreme forms of collectivism in economic and social affairs, and a tendency to reject Soviet hegemony in inter-party relations. Clearly there are battles still to be fought on the ideological front.

2.3 The Ideological Division of Labour

As our reference to the British Foreign Secretary and his attack on Eurocommunism made originally at Cambridge in November 1977 shows, the distinction between containment theorists and fundamental anti-Communists is not merely an account of individual differences. Rather it leads to an analysis of the different roles in ideological production taken by specific groups of ideological agents. Whereas containment theories appeared mainly in international relations journals published by institutes and organisations closely involved in the development of foreign policy, fundamental anti-Communism has been published in more accessible, quasi-commercial journals like *Commentary* and *Encounter*. The foundation of both the *Policy Review* and the *Washington Review* appear to be attempts to counter containment theorists in the foreign policy field. *Commentary* and *Encounter*, however, belong much more to the public sphere, with the role of providing interpretations of developments for further dissemination by politicians and journalists addressing a wider public.

In Britain the main political interventions by Harold Wilson, David Owen and, at an earlier stage, Margaret Thatcher, have all followed an anti-Communist line. The only exception has been Eric Heffer, whose version of the social-democratisation thesis was published in the *Times* (7 November 1977) and the *Guardian* (29 November 1977). Heffer's *Times* article coincided with Wilson's attack on 'the political plague with no boundaries' in the *Guardian* (7 November 1977) and is evidence of a debate within the labour movement. It is a debate, however, in which those advocating containment or acceptance are largely restricted to working through party journals or left-wing publishing houses, while those taking the traditional anti-Communist line may be confident of reaching a wider audience through wider circulation media. Thus Stuart Holland in his preface to Sassoon's collection of PCI speeches published in 1978 (by Spokesman Books of Nottingham, funded by the Bertrand Russell Foundation) commends it as essential reading for 'people with tired minds, little information or both for whom "Eurocommunism" is an infection of the democratic body politic' and for 'more openminded members of the public who want to know before they judge' (p. 7).

This illustrates a crucial point about the nature of the Western cultural system, namely the disjunction which exists between the elite and popular levels, between what might be termed administrative and electoral politics. At the elite level there are grounds for arguing that containment theory was in the ascendant in 1976 and 1977. During this time it apparently coincided with US government policy, founded on the foreign policy consideration that it would do 'them' more harm than it would 'us'. 'Eurocommunism' has hardly been popularised, at least in the English-speaking world, beyond the level of the news magazine and quality newspaper. In so far as it has, what has been involved has been less a diffusion of the debate at the elite level and more of a counter-attack from the fundamental anti-Communists. *Time* and *Newsweek*, for example, while they featured Carrillo's book for its anti-Soviet implications, also featured various anti-Communist tracts and exposés published in France and Spain.

An extended review of 'Eurocommunist' developments in *The Economist* (5 November 1977) quoted only Annie Kriegel, Andre Glucksmann and Kissinger among Western commentators, all of them prominent anti-Communists. Press reporting of political developments in Europe has accepted the term as a journalistic convenience and so given it currency. Reference has already been made to some of the concern this has provoked among anti-Communists. Michael Ledeen, Laqueur's associate, attacked American reporting of Eurocommunism in *Commentary* in 1977. His article clearly illustrates the counter-attack which was being mounted at that time. Ledeen complained that a term coined to expose Berlinguer's propaganda had come to be treated at face value. But such press reporting, of limited interest to financial and political elites, has to be set against the more popular preoccupation with violence as *the story* coming from the 'Eurocommunist' countries, a story which fits very easily into the paradigm of totalitarianism.

Henry Kissinger, the most prominent anti-Communist of all, has provided a point of reference for almost everyone involved in the debate. He has had access to elite circles such as the International Institute for Strategic Studies, London, the American Enterprise Institute for Public Policy Research and the Hoover Institution on War, Revolution and Peace, and to elite media such as the *Atlantic Quarterly* and *Across the Board*. But his chief importance has been as a publicist and symbol of the essentialist anti-Communist position. In January 1978, this achieved full recognition in a television spectacular, originally made by NBC, and seen in the US by millions of viewers, according to the BBC which broadcast an extended version on BBC2 on a Sunday night in what is usually the arts programme slot. Coincidentally, the Carter administration took a public stance against PCI participation in the Italian government at virtually the same time.

'Eurocommunism', Kissinger announced, is Communism in Europe, a definition which enabled him to start his exposition with film of the Berlin wall, the limit of what Communism had been able to achieve by force in the West. But now, Kissinger warned, it had found a new way of threatening the West. Through elections it was crossing the wall which had held it in. The programme went on to provide a country by country survey in which good points about CP developments were cancelled by bad and in which Kissinger continually repeated a series of slogans to drive home his points. These covered the familiar ground that 'Eurocommunism' was no more than a Machiavellian tactic to gain power, that it would act as a Trojan horse in Western defence, that there was no internal democracy in the parties, that Communist economies were always less productive than capitalist ones, that terror and violence worked in the Communists' favour by provoking a demand for order at any price. Throughout it all there were references to what Kissinger was pleased to call his paradox. Why should Communism attract support in the West given the contrast between the prosperity to be found there and the bureaucratic backwardness of Communist states in the East? There, Communism had been tried in practice and found wanting.

Our tentative conclusion to the first part of this chapter, therefore, is that, far from the Western media and cultural system allowing a free flow of debate and opinion, there is a division of labour with important consequences for political communication. Ideological elites, on the one hand, may engage when appropriate in what we termed ideological retooling. On the other hand, at a more general level such innovation is unlikely to change the reliance which the dominant culture and its spokesmen place in their original capital investment, in this case in the essentialism of the Cold War.

3 From Bourgeois to Communist Analysis

In the rest of the chapter our primary interest is to chart the manner in which the term 'Eurocommunism' was appropriated by the leadership of the appropriate CPs and to suggest why this occurred. We shall seek to show that a process of theoretical development was already in train to which the label could be assimilated, although not entirely without difficulties. The most striking counterpoint between the bourgeois analysis just examined and the Communist accounts concerns the degree of complexity of the latter, and the different range of symbolic reference points each displays. Our argument is that the bourgeois analysis of 'Eurocommunism' is, broadly speaking, impoverished. While the anti-Communists continually reiterate the lessons of history viewed from the perspective of totalitarian theory, containment theorists start from the politico-strategic question: 'How can the transformation of capitalism be prevented?' Neither stream of analysis takes seriously the current parameters of debate within Marxism.

On turning to the Marxist writing, we find a range of issues being canvassed and debated which are simply not reflected in the ideological mediations we have considered, for instance the dictatorship of the proletariat, the problem of the state, the theory of state monopoly capitalism, the analysis of class structure and the problem of alliances, the critique of the Soviet Union and 'proletarian internationalism', and the relationship between theory and practice in Marxism. In addition, there are a series of historical reference points to the works of Marx, Engels, Lenin, Kautsky, Luxemburg, Gramsci and, in particular, to the whole question of social democratic revisionism at the turn of the century. Now, the West European Communist parties are of course concerned with the problem of power as it relates to the transition to socialism. But this problem is situated in a developing mode of analysis and cannot, in our view, simply be reduced to a question of Machiavellianism.

However, to illustrate out point that bourgeois discourse does not take Marxism seriously consider what Ronald Tiersky – without doubt one of the shrewdest analysts of the PCF – says about the recent debate on the dictatorship of the proletariat within the PCF: 'Though some might find this of monumental importance it is only window dressing' (Tiersky, 1976, p. 42). Popov (1976) similarly maintains that the dropping of the concept is 'merely presentational'. For Aron, the manner in which it was done merely served to confirm that the worst excesses of democratic centralism still obtained. These reactions are trivialising ones, when what is at stake – as those who have considered Althusser's and Balibar's theoretical interventions will know – is a serious debate about the nature of class rule, the class nature of the state, the validity of the theory of state monopoly capitalism and the CPs' consequent alliance strategy. The material presented earlier hardly indicates that there is an orthodox PCF text *Les Communistes et L'Etat* which, as it were, codifies the official positions of the Twenty-Second Congress of the PCF of early 1976, and which argues that the bourgeois state need not be destroyed but rather only its oppressive characteristics removed in the creation of an 'advanced democracy', the first 'real' step towards socialism (Fabre *et al.*, 1977). Against this one finds the arguments of Balibar (1977) and leftists outside the CP, who have argued that this is an unacceptable form of revisionism.

3.1 The Appropriation and Transformation of 'Eurocommunism'

If the accounts we gave earlier are to be accepted, 'Eurocommunism' was coined in mid-1975 (Barbieri) or late 1975 (Levi). These datings seem to be more acceptable than that offered by Fernando Claudín in his book *Eurocommunism and Socialism*, who says:

> Towards the end of 1970 a new word hit the front pages of the international press and rapidly passed into political currency: Eurocommunism. *Originating outside the Communist parties to which it referred*, the term originally inspired reservations in the leaderships of these parties (Claudín, 1978, p. 7; emphasis added).

As we shall see, these reservations were, with reservations, overcome. For the moment, what is of interest is the vagueness of Claudín's remarks. The term 'Eurocommunism' has been embraced most wholeheartedly by Santiago Carrillo of the PCE, although, even in his celebrated text *'Eurocommunism' and the State*, he has felt obliged to retain the quotation marks. Carrillo's remarks concerning the term are illuminating about the way in which its anti-Communist meaning is transformed and rendered positive:

> the term 'Eurocommunism' . . . is very fashionable, *and though it was not coined by the Communists and its scientific value may be doubtful*, it has acquired a meaning among the public and, in general terms, serves to designate one of the current communist trends . . . the policy and theoretical elaboration which justify 'Eurocommunism' describe a tendency in the modern progressive and revolutionary movement that is endeavouring to get to grips with the realities of our continent – though in essence it is valid for all developed capitalist countries – and adapt to them the development of the world revolutionary process characteristic of our time. . . . So 'Eurocommunism' forces itself upon us as a reality, *as long as we cannot find a better definition* (Carrillo, 1977, pp. 8–9).

There has been some doubt about when the three CPs in question began to call themselves 'Eurocommunist'. This is understandable, since the process has been an uneven one: there is some basis for arguing it was in 1976, and some for saying it was in 1977. At the time of the East Berlin conference of European CPs in June 1976, Carrillo was definitely reluctant to use the term, the PCF firmly avoided it, and the PCI made only very qualified use of it. The ideological initiative directed against the CPs in question had been under way for well over half a year, and clearly Berlinguer in his speech at the Berlin conference felt some riposte was necessary in a context which would gain maximum publicity. After asserting that the West must find its own road to socialism, Berlinguer referred to convergences between the PCI, PCF, CPGB and PCE, and observed:

> It is this new type of elaboration and searching that some people have referred to as 'Eurocommunism'. Obviously, we were not the ones to coin this term, but the very fact that it has gained such wide circulation indicates the depth and extent of an aspiration to see solutions of a new type in the transformation of

society in the socialist direction take root and advance in the countries of Western Europe (Berlinguer, 1976, p. 61).

What is interesting about Berlinguer's handling of the term is the manner in which he appropriated it and gave it a positive meaning: it was linked to the convergent developments already taking place in several Western CPs. Berlinguer's studied vagueness about its origins and his suggestion that its currency expressed *socialist* aspirations must be calculated moves given the evidence of the earlier part of the chapter.

The quotation above from Carrillo shows him engaged in the same process of appropriation, in presenting its first major popularisation by a Western CP leader. According to Claudín, Carrillo first began to use the term in a qualified manner in July 1976 in a report to the Central Committee of the PCE (in terms which exactly echoed Berlinguer's). The decisive public moment came in December 1976 when Carrillo launched the slogan 'the "Eurocommunist" road to power' (Claudín, 1978, p. 8). Carrillo's full endorsement is independently confirmed from the date in the preface to his book. One can see, therefore, why some commentators have suggested that the Berlin conference saw the formal launching of 'Eurocommunism' by the CPs themselves (e.g. Gati, 1977).

The other date given, which we would consider more acceptable, is the March 1977 meeting of the PCI, PCF and PCE in Madrid. This was labelled the 'Eurocommunist summit' in the press. On this occasion Marchais of the PCF gave an extensive gloss on the term, once again pointing out that the CPs themselves had not invented it. According to the *Morning Star*, 17 March 1977, Marchais said:

> while taking into account the differences that exist between our three countries, our socialist democracy will differ from that which at present exists in those countries which have gone over to socialism. If that is what is meant by Eurocommunism, then we agree. But if it was thought, which none of us did, that Eurocommunism envisaged the establishment of a new international centre, then our reply is a categorical No.

The PCF has never been keen on the term, and some of this reluctance emerges in Marchais's qualifications. However, according to Goldsborough, he had become convinced that the term was working to the CPs' advantage rather than to their detriment.

The next major step in the appropriation of the term by Communists came with the publication of Santiago Carrillo's book. Carrillo's critique of Soviet 'socialism' provoked outraged diatribes from the CPSU through the medium of the journal *New Times* (June 1977). The *New Times*'s attack on Carrillo pointed up the unwillingness of the major Western CPs to identify themselves as 'Eurocommunist', although this is a point which has received little attention. The CPs which defended Carrillo did so individually, by defending his right to his views, but without endorsing them – in particular his criticisms of the nature of the Soviet Union. An editorial in *L'Unità* (28 June 1977) defended the line taken by the major Western CPs, but was extremely careful in its use of the term 'Eurocommunism', placing it in quotation marks, and using the prefix 'so-called'. Carrillo's book was described as not being

> a finished exposition of a 'doctrine' of 'Eurocommunism': a doctrine which does not exist, so much so that there is no organizational centre nor any comprehensive codification, although very significant documents have been underwritten by the interested parties on a bilateral basis.

Later, however, the article singled out a key feature of 'what is called Euro-communism', namely, 'the relationship between the process of development of political democracy and the big social transformations'.

In the bourgeois accounts considered earlier, the main interest in Western CP – USSR relations was either to assess to what extent Western developments could destabilise the Soviet bloc without endangering the future of capitalism, to assert that the CPs do have a certain autonomy, or to argue that they are unwitting agents of Soviet totalitarianism. Such debate as exists between the Soviet bloc and Western CPs is reduced to a problem of the political domination of the former over the entire Communist movement. Now that is certainly important, but there are, over and beyond this, genuine questions of Marxist theory involved. Whatever one may think of Moscow's rather arid dogmatising on the question of revolution (in particular, its view that only the Soviet road through the dictatorship of the proletariat should be followed), serious theoretical implications do follow from this which are the subject of much debate among Western Marxists.

Clearly, some explanation needs to be sought concerning the different attitudes of the PCI, PCE and PCF towards using the term. The PCE, we would argue, had a most pressing need to achieve national recognition at a time when Francoism was finally collapsing, and had to assert its own democratic credentials. This was most easily done by an attack on Soviet shortcomings. It is noticeable that the PCE flourished 'Eurocommunism' in a very distinctive way. It also attracted most of the public attacks on 'Eurocommunism' by the CPSU. Manuel Azcárate (1977), the Head of the PCE's International Department and the target of a second attack in *New Times*, chose to argue that the Madrid summit 'has imparted a definite form to the term Eurocommunism', and to reaffirm the need to criticise the Soviet bloc – an emphasis notably lacking from the approaches of PCI and PCF. Claudín has also observed that, while for Carrillo going out on a limb is easier, the other CPs are now closer to power, so 'the maintenance of good relations with Moscow is starting to become a matter of state interest for the two parties'.

The PCI has no problem of identity, and hence little need of the term 'Eurocommunist'. It is the largest West European CP, with a well established and distinctive road and a long history of expounding it. Berlinguer and other major figures such as Napolitano have, on the whole, tended to limit themselves to appropriating the term, without placing very great emphasis on its diffusion. None the less, it is clear that Berlinguer has been careful to retain some title to the term whereas other members of his party have failed to see the advantage in this. For instance, at the 1977 *Unità* festival in Modena, after a senior party historian had argued that 'Eurocommunism' did not exist, Berlinguer specifically took up this point in his concluding speech on 18 September. He stressed the convergences between the Spanish, French and Italian parties, carefully noting that they did not constitute a regional organisation, and argued that this might properly be called 'Eurocommunism' (Radice, 1978). On the other hand, some leaders of the PCI, such as Amendola, have especially stressed the *Italian* specificity of their policies. In a style reminiscent of Marchais, Amendola says:

I think that when people speak of 'Eurocommunism' they are wrong, because there is no such thing – there are as many specific strategies as there are Communist parties. We are opposed to the re-establishment of a single world centre for the communist movement in Moscow – and we are not going to establish a single centre of 'Eurocommunism' in Rome or Paris.

It is also notable that in the interviews Eric Hobsbawm conducted with Giorgio Napolitano (Napolitano/Hobsbawm, 1977), a book widely debated and translated in Western Europe, there is no mention at all of the term 'Eurocommunism' in the first interview (dated October 1975), and that it only enters during Hobsbawm's second interview (which took place just after the Madrid summit). Napolitano gives the term a rather vague definition and is quick to point out that the same analysis extends to CPs outside Europe, such as the Japanese.

The PCF has been more consistent and emphatic in its nationalism, and in its hostility to NATO and the EEC than the other two parties. Marchais's line at Madrid was anticipated in one of the party journals (*France Nouvelle*, 28 February 1977) by Gérard Streiff of the PCF International Department, who acknowledged the 'broad common themes' being developed by the CPs in advanced capitalist states, but was careful to state that '"Eurocommunism" is not part of our political vocabulary. In fact we do not believe that there are any universal or regional "models" of socialism'. More recently, Jean Kanapa of the party's political bureau enumerated 'the characteristics of Eurocommunism' at the Fondation Nationale des Sciences Politiques in Paris during November 1977. Kanapa observed:

To conclude, the word Eurocommunism is badly chosen. In effect, it designates a reality which concerns not only the communist parties of Europe, nor all the communist parties of Europe. But we haven't the relish for a war of words . . .. The expression Eurocommunism – in the way that we use it – has nowadays, for us, acquired a positive, an offensive meaning; it renders the aspiration of those working for socialism *in* liberty. And it is in that way that it is accepted. No doubt this explains why nowadays the term embarrasses those very ones who invented it (Kanapa, 1976).

Kanapa's remarks show a clear (and somewhat tongue-in-cheek) awareness of the benefits for the Communist parties which derived from the appropriation of the term, while still keeping a certain wary distance from it.

In sum, our argument is that the term 'Eurocommunism' came to be used by the various CPs (with varying emphases) because it was important for them not to permit a major ideological initiative to be successful. In their response they managed to appropriate the term and develop a positive meaning, thus creating difficulties for those who had initially used the term in a hostile sense. What is noticeable is the extremely rapid diffusion of 'Eurocommunist' texts – through translation – into Western Marxist culture. In this respect the PCI and the PCE must be judged especially good publicists.

An interesting question is whether the CPs are likely to use the term 'Eurocommunist' in the future. With the breakdown of the Common Programme in France, and the failure of the left to form a new majority, only the PCI is left poised on the threshold of power in the immediate future. There has been a definite tendency for the term 'Eurocommunist' to lose currency in bourgeois discourse. With only one CP posing a threat to capitalism, and that less serious than appeared in 1974–6, the 'Euro' designation has rather less work to do. The outcome may be that it is dropped – at least for the time being – by bourgeois ideologists. Given the reluctant record of the PCI and PCF, its future within Marxist discourse also looks uncertain. The only new area in which it has been espoused recently is amongst East European dissidents – as for instance in the manifesto of the SED opposition which appeared early in 1978 in *Der Spiegel* (2 and 9 January 1978).

4 Conclusion

In this chapter we have presented some of the main types of ideological work which have been done on the growth of Communism in Western Europe in recent years. We would not claim that the review is complete, but it is sufficiently comprehensive to make a number of concluding points about the way such ideological work is carried on.

The first and most important point is that the ideology has been developed in two different cultural systems, networks of meaning in the Geertzian sense. Each of these is underpinned by different sets of ideologists, organisations and communicating media. Each is available to the other. The ideologues working in one tradition take and make use of material produced in the other. But the relationship between the two is not one of interpenetration and overlap founded on shared meanings. Rather there is a boundary between the two which is crossed only in ways analogous to warfare. Information and ideas are used for intelligence on developments within the opposing camp, captured and converted into the terms of the opposing system or used simply as propaganda with which to engage the other side in battle. The extent of the difference between the two systems is brought out very clearly in Maurice Cornforth's *The Open Philosophy and the Open Society.* Writing 'for Marx' against Karl Popper, Cornforth illustrates how individual differences over particular topics are all part and parcel of a fundamental difference of approach, a recording of appearances confronting a science of observation and analysis. As is clear from the title, in the course of his book Cornforth attempts to realign some key symbols.

In the case of 'Eurocommunism', the difference between the content of the two systems can be seen in the different attention given to constitutional, political forms as against economic and class relationships. It was the possibility of Communists achieving political power through electoral means which first put 'Eurocommunism' on the Western agenda. But what in bourgeois terms appeared to be a Machiavellian tactic to gain political power rested in Marxist terms on a re-analysis of contemporary developments in economic relationships and the class struggle. Each system has a different account of political power.

This brings us to a second important concluding point, one about 'Eurocommunism' itself as an ideological figure. There is more to the development of a new sign than its content. Of particular significance is the relationship between the new sign and those which have covered the same subject before. Part of our argument has been to show how the ideological initiative in the creation and development of this figure passed from side to side. In the West, Communism is necessarily a counter-culture which seeks to exploit what Vološinov has called the 'multi-accentuality' of ideological signs. Multi-accentuality was particularly apparent in the case of 'Eurocommunism' because of the way it developed the understanding of Communism available in the West. It disturbed the uni-accentual account of Communism established in the dominant ideology. Not only was there the suggestion that there might be 'good Communists' who accepted democratic values, but, more fundamentally, it allowed that there might be a different type of Communism, different in the crucial respect that it fell outside the boundaries of totalitarianism theory. The conclusion of that theory has been that all democracy's enemies are fundamentally the same.[9]

It is interesting to recall that until recently all forms of socialism, including social democracy, appeared on the other side of the divide. In his celebrated work, *Capitalism, Socialism and Democracy*, Joseph Schumpeter discusses the relationships between socialism and democracy in sceptical terms closely akin to those cited earlier. For example, Schumpeter argues that there is nothing essential to socialism which makes it democratic, and 'the only question is whether and in what sense it *can* be democratic'. While denying that he is accusing the classical German and Austrian social democrats of the Second International of Machiavellianism or insincerity, Schumpeter does lay emphasis on the opportunism he detects:

> They lived in environments that would have strongly resented undemocratic talk and practice . . . In some cases they had every reason to espouse democratic principles that sheltered them and their activity. In other cases most of them were satisfied with the results, political and other, that advance on democratic lines promised to yield . . . Thus in professing allegiance to democracy, they simply did the obvious thing all along (Schumpeter, 1970, pp. 238–9).

The question of whether all forms of socialism are inherently anti-democratic is still a live issue. It has been taken up recently by many of the ideologues involved in the crusade against Eurocommunism. In 1978 *Commentary* devoted its August issue to a symposium of 26 replies to the question of whether there was an 'inescapable connection between capitalism and democracy'? The preamble suggested that many intellectuals now accepted as plausible what they had once rejected as wrong and politically dangerous, that there 'may be something intrinsic to socialism which exposes it ineluctably to the "totalitarian temptation"'. As well as this implicit reference to Revel,

Commentary referred explicitly to the 'new philosophers' in
France and 'Paul Johnson and others' in England as examples of
those holding such ideas in Europe. It is safe to assume that
among the 'others' in England was Stephen Haseler, who in 1977
had contributed a piece to *Commentary* on 'The Collapse of the
Social Democrats' in which he had cited Revel, the *nouveaux
philosophes* and Johnson as signs of hope that some had already
warned against the slide of social democracy into socialism.

At this point the ideological battle shifts from totalitarian
theory's critique of Communism to an effort to develop a
particular conception of 'social democracy' as the only possible
form of democratic socialism and thereby to monopolise
ideological space. This brings us back to 'Eurocommunism', for in
another spin-off from his book Haseler argued that 'differences
of style and intellectual vitality (apart), the British Labour left is
a branch of the "Eurocommunist" movement of Western
Europe. It certainly has more in common with 'Eurocommunism'
than with Northern European parties of social democracy' (*The
Times*, 27 October 1978). The danger which follows, according to
Haseler in this article, is the break-up of the Atlantic alliance and
the unity of NATO. But if Haseler, Secretary of the Social
Democratic Alliance, a ginger group on the Labour Party's right
wing, is content with a single condemnatory point on defence
policy, Paul Johnson, ex-editor of the *New Statesman* and
currently contributor to the *Sunday Telegraph* and the *Evening
Standard*, fights the battle on a wider front. In a piece in the
Standard (5 December 1978) he welcomed the publication of a
new volume of right-wing essays, *Confrontation: Will the Open
Society Survive until 1989?*, which poses the choice between
collectivism and individual freedom. Johnson applauds the
growth of a new dynamic orthodoxy on the right. This includes
the *nouveaux philosophes*, 'Fritz' Hayek, author of *The Road to
Serfdom*, one of the early texts of totalitarian theory and
favourite reading of Margaret Thatcher and, on America's east
coast, *Commentary*. In the gathering gloom of their own
predictions, this group of ideologues are not only whistling to
keep up their spirits but passing the music round as well.

Returning to the case of 'Eurocommunism', the recognition of
a distinctive new type of Communism ran counter to the
fundamentally essentialist notion that Communism is one,
indivisible and identifiable as the enemy. The problems this

created were particularly apparent the more discussion of 'Eurocommunism' moved out of elite circles into popular consumption. This brings us to our third concluding point, the light the 'Eurocommunist' case throws on the division of labour which exists between ideological elites in the West.

Problems with public opinion already lay behind *détente*. According to Kissinger's own account, ideological adjustments were necessary to reassure Western publics confused by events in Czechoslovakia, Vietnam, Chile and elsewhere. The problem since has been how to achieve this ideological realignment without abandoning confrontation. One initial attraction of 'Eurocommunism' may have been its anti-Soviet potential. Certainly this was what first impressed the Communist ideologues who attacked it as an anti-Soviet construct. But within the context of the West, its value was much more ambiguous, a new form of Communism linked to symbols like Dubcek, of the human face, and Allende, of the democratic road, which had already proved troublesome. It meant that in the West anti-Communists were all the time fighting off the back foot, seeking to show that what they had identified as different was in fact similar, that 'Eurocommunists' were not to be trusted.

In summary, we may conclude that 'Eurocommunism' had four values as a figure in the Western system. Its first was to signal an old danger in a new form. Its second, the foreign policy potential, suggested further disorder in the enemy's ranks with the added attraction that it might provoke dissent in Eastern Europe. A third was the economic potential. If PCI participation in Italian government should prove necessary to help capitalism in that country overcome the crisis, then it was as well that it should be clear that it was not just any old Communism but something new, distinct and technocratically flavoured.

The fourth advantage developed in use, from the experience of fighting off the ideological back foot. As a compendious term 'Eurocommunism' made possible a form of argument by contra-example. Any 'good' phenomenon in one country could be countered by evidence of 'bad' practice in another with the suggestion, implicit or explicit, that only the 'bad' was real. The technique reached its apotheosis in Kissinger's broadcast, when he included a section on the Portuguese party, a party which may be 'European' but which no one hitherto had had the nerve to suggest was 'Euro'. The foreign policy value lost credibility when the Carter administration changed its assessment in January 1978. The economic value was always better served by isolating the Italians for special treatment rather than some more general group of Europeans. 'Eurocommunism' is unlikely to survive simply as a convenient compendium. That is essentially a method of defence rather than attack and there is no reason to suppose that spokesmen for the dominant culture will make a virtue of a defensive posture.

As for the CPs, our argument is that 'Eurocommunism' has been used more to appropriate an ideological initiative than as a term of Marxist analysis. Just as the term has 'run away' from its original creators, so it has 'run away' from its appropriators in the CP leaderships. In spite of the care they have taken to distance themselves from the concept, such leaders are commonly identified as 'Eurocommunist' in discussions on the left, where the term has acquired as much currency as in bourgeois political discussion. A full analysis of this process will be the task of our next paper.

Notes

1. This is a revised and extended version of a paper first published in the *Sociological Review*, vol. 27, no. 1 (February 1979) under the title 'On the Stratification of Political Knowledge: Studying "Eurocommunism", an Unfolding Ideology'. We are grateful to the editors of the *Review* for permission to reprint it here.

2. These claims are also set out in the definitive book by Wolfgang Leonhard, *Eurokommunismus: Herausforderung für Ost und West* (1978, p. 9). This account, which became available to use only after the first version of this paper had been written, bases its assessment largely on the same sources as ours. While Barbieri's claim is taken most seriously, Leonhard does not consider the origins of the term, or its ideological ramifications, to be of especial importance, since his main interest is in exploring the practical, political consequences for the left of the recent developments.

3. In recent history 'white' has been associated generally with royalist, legitimist and conservative causes, such as the monarchists of France, Spain and Russia. 'Neo' appears to be a more neutral prefix, but in an Italian context there is a particular connection, this time with the contemporary usage of 'neo-Fascist' for parties which are reincarnations of a movement once defeated. 'Euro', however, says something about international co-operation, international capitalism, technocracy and development. It is hard to resist the conclusion that all were fundamentally unsatisfactory to serve as an ideological figure to encapsulate opposition to the growth of the Communist parties in the West, since any such specific designation allowed the possibility that Communism might take *different forms*. This runs counter to the established anti-Communist

position, founded on totalitarianism theory, and popularised through the Cold War, which takes an essentialist view of Communism as one and indivisible.
Cf. Clifford Geertz's analysis of another unsatisfactory ideological figure: 'slave labour law' as applied to the Taft-Hartley Act (Geertz, 1975).
4. An apparently favourable assessment of the PCI after the June 1976 elections is available from Euroeconomics, a research combine of major Western banks for FF500, providing its contents are not made public.
5. *Commentary*, like *Encounter*, has been active in countering the threat of 'Eurocommunism', as is detailed below.
6. It is not just at the foreign policy elite level at which the war is waged. Aron and Revel occupy crucial roles in the important French political weekly *L'Express*. Aron is president of the editorial board and Revel the magazine's director. *L'Express* currently specialises in anti-Communist crusading. See Walter Schwartz, '£200,000 damages for Editor', *Guardian*, 23 February 1979.
7. The *Policy Review* was founded in 1977, and the very first article to appear in it concerned the 'spectre of Eurocommunism'. Its author, who is also a member of the editorial board, was Robert Moss, a British journalist who edits the *Economist*'s confidential *Foreign Report*. Moss is well known in Britain for his prominent role in the Institute for the Study of Conflict, a body which specialises in counter-insurgency literature (Schlesinger, 1978).
8. Sonnenfeldt has already given his name to the 'Brezhfeldt doctrine', associated with the previous American administration, that the spheres of influence of the USSR and the USA should remain stable. 'Brezhfeldt doctrine' is *Le Monde*'s term conflating the doctrines of Brezhnev with those of Helmut Sonnenfeldt as expressed at a meeting of American diplomats in London in December 1975.
9. Cf. the title of Annie Kriegel's polemic against 'Eurocommunism', *Un Autre Communisme?* Kriegel's answer is an unhesitating 'Non, çest la même chose!'

References

Amendola, G., interviewed by H. Weber, 1977. The Italian Road to Socialism. *New Left Review* (November–December), 39–50
Aron, R. 1977. *Plaidoyer pour l'europe décadente*. Paris: Editions Robert Laffont. Extracts translated as 'My Defence of Our Decadent Europe'. *Encounter* (September and October) 1977
Azcárate, M. 1977. Eurocommunism: a Reality, a Hope. *Mundo Obrero* (March), reprinted in *Euro-Red*, 4, 4–5
Balibar, E. 1977. *On the Dictatorship of the Proletariat*. London: New Left Books
Berlinguer, E. 1976. For New Roads towards Socialism in Italy and Europe. *The Italian Communists*, 2/3
Bettiza, Enzo 1978. Great Illusions in the Face of Danger. *Encounter* (January), 21–3
Carli, G. 1976. Italy's Malaise. *Foreign Affairs* (July), 708–18
Carrillo, S. 1977. *'Eurocommunism' and the State*. London: Lawrence and Wishart
Chirac, J. 1978. France: Illusions, Temptations, Ambitions. *Foreign Affairs* (April), **56**, 3, 489–99
Claudín, F. 1978. *Eurocommunism and Socialism*. London: New Left Books (Spanish original published 1977)
Cornforth, M. 1977. *The Open Philosophy and the Open Society*. London: Lawrence and Wishart, rev. edn.
Dalma, A. *et al*. 1977. *Euro-Kommunismus*. Zurich: Edition Interfrom A.G., 7

Devlin, K. 1977. The Challenge of Eurocommunism. *Problems of Communism*, **XXVI** (Jan–Feb.), 1977

Domhoff, G. William. 1969. Who Made American Foreign Policy, 1945–1963? In D. Horowitz (ed.), *Corporations and the Cold War*. New York: Monthly Review Press

Earle, J. 1976. The Italian Economy: a Diagnosis. *The World Today*, **32**, 6 (June) 214–21

Elliott, P. and Schlesinger, P. 1979. Some Aspects of Communism as a Cultural Category. *Media, Culture and Society*, **1**, 2 (April)

Fabre, J. Hincker, F. and Sève, L. 1977. *Les Communistes et L'Etat*. Paris: Editions Sociales

Gati, C. 1977. The 'Europeanization' of Communism. *Foreign Affairs*, **55**, 3 (April)

Geertz, C. 1975. Ideology as a Cultural System. In *The Interpretation of Cultures*. London: Hutchinson

Goldsborough, J.O. 1977. Eurocommunism after Madrid. *Foreign Affairs*, **55** (July)

Haseler, S. 1977. Europe: the Collapse of the Social Democrats. *Commentary*, **64**, 6

Haseler, S. and Godson, R. 1978. *Euro Communism: Implications for East and West*. London: Macmillan. Copyright, National Strategy Information Centre Inc.

Hayek, F. 1944. *The Road to Serfdom*. London: Routledge and Kegan Paul

Institute of Economic Research. 1978. *Confrontation: Will the Open Society Survive until 1989?* Hobart

Kanapa, J. 1976a. A 'New Policy' of the French Communists? *Foreign Affairs*, **55**, 2 (January)

Kanapa, J. 1976b. Les caractéristiques de l'eurocommunisme. *Recherches Internationales à la lumière du marxisme*, no. 88–9 (L'eurocommunisme) Vol. 3–4 (published in 1978)

Kissinger, H. A. 1977a. Communist Parties in West Europe: Challenge to the West. *Atlantic City Quarterly*, **15**, 3 (Autumn)

Kissinger, H. A. 1977b. Eurocommunism – Kissinger's Warning. *Across the Board*, **14**, Part 4 (September)

Kolakowski, L. 1977. The Euro-Communist Schism. *Encounter*, **XLIX**, 2 (August)

Kolakowski, L. 1978. *Main Currents in Marxism*. Oxford: Clarendon Press, 3 volumes

Kriegel, A. 1977. *Un autre communisme*? Paris, Hachette:

La Malfa, U. 1978. Communism and Democracy in Italy. *Foreign Affairs*, **56**, 3 (April)

Lange, P. 1976. What is to be Done – about Italian Communism? *Foreign Policy*, **62**, Part 2 (August)

Laqueur, W. 1976. Eurocommunism and its Friends. *Commentary* (August)

Laqueur, W. 1978. The Eurocommunist Debate (editorial statement). *The Washington Review of Strategic and International Studies*, **1**, 2 (April)

Ledeen, M. 1977. The 'News' about Eurocommunism. *Commentary* (October)

Leonhard, W. 1978. *Eurokommunismus: Herausforderung für Ost und West*. Munich: C. Bertelsmann

Levi, A. 1977a. Eurocommunism, the Italian experience So Far. *Across the Board* (July)

Levi, A. 1977b. Italy's 'New' Communism. *Foreign Policy* (Spring)

Lieber, R.J. 1977. The Pendulum Swings to Europe. *Foreign Policy*, 26 (Spring)

Löwenthal, R. 1977. Can Communism Offer an Alternative World Order? Some Lessons of 20th Century Politics. *Encounter*, **XLVIII**, 7 (April)

McInnes, N. 1975. *The Communist Parties of Western Europe*. Oxford University Press: London
McInnes, N. 1976. *Eurocommunism*. The Washington Papers, no. 37. London: Sage
Marchetti, X. 1978. The French Left and March Elections. *The Washington Review of Strategic and International studies*, **1**, 1 (January)
Moss, R. 1977. The Spectre of Eurocommunism. *Policy Review*, **1**, 1 (Summer)
Moynihan, D. 1978. The American Political Elite: a Conversation with Michael A. Ledeen. *The Washington Review of Strategic and International Studies*, **1**, 1 (January)
Napolitano, G. 1978. The Italian Crisis: a Communist Perspective. *Foreign Affairs*, **56**, 4 (July), 790–9
Napolitano, G. Hobsbawm, E. 1977. *The Italian Road to Socialism*. Nottingham: Journeyman
Nichols, P. 1976. On the Italian Crisis. *Foreign Affairs*, **54**
Owen, D. 1978. Communism, Socialism and Democracy. *The Washington Review of Strategic and International Studies*, **1**, 2 (April)
Popov, M. 1976. 'Eurocommunism' and the pan-European Conference. *The World Today*, **32**, 10 (October)
Radice, L. Lombardo 1978. Un Socialismo da inventare. *Critica Marxista*, 4 (July–August)
Revel, J.-F. 1976. *Le Tentation Totalitaire*. Paris: Laffont
Revel, J.-F. 1978. The Myths of Eurocommunism. *Foreign Affairs*, **56**, 2
Romeo, R. 1978. 'Rome 1984?' A Conversation with G. Urban. *The Washington Review of Strategic and International Studies*, **1**, 1 (January)
Sassoon, D. (ed.). 1978. *The Italian Communists Speak for Themselves*. Nottingham: Spokesman Books.
Schlesinger, P. 1978. On the Shape and Scope of Counter-Insurgency Thought. G. Littlejohn *et al*. (eds.), *Power and the State*. London: Croom Helm
Schumpeter, J. A. 1970. *Capitalism, Socialism and Democracy*. London: Unwin University Books.
Segre, S. 1976. The 'Communist Question' in Italy. *Foreign Affairs*, **54**, 4 (July)
Silberman, L. 1977. Yugoslavia's 'Old' Communism. *Foreign Policy* (Spring)
Sonnenfeldt, H. 1978. 'The Sonnenfeldt Doctrine revisited'. A Conversation with Michael A. Ledeen. *The Washington Review of Strategic and International Studies*, **1**, 2 (April)
Stehle, H. 1977. The Italian Experiment and the Communists. *The World Today*, **33**, 7–16
Stehle, H. 1978. The Italian Communists on the Parliamentary Road to Power. *The World Today*, **34**, 5, 135–83
Steinkühler, M. (ed.). 1977a. *Eurokommunismus im Widerspruch: Analyse und Dokumentation*. Cologne: Verlag Wissenschaft und Politik
Steinkühler, M. 1977b. Ursprung und Konzept des Eurokommunismus; Gespräch mit Frane Barbieri. *Deutschland-Archiv*, Part 4 (April 1977)
Tiersky, R. 1974. *French Communism, 1920–1972*. London: Columbia University Press
Tiersky, R. 1976. French Communism in 1976. *Problems of Communism*, **25**, 1 (January–February)
Timmermann, H. 1977. Eurocommunism: Moscow's Reaction and the Implications for Eastern Europe. *The World Today*, **33**, 10 (October)
Urban, G. 1977. Communism with an Italian Face? A Conversation with Lucio Lombardo Radice. *Encounter*, **XLVIII**, 5 (May)
Urban, G. (ed.). 1978a. *Eurocommunism: its Roots and Future in Italy and Elsewhere*. London: Temple Smith

Urban G. 1978b. Have they Really Changed? A Conversation with Altiero Spinelli. Eurocommunism, Again. *Encounter*, **1**, 1 (January).

Vološinov, V.N. 1973. *Marxism and the Philosophy of Language*. London: Seminar Press

3 THE PCE IN SPANISH POLITICS

Eusebio Muhal-Leon

Little more than a year after participating in the first free Spanish parliamentary elections in over forty years, the Partido Comunista de España (PCE) stands at a crossroads. The most avowedly Eurocommunist party on the Continent, the PCE has so far been unable to translate into electoral success the influence it had exerted as the best organised opposition force in the country during Francisco Franco's last years and the attention gained from the often virulent quarrels it has had with the Soviet Union.

In the elections of June 1977, the Communist Party captured 9.2 per cent of the national ballots, or nearly 1.7 million votes, but the PCE still trailed far behind the Unión de Centro Democrático (UCD) led by incumbent Premier Adolfo Suárez and Partido Socialista Obrero Español (PSOE) – which garnered 34 and 29 per cent of the vote respectively. Although in one sense these results came as no surprise (various opinion polls released in the four or five months prior to the elections had forecast that the PCE would win between 8 and 12 per cent of the ballots), they nevertheless represented quite a setback to a party whose leaders had been predicting that any effort to reform the Francoist system would inevitably fail and whose militants had only the year before been exhorted to lay claim to 'a hegemonic role in the process of change'.[1] As it was, the showing of the Spanish Communists compared rather unfavourably with those of the French and Italian Communists in the immediate post-Second World War period and with the 15 per cent of the vote that their Portuguese counterparts had polled in April 1976.

New parliamentary elections are likely next year in Spain, and the PCE clearly recognises that improving on its performance of a year ago will be essential in these elections. Otherwise, the party will risk having the political/electoral boundaries on the left frozen and might find itself relegated to an essentially marginal position in the political system.

This chapter will explore some of the reasons for the Communist failure in June 1977 and the efforts undertaken by the PCE in the months after the elections to increase its influence in Spanish politics. The concluding section will assess the short and medium-term prospects for the party in the post-Franco era.

Operating illegally after the end of the Civil War in 1939, the PCE developed into the most effective component of the opposition to the Franco regime. Furthermore, in the years after 1956 and under the leadership of Secretary-General Santiago Carrillo, the Spanish Communists shifted policy in many areas. The PCE not only abandoned its traditional anticlericalism, but also, taking advantage of regime-sponsored syndical elections, built a political base around the unofficial, parallel trade union movement known as the Comisiones Obreras (CCOO). Rejecting the Soviet model for Spanish and other Western European societies, the Spanish Communists discarded the traditional Leninist notion that so-called bourgeois liberties were at best formal and indicated that they had come around to the view that political, civil and religious liberties were fundamental rights in any political system.[2] Particularly after the Warsaw Pact invasion of Czechoslovakia in August 1968, party leaders became increasingly vocal in their criticism of the Soviet Union and other Eastern bloc countries.

The success with which the PCE had managed to cope with the rigours of clandestinity and the party's moderate domestic and independent international policies seemed to suggest that the Communists would without great difficulty assume an important role in Spanish politics. But the results of the June 1977 elections indicated such an assessment to have been overdrawn.

There are any number of explanations which one can adduce to help account for the results. Some observers would underscore the fact that the PCE, illegal until less than two months before the election, could not in the space of a few weeks overcome the effects of forty years of hostile anti-Communist propaganda and the memories of its own at times ruthless tactics during the 1936–9 Civil War. Moreover, there was the nature of the electoral law under which the balloting took place, The Suárez government fashioned a law which quite clearly discriminated against the left. For one thing, specific provisions in the law made it less than directly proportional and thus worked to the advantage of the larger parties. The electoral law was discriminatory in other ways as well. For example, it over-represented the more conservative agricultural parts of the country. It also kept the voting age limit at 21 years (thus eliminating from the rolls some 2 million young people among whom the opposition had gained quite an audience) and placed numerous obstacles in the way of the more than half a million emigrant workers who theoretically could have participated in the elections. There was, in addition, the presence of an invigorated and youthful PSOE, which, although laying claim to the mantle of Marxism and class struggle, had neither a history of subservience to the Soviet Union nor a reputation for intolerance. The Communist decision to direct the brunt of criticism during the electoral campaign at the collection of Francoist notables in Alianza Popular (AP) and not at Suárez and the UCD may also have backfired. It permitted the PSOE to present itself as an intransigent opponent of Francoism, opposed not only to the Alianza but to the more seductive image offered by Suárez.

These explanations are correct as far as they go. They are insufficient, however, to the degree that they do not explicitly recognise that the poor Communist performance in June 1977 reflected above all the success of King Juan Carlos and Premier Adolfo Suárez in keeping the political initiative from the PCE in the years after Francisco Franco's death. The Communists could not galvanise the forces necessary to impose a *ruptura* between the Francoist past and the democratic future and were thus unable to capitalise on their political/organisational superiority. Adolfo Suárez accomplished the *reforma* within the framework, if not the spirit, of the laws and institutions bequeathed by Franco. He consummated the *ruptura* but at a pace which, because it was deliberate, permitted the emergence of the PSOE as a challenger to the Communists on the left.

The struggle for power in the post-Franco era really began nearly two years before the death of the caudillo with the assassination of Admiral Luis Carrero Blanco in December 1973. That brutally efficient act of political violence, attributed to a branch of the Basque terrorist organisation Euskadi ta Askatasuna (ETA), marked the death knell of the Franco regime.

While opposition organisations like the Communist Party had long been active in the struggle against the dictatorship, their predictions of its imminent downfall had become marked by an air of unreality. In the 1940s, the regime had defeated the opposition-sponsored guerrilla movement and had weathered the international isolation into which the defeat of the Axis powers in 1945 had thrust it. More recently, it had withstood the resurgence of powerful strike movements. In late 1973, it gave every indication of being able to assure its permanence.

Carrero Blanco's assassination changed all that. Not only was he the titular head of state and Franco's close confidant, but the ageing leader had charged him with ensuring the continuity of the system. His physical disappearance meant the elimination of a key piece from the political chessboard. The Spanish political elite understood as much, and on 12 February 1974 even Carrero Blanco's extremely conservative successor, Carlos Arias Navarro, promised the establishment of 'national political associations' and a general liberalisation of the political system. The speech aroused the hopes of many moderate opponents of the regime, but it did not take long for disillusionment to set in. Government efforts to exile the bishop of Bilbao for including a call for Basque civil rights in a homily, and the decision to execute anarchist Puig Antich in Barcelona came only a few weeks after Arias's speech and indicated that the new premier would have a difficult time shedding the habits and background he had acquired as Minister of the Interior.

A psychologically invigorated – albeit not terribly well organised – opposition faced the Arias government in early 1974. Most of these as yet fledgling groups could be said to belong to one or another of four families.

Among the socialists could be numbered the Felipe González-led PSOE, the Partido Socialista Popular (PSP), and a rapidly growing assortment of regional socialist groups. The PSOE had been the premier organisation on the Spanish left in the years preceding and during the Civil War. During the two decades following the end of that conflict, the PSOE endured the harsh repression unleashed by the regime, and by the early 1960s it had lost much of its influence among opponents of Franco. Under the exiled leadership of Rodolfo Llopis, the party increasingly lost touch with the changes taking place in Spain and proved progressively unable to rally the new generations of Spaniards to the PSOE banner. One manifestation of this loss of influence was the growth of a variety of groups, each hoping to become the occupant of historic socialism's space in the Spanish political spectrum. This was the case, for example, of the Partido Socialista del Interior (later to become the PSP), headed by a prestigious university professor, Enrique Tierno Galván. Other socialist groups developed, particularly in Cataluña, Galicia, the Basque country, Aragón and Andalucia, but these had a markedly regional cast. We should also note here the presence of the Unión Social Demócrata Española (USDE), led by Dionisio Ridruejo and Antonio Garcia López, which aimed at shifting the axis of Spanish socialism away from its Jacobin tradition and towards social democracy. At any rate, the PSOE languished under the asphyxiating control of the Llopis exiled leadership until its Twelfth congress in October 1972, at which time militants from the interior (most notably Pablo Catellanos, Felipe González and Enrique Múgica) captured control of the party. In 1973, the Socialist International gave its blessing to the younger leaders.[3] This decision was to have important longer-term consequences, for it ensured West German and Swedish moral, organisational and financial support for the PSOE.

Another opposition component was the various Christian democratic groups. Potentially the most important of these organisations were the Federación Popular Democrática (FPD) of José Maria Gil Robles and the Izquierda Democrática (ID) of Joaquín Ruiz Giménez. Regional Christian democratic movements existed to one degree or another in Cataluña, Galicia, Valencia and the Basque country, but it was only the pre-Civil War Partido Nacionalista Vasco (PNV) from the last region that had anything resembling a mass audience. Most of the Christian democratic groups were what the Spanish call 'grupos testimoniales', coalescing around individuals of great personal prestige but having little effective political organisation. Their political future lay (despite Ruiz Giménez's proclivities for alliance with the left) in the yet-to-be-established centre, but whether they would occupy that part of the political spectrum depended not only on how the transformation of the regime came about, but also on the decision of the Spanish episcopate to help actively in the organisation of a mass Christian democratic party.

So-called extreme left groups made up a third sector of the opposition.[4] These organisations had proliferated during the 1960s in reaction to what they perceived as the abandonment of revolutionary principles by the PCE. Some of the groups, like the Partido Comunista de España – Marxista Leninista (PCE-ML) and the Partido del Trabajo (PT), were avowedly Maoist and had split off from the PCE because and in the wake of the Sino-Soviet rift. By contrast, others, like the Organización Revolucionaria de Trabajadores (ORT) and Bandera Roja (BR), had had their origins in the radicalisation of the apostolic labour organisations in the early 1960s, but had eventually come to assume rigidly dogmatic Marxist-Leninist positions.

None of the various groups could match the strength of the PCE, the fourth component of the opposition. In 1974, the Spanish Communist Party was the only one of the organisations challenging the regime which, it may be said without great fear of contradiction, had a genuinely national audience, could be considered an authentic political party, and could present a real, if not altogether attractive, alternative to the regime.

Rebuffed over the years in its efforts to create a broad front against the Franco regime (the last call in 1969 for the conclusion of a *'pacto para la libertad'* had not found many supporters), the Spanish Communists redoubled their efforts to bring the opposition together in the months after Carrero Blanco's assassination. Encouraged further by the April 1974 revolution in Portugal, the PCE entered into contacts and negotiations with Don Juan de Borbón (the son of Spain's last monarch and father of Prince Juan Carlos) and with the PSOE, PSP, USDE and various Christian democratic organisations. These were all under way when news about a Franco illness broke in June 1974. The Communists, convinced that Franco would not physically last out the summer and that his regime would disintegrate rapidly after his death, insisted on the rapid creation of a unitary opposition front. Don Juan declined the offer, as did most of the other groups, including the PSOE. The socialists saw an undue haste in the project and felt, not unreasonably, that they were being asked to join in an endeavour which would help establish a Communist preponderance over the rest of the opposition.[5]

Sure that the other groups were making a historic error from which they were unlikely to recover, the Communists went ahead with their plans and in late July 1974, just as Franco left the hospital, announced the creation of a Junta Democrática. The Junta was an unlikely coalition. It included, besides the Communists and the Comisiones Obreras, groups like the PSP, the Partido Carlista (supporters of the pretender to the throne, Carlos Hugo de Borbón Parma, and advocates of autogestion or workers' self-management), the Alianza Socialista Andaluza, and independent personalities. All of them rallied around a 12-point programme (to which they were committed only until constituent assembly elections could be held) calling for the establishment of a provisional government, total amnesty, the legalisation of all political parties, syndical liberties, separation of Church and state, and eventual Spanish entry into the European Economic Community.[6]

Strictly speaking, the Junta did not represent much beyond the PCE. Yet, from a public relations point of view, it was an outstanding success. Impressive confirmation of this fact came with the revelation that in August 1974 Nicolás Franco, nephew of the Generalíssmo, had travelled to Paris for a meeting with Carrillo and other representatives of the Junta. It benefited, moreover, from the enormous psychological advantage of being the only functioning opposition front for nearly a year.

The Junta appeared on the Spanish political scene at a particularly fortuitous moment. One did not need to be an overly perceptive observer of Spanish politics to grasp that the country's political structures were slowly but surely losing their legitimacy. This is not the place to enter into an extended discussion of the reasons for the shift in public opinion. Suffice it to point out that there was a growing awareness among Spaniards of all classes that the *status quo* could not long endure.

Symptomatically, the changes taking place in Spanish society had begun to undermine even as staunch a pillar of the regime as the armed forces. After Carrero Blanco's assassination, it had become manifest in particular that a generational cleavage existed in the military between those officers who had fought in the Civil War and wanted the army to function as a partisan political instrument with the principal objective of ensuring the state's fidelity to the Francoist heritage, and other, younger officers who opposed such an orientation and wanted the professionalisation of the military. Some of the latter joined in the clandestine Union Militar Democrática (UMD). The UMD advocated the democratisation of the Spanish political system, but, in contrast to the Portuguese Movimento das Forças Armades (MFA), most of the officers involved in the movement believed the military should not play a major role in the process of change. The government arrested eight officers affiliated with the UMD in June 1975; however, exact figures on the organisation's strength were never revealed, and the extent of its influence can only be surmised. Luckily for the regime, the Spanish army was not involved in any disastrous colonial venture, and when hard-line officers called for intervention in the Spanish Sahara in October 1975, the government decisively rejected that alternative.[7]

Hardly an issue of the PCE's bi-weekly *Mundo Obrero* went by in 1974 and 1975 that did not cite some new evidence of discontent within the regime or indicate that the end of Francoism was in sight. In retrospect, however, Communist assertions that the '*huelga nacional*' would take place under the direction of the Junta, that the Junta alone could unleash a strike movement powerful enough to neutralise the army and the 50,000-man Guardia Civil, appear to have been far off the mark. In fact, a trial-run '*acción democrática nacional*' called by the Junta in June 1975 had little success. The Communists not only overestimated their own strength and that of the opposition in general but also undervalued that of the regime.

With the wisdom of hindsight, we can see that the Junta did not bring together a sufficiently broad spectrum of the opposition to force a radicalisation of the pre-revolutionary situation developing in the country after December 1973. A judgement as to whether responsibility for this fact should be assigned to the Communists for their obstinacy in insisting on a Junta including individuals and organisations to which the PSOE objected, or to the socialists for making these objections, depends in large measure on one's ideological perspectives and political preferences.

To focus exclusively on the disunity of the opposition as the factor responsible for the failure of efforts to bring Franco down would be incorrect, however. The other side of the coin was that few of the groups which had been economically or politically favoured since 1939 were willing to break with the regime. Discontent was one thing; active opposition, quite another. Many incipient oppositionists still held out the hope that upon his accession to the throne Juan Carlos would move to force a real liberalisation of the regime and thus pave the way for its economic and political integration into Western Europe. They had been deeply disturbed by the radicalisation of the Portuguese revolution, and while they understood the need for reform of the system, they also feared what would happen were the situation to get out of hand in Spain. The great majority of the population, moreover, still suffered from the depoliticisation and demobilisation encouraged by the authoritarian Francoist regime, and the experience of the Civil War, although a vanishing memory, still lingered in the popular consciousness, inhibiting political activity.

The PCE, in any case, was not as finely honed a political weapon as its leaders might have supposed or let on. The party's organisational strength was impressive if measured relative to that of other groups, but the PCE was not exempt from problems. This was particularly true in Madrid, where the party organisation received severe criticism from Carrillo for its political work and where in 1974 the party had suffered a heavy blow with the arrest of Executive Committee member Francisco Romero Marín. His arrest brought with it the confiscation of an important part of the propaganda apparatus and forced the restructuring of the entire organisation. This was a difficult enough thing to do without having to prepare at the same time for an assault on the citadels of power.

Furthermore, there were important sectors of the party (not just *gauchiste* intellectuals but working-class activists) who were not enthusiastic about the idea of a *pacto para la libertad* in so far as it meant setting up an alliance, however temporary, with the representatives of 'monopoly capital'. Leftist dissidents in Madrid and Valencia had sought to draw these discontented elements from the party by forming an organisation called the Oposición de Izquierda al Partido Comunista (OPI).[8]

In the labour sphere, too, the party had its share of problems. Through its influence in the Comisiones Obreras, the PCE had developed into the preponderant force in the Spanish labour movement, but while the CCOO had originally benefited from an ambiguous juridical status, by the late 1960s and early 1970s the regime had begun to crack down harshly on labour dissidence. One particularly successful raid in June 1972 netted Marcelino Camacho, Nicolás Sartorius, Francisco Garcia Salve and other top leaders of the movement during a meeting of the Coordinador General and effectively decapitated the Comisiones. Control of the national movement had to pass to the Catalan branch, whose leader Cipriano Garcia had not been at the ill-fated session.

While Franco lived, the struggle between the various groups and factions in the opposition and the establishment, it turned out, was largely limited to one for position. Only when Franco died in November 1975, after a prolonged agony lasting well over a month and involving no fewer than half a dozen major operations, did the battle for control of the tempo and substance of change in the political system truly get under way.

Some had feared and others had hoped that his death would open the floodgates, but it appears that the lengthiness of the wait helped make the moment of his passing anticlimactic and probably contributed to a smooth transmission of power to Prince Juan Carlos.

The first government of the monarchy assumed office in December 1975. Those who had wished for a rather clear break with the past were disappointed. Unsure of where real power lay within the regime and unwilling to test the extent of the powers Franco had delegated to him, Juan Carlos kept on the incumbent premier, Carlos Arias Navarro, a man of deep conservative instincts. The Cabinet, on the other hand, included a group of reformers, the most important of whom, José María Areilza and Manuel Fraga Iribarne, were appointed to the Ministry of Foreign Affairs and the Ministry of the Interior respectively.

While Fraga and Areilza held strategically and symbolically important Ministries, the government as a whole was only slightly more 'liberal' than traditional Francoist governments. Moreover, the term of the first government of the monarchy was characterised by a struggle between reformers and their opponents. Conservatives, drawing support from ultras entrenched in the Cortes, in the state bureaucracy and in the highest ranks of the military, successfully weakened reform measures and in general managed to obstruct and delay. Arias sought to convey the impression that he stood above the fray, but, in fact, the bunker, as Santiago Carrillo and others on the left pointedly called the most conservative elements,[9] knew very well that the premier was their ally.

Although the Communists remained convinced that all efforts to reform the political structures of the regime would fail, the entry of the 'reformist' wing into the government in December 1975 visibly complicated the situation for the PCE. The Communists feared that other groups in the opposition, particularly the PSOE, would betray them and accept preferential treatment, perhaps even legalisation, from the government. These circumstances made it imperative, from the Communist point of view, that a showdown with the regime come as quickly as possible.

Originally, the PCE had envisioned the formation of a united opposition front that would be able to go on the offensive immediately after Franco's death. Soon after the constitution of a rival Plataforma de Convergencia by the PSOE and others in June 1975, the Junta had entered into conversations with those groups with a view to bringing about the rapid unification of the two organisations. The talks, although spurred by the proclamation in August 1975 of a decree law suspending habeas corpus for two years and the subsequent execution of several terrorists in September, did not progress as the PCE wished, and the opposition faced the first government of the monarchy still divided.[10]

With a united opposition front impossible for the short term, the PCE opted to shift its emphasis to mass mobilisation. Such an approach would not only serve to channel growing popular discontent with the deteriorating economic situation (over 20 per cent inflation and rising unemployment) against the regime but also, by helping to destabilise the political situation, might prevent any *rapprochement* between the government and the moderate opposition. The 'jornadas de lucha' began in December 1975 with the Communists instructing their militants and sympathisers in the Comisiones Obreras and neighbourhood and housewife associations to organise protests against the suspension of collective bargaining and the wage freezes imposed by the government.

The movement was launched where the party was strongest, among transport, metallurgical and construction workers, and in the industrial belts around Madrid and Barcelona, but it soon spread. At its apogee in January and February 1976, it involved more than 300,000 workers in Madrid alone and virtually paralysed both the capital and Barcelona.[11] In the former, the government had to order the militarisation of the Metro and mail services; in the latter, the militarisation of municipal employees.

The success of these strikes and the tragic deaths of five demonstrators during a peaceful march in favour of amnesty in the city of Vitoria impelled the opposition towards a general agreement. By early April 1976, the PCE could at last see the fruit of its long-standing efforts: representatives of the Junta and Plataforma held a press conference at a prominent Madrid hotel and announced the fusion of the two organisations and the formation of Coordinación Democrática.

It was a pyrrhic victory. Although Coordinación brought together a multiplicity of opposition currents, the very extension of the coalition (which now included organisations ranging from Maoist groups like the ORT to liberal and Christian Democratic groups) made concerted action difficult, The PCE could and did congratulate itself about outbidding the government for the temporary allegiance of moderate groups, but in order for Coordinación to become a reality, the Communists had had to abandon some of their most cherished notions. The new coalition's declaration of principles issued no call for a provisional government and made no reference to Juan Carlos or the monarchy.[12] Moreover, despite the relative success of the Jornadas, few groups in the opposition saw mass mobilisation as the way to change the political system.

The constitution of Coordinación and its acceptance of the need for a *ruptura pactada* (agreement for a break) in effect meant the defeat of the mass mobilisation tactics supported by the Communists and the extreme left and the victory of those groups which argued that the opposition should eschew confrontation. Ruiz Giménez's Izquierda Democrática had defended the latter position with particular vehemence, and ID had conditioned its entry into Coordinación on prior agreement that there would be no call for a provisional government and that the other elements in the opposition would consider the holding of free elections to be the equivalent of a *ruptura*.[13]

The governmental policy of selective toleration so evident in the authorisation of meetings of the Christian Democratic Equipo in January 1976 and of congresses like those of the PSP, the PSOE-affiliated trade union movement known as the Unión

General de Trabajadores, and the Federación de Partidos Socialistas in May and June, and in the prohibition of events like the provincial and regional assemblies of the Comisiones Obreras and of organisations affiliated with the PCE increased the friction between the Communists and the moderate opposition groups. Yet, the government headed by Arias Navarro proved incapable of taking advantage of these divisions. Indeed it was either unable or unwilling to crack the whip at a surprisingly defiant Cortes that was threatening to emasculate what were already little more than cosmetic government-proposed revisions of the penal code and political associations law. Juan Carlos voiced his disappointment with the premier's performance (he called Arias an 'unmitigated disaster') in the course of an interview he granted a *Newsweek* correspondent in late April.[14] The debility of the Arias government threatened to imperil the future of the monarchy itself, and shortly after the King returned from an official visit to the United States he finally acted, asking for and receiving the resignation of the premier.

If Juan Carlos had held back in replacing Arias, it was primarily because he was unsure who his new premier would be. The appointment of a new premier was no simple matter, for, among the procedural obstacles Franco had placed in his successor's way, the most important was that the Council of the Realm had the power to select a *terna* of three candidates from which the King could choose. From the *terna* presented to him in July 1976, Juan Carlos selected Adolfo Suárez, a relatively young man who had previously been Secretary-General of the only legal party, Movimiento Nacional, under Arias.

Few people in Spain in July 1976 believed that this decision was a good one. The Communist economist Ramon Tamames called the appointment 'a historic error', and *Mundo Obrero* dismissed Suárez's first nation-wide telecast as purely verbal reformism.[15] They were not alone. Only the more conservative elements applauded the choice, and then primarily because Suárez had made his career as an *apparatchik* in the Falange and seemed a fairly conservative sort.

That Suárez would last out the summer, much less that he would preside over a historically almost unprecedented transition from authoritarianism to democracy, was a thought that entered few minds. And yet the new premier, young enough to have a political future still before him and not lacking opportunism, did just that. He understood that decisive action by the government was necessary to break the false unity of the opposition and impose the 'reformist' solution. Indeed, in retrospect, there appears to have been little that separated the Suárez reform plan from that of someone like Fraga, except that the new premier grasped the importance of style. As some wits put it in explaining the difference between Arias and his successor, the former did not bother to listen, while Suárez listened and then went his own way.

Suárez faced an opposition which at first glance appeared more united than ever. Indeed, in October 1976, a new opposition coalition named the Plataforma de Organizaciones Democráticas (POD) would appear on the political scene. However, beneath the surface tranquillity, the opposition was, in fact, deeply split. Although the more moderate groups like the Christian democrats, the PSP and the liberals saw the political reform programme which Suárez offered as insufficient in many aspects, they thought it offered a solid basis for negotiations, particularly with respect to certain aspects of the electoral law.[16]

By contrast, the Communists (and others to their left) bluntly rejected the *reforma*.[17] The PCE Executive Committee in a September 1976 statement called it a 'fraud' and 'undemocratic'.[18] As a pre-condition for any discussion about the electoral process, the Communists demanded the prior legalisation of all political parties and the neutralisation of the state apparatus.

Publicly, then, the PCE remained committed to a *ruptura*, but one wonders how much of the intransigence was simply posturing with a view to strengthening the party's hand in an eventual negotiation or to ensuring its legalisation at or about the same time as other opposition groups. In any case, the PCE could hardly keep repeating that things had not changed. They had, and substantially so. There was a *de facto* toleration of the party which could not have been imagined a year before. The unofficial headquarters of the PCE had been installed in downtown Madrid, less than a half mile from the Dirección General de Seguridad where Central Committee member Julian Grimau had been tortured in 1964.

It should not surprise us that the rather rapid changes Spanish society experienced in the year after Franco's death had an impact on the PCE as well. After all, those changes were taking place along lines that were quite different from those that the Spanish Communist leadership had predicted. A close reading of Communist documents from that period suggests the existence of a strong internal debate on the political implications of the controlled decompression initiated by the King and Adolfo Suárez. Although the materials for an exhaustive analysis of trends within the party and the unravelling of the political and personal elements that helped create them are not available, it may be useful to focus on the different perceptions which manifested themselves in connection with the nationality question and the labour movement.

The PCE had traditionally presented itself as the most vigorous proponent of autonomy and self-determination for the various regions, declaring its advocacy of federalism but calling for referenda in Cataluña, Galicia and the Basque country to determine whether the local populations wanted outright independence or some form of association with the Spanish state.[19] There was little disagreement within the party as to these general propositions, but difficulties arose when one sector of the party (some Basques and representatives of the Valencia branch of the PCE, among others) demanded that in the program for the *ruptura* the leadership include a demand for self-government for all regions, not simply those mentioned above, and for the establishment of regional provisional governments the moment the left consummated the *ruptura* at the national level.[20] This policy, in many ways consistent with traditional party demands, seemed dangerously utopian to a rival faction, whose public voice was Executive Committee member Pilar Brabo, and who argued against *rupturas parciales*.[21] The call for regional governments in the short term, Brabo declared, would only serve to obstruct the drive for a national *ruptura* and would lend a certain credence to the views of those who said the Communists advocated the dismemberment of the national state. The PCE already had its hands full dealing with those like Catalan politicians Josep Pallach and Josep Tarradellas, who advocated separate negotiations with Suárez, and did not need a similar problem in every region.

Comparable differences between maximalist and minimalist opinions developed in the labour movement, based on factory assemblies, whose militants took advantage of regime-sponsored syndical elections to infiltrate the official Organización Sindical (OS).[22] The mixture of legal and illegal work had helped the movement deal with the rigours of repression. By the latter part of the 1960s, it had become the principal labour organisation in the country. Its success appeared to suggest that it would one day simply take over the OS. So long as other groups in the labour movement were organisationally weak, the CCOO could eschew traditional labour union structures, with their bureaucracies and membership rolls, and maintain the fiction that as a *movimiento socio-político* it was a trade union of a new type, composed of all the workers in a factory and independent of all political parties. Basing himself on this notion, Marcelino Camacho in the winter of 1975 called for a constituent workers' congress and offered Comisiones as the vehicle within which other trade unions, like the UGT, could participate.[23] By the summer, the rapid growth of the other labour organisations led to a reassessment of that strategy on the part of the Communist leadership and instructions to Communist militants in the labour movement to push for the transformation of Comisiones. Proposals along these lines were submitted and approved at the July 1976 General Assembly of the CCOO, but the move, despite its inevitability, caused consternation among some in the party who continued to talk about the need and possibility for a *ruptura* at both the political and syndical levels.

By the time the government held its long-awaited referendum on the political reform programme in December 1976, the PCE had abandoned all hope it might be able to impose a *ruptura*. While the party urged a negative vote in the referendum, this was more or less *pro forma*. The Executive Committee had already issued several statements indicating that the PCE had dropped its long list of demands and would participate 'in a positive way' in the political process if there were political liberties.

The focus of Spanish Communist efforts now shifted to bringing about legal recognition of the PCE's presence in the country. Before its legalisation on 10 April, the party had to withstand several acts of violence perpetrated by the extreme right: the most cold-blooded was the murder of five people, including four Communist lawyers, at their offices in late January 1977. This assassination came on the evening of the day an extreme leftist commando kidnapped the head of the Supreme Military

Tribunal, but the crisis only served to draw opposition and government together. Thus, a potentially disastrous military intervention did not materialise.

Less than a week after the PCE's legalisation, the party's Central Committee met for the first time in 39 years in the Spanish capital. With only Dolores Ibárruri absent (she was still in Moscow but would return a short while later), the ranking leaders of Spanish Communism met to prepare the strategy for the forthcoming parliamentary elections. Santiago Carrillo's report to the session emphasised the need for the PCE to follow a moderate course so as not to provoke political destabilisation. He called for the establishment of a *pacto constitucional* among all the parties of the centre and left and repeated the party's oft-stated position that the new Cortes should draft a new constitution to replace the Leyes Fundamentales and then be dissolved.[24]

The same Central Committee session approved the party's electoral programme: This called for the constitution to make specific references to the legalisation of all parties, to establish the supremacy of Parliament over other branches of government, to set the vote at 18, to grant autonomy for nationalities and regions, and to enshrine the principle of Church-state separation. In its economic aspects, the document called for fiscal amnesty and reform, the extension of unemployment insurance to those without jobs in the agricultural sector (a particularly serious problem in Extremadura and Andalucía), greater state participation in the social security system, and the creation of a *consejo económico y social* to function as the national planning board. The party did not advocate any major nationalisations, and on the whole its short-term economic programme was remarkably similar to that of the UCD.

Perhaps the most polemical aspects of the plenum were the decisions it took to shift the party's historical allegiance from the tricolour Republican flag to the traditional bicolour one associated with the monarchy and re-imposed by Franco after 1939, and to drop its insistence on a republican form of government. These decisions caused some commotion in sectors of the party, and at the plenum 11 members of the Central Committee showed their opposition by abstaining.[25]

The campaign officially began three weeks before election day, but for the Communists, keenly aware that most polls gave the party a rather low percentage, it started immediately after the Central Committee meeting. The party's primordial objective was to minimise the electoral support for Alianza Popular. Fraga and his associates there became a favorite target of Communist orators, who dubbed the group the *alianza impopular*, and, in fact, the only real flashes in an otherwise restrained campaign came when the two arch-rivals crossed verbal swords. At the same time, the Communists also directed much criticism at the PSOE. The PCE held several things against Felipe González and his party, but perhaps the most important was that the PSOE, through a combination of skill and luck, seemed likely to reap many of the fruits of what the PCE considered to be its unique contributions to the democratisation process. Sparring for hegemony on the left, each one accused the other of invading its political space. Indeed, the critical remarks the Communists made about Felipe González on numerous occasions contrasted with their generally neutral or sometimes even favourable comments about Suárez.

The Spanish Communists emerged from the June 1977 elections in a clear minority position: they had only 20 seats in the Chamber of Deputies as compared with the 165 of the UCD and 118 of the PSOE. When the UCD and PSOE came to agreement on a specific issue, as they did on several occasions in the first few weeks of the new Cortes's term, no one could stop them.

PCE leaders attributed the results of the election primarily to the lingering effects of forty years of anti-Communist propaganda, and Communist analyses in general sought to minimise the defeat suffered by the party. They instead emphasised that the results clearly favoured those forces interested in building democracy in Spain and had gone against Alianza Popular and other, more overtly Francoist groups like the Frente Nacional, which yearned for a return to the past.

In keeping with the theme of consolidating democracy, the thrust of Spanish Communist efforts after 15 June was to encourage the creation of a *gobierno de concentración nacional* with the participation of the UCD, Catalan and Basque minority groups, and parties to their left, including possibly the Communists. All would come to terms on a constitutional pact and an economic recuperation programme to last four or five years.[26] The Communists insisted again and again during the summer and autumn of 1977 that only such a government could rally the popular support necessary to stop those interested in destabilising Spanish democracy, but behind their warning about the dangers of polarisation — Marcelino Camacho cautioned about the possible rise of a Pinochet as in Chile, and Carrillo railed against those 'who do not see what is right in front of their noses'[27] — the Communists were also laying the foundation for closer collaboration with the UCD, collaboration which would in part be directed against the PSOE.

The proposal for a *gobierno de concentración nacional* did not elicit an overly enthusiastic response from the socialists. Flush from their electoral triumph, socialist leaders were staking out for their party a claim as immediate left alternative to the government and had begun to envision the development of a two-party system in Spain: PSOE-UCD or PSOE and whatever the centre-right might come up with. The PSOE expected that after new general elections it would be able to form a government on its own terms and saw in the Communist call for a broad coalition government a rather transparent effort to weaken the socialists.[28]

As might be expected, the idea of a socialist government did not sit well with either the Communists or the UCD. Sparring between the PCE and PSOE had been constant much before the June 1977 election, but in the aftermath of the contest relations deteriorated, with leaders of the two parties engaging in rather personal attacks.[29] The socialists' relations with the UCD were not much better. Suárez and his associates had been bitterly attacked by the PSOE during the campaign, and although the virulence of the attacks diminished after the elections and the UCD and the PSOE sometimes voted together in the first session of the Cortes, the honeymoon was brief.

By late summer 1977, and particularly after the socialists forced through a motion of confidence vote in the Cortes in September (which they lost and on which the PCE abstained), the UCD and PCE were ready to draw together in an attempt to trim the socialists' sails. The Pacto de la Moncloa, an economic and political agreement signed in late October whose name derives from the residence of the premier near the University of Madrid, was the most explicit manifestation of this confluence of interests between the centre and the Communists. While the PSOE signed the agreement only reluctantly and warned it would be up to the government to make the Pacto work, the PCE hailed the agreement as a vindication of its policies and as the first step towards shifting the axis of Spanish politics from the parliamentary sphere (where the party was so weak) to other terrain where the Communists' ability to manoeuvre was greater and their influence in the labour movement could be more effectively employed.[30]

Although the signing of the Pacto was a victory for the PCE, the party was not able to exploit the move fully.[31] The socialists would not accept the Communist suggestion that a supraparliamentary commission be set up to oversee implementation of the accords, and the PCE just did not have the leverage necessary to compel the Suárez government to live up to its end of the bargain. Indeed, it became especially clear after a Ministerial reshuffle in February 1978 that the government interpreted the accords quite differently from the PCE.

The struggle for hegemony on the left between the PCE and PSOE centred during this period (and still does) in the labour movement. The Communists, as we have already noted, had developed an important presence in Spanish labour in the 1960s and early 1970s through the influence they exerted in the Comisiones Obreras. PCE leaders had confidently expected that their party would turn its long-standing efforts at penetration of the official Organización Sindical to advantage and would one day simply assume control of the national labour structure. The success of the Suárez *reforma política* and the lengthiness of the transition to the post-Franco era foiled these plans. In the months after Franco's death, the Comisiones Obreras was shown to be an organisation which, despite its claims to independence and autonomy, was firmly under the control of the Communist Party. (In mid-summer 1976, it came out that 21 out of 27 individuals on the CCOO National Secretariat were members of the PCE, and later that summer, during a visit to the USSR, Marcelino Camacho blundered by giving an interview to Tass in which he extolled life in that country.[32]) Moreover, the lengthy transition to the post-Franco era gave the socialist-inspired UGT the opportunity to build a much needed infrastructure. The sterling PSOE performance in June 1977 (the socialists, it should be emphasised, received triple the Communists' number of votes) provided a further shot in the arm to the UGT. Many

Socialist labour activists, eager to give their party an advantage in dealing with the Communists which no other Latin European socialist party had had since the end of the Second World War, anticipated the UGT would develop a hegemony in the labour movement analogous to the one the PSOE had begun to build in the political sphere. The Communists, for their part, were keenly aware of the need to hold the line in the working class: a UGT triumph in the forthcoming syndical elections would be a serious blow to any hopes the PCE had of reversing the correlation of forces on the left.

The animosity between Communists and socialists that had already become evident in the Cortes and had been exacerbated by the Moncloa agreement grew even more acute as a result of competition in connection with the syndical elections. For example Nicolas Redondo, a socialist deputy and head of the UGT, kicked off the syndical campaign in Barcelona by telling his audience that CCOO was 'a reformist union at the service of the UCD and of the bourgeoisie'.[33]

Many issues separated the two unions. For instance, UGT and Comisiones were sharply divided on the issue of the Pacto de la Moncloa, with the former criticising the agreement (more harshly than the PSOE, in fact) and the latter expressing whole-hearted approval of it from early on. They were also at odds regarding the claims the UGT made to the *patrimonio sindical* confiscated by the Franco regime in 1939 and on the question of whether the delegate lists for the syndical elections should be closed or open.

With respect to the last issue, the UGT favoured closed lists. It argued that such a procedure would encourage the identification of the worker with a union instead of an individual and would therefore not only provide an accurate reading of the strength of particular unions but also encourage the creation of a stable industrial relations system in the country. Behind this argument, of course, lay more than the conviction that trade unions were the best instrument for the defence of the rights of the working class. The UGT believed that closed lists would help it to attract those workers' votes which had gone to the PSOE in June 1977.

Comisiones had a different point of view on this issue. Drawing on a lengthy tradition of workplace *asambleas* and a disdain (tempered over time, however, by the necessity to consolidate control of the union) for traditional trade union structures, the CCOO called instead for a system of open lists and for the *comites de empresas* (or workers' councils) to have bargaining power over trade union sections in the factories.

The dispute over which system should be introduced intensified as the UGT accused the government of favouring comisiones by seeking to adopt the system the CCOO desired. That the government did not want a UGT victory in the syndical elections is quite clear; that it wanted CCOO to win is much less so. Some individuals in the government (primarily Minister of Labour Jiménez de Parga, whose brother worked for the comisiones and was Vice-President of the Soviet-Hispanic Friendship Association) may have preferred such an outcome, but those close to Suárez and with real influence in the government were less interested in promoting the Communist-led union than in keeping the UGT down and in confusing the labour situation to the point where the UCD could promote its own trade union alternative.

That such was the underlying objective of government labour policy became readily apparent when the Suárez government issued its decree regulating the syndical elections.[34] The law set up a system of closed lists in enterprises with more than 250 workers (approximately 30 per cent of the electorate) and open ones in factories with fewer than that number. In the latter, moreover, there was no requirement that the prospective delegate's syndical affiliation appear on the ballot. This permitted the government subsequently to claim that many of the delegates in those factories were independents.

After several months of delay, negotiation and procedural squabbling, the syndical elections began in early 1978. The voting lasted well over three months. Available provisional results indicate that comisiones came in first nationally with between 38 and 44 per cent of the delegates elected compared to between 27 and 31 per cent for the UGT.[35] Comisiones won most clearly in the regions of Cataluña (particularly in Barcelona), Asturias and Madrid, and in parts of Andalucía. CCOO did best in factories with less than 50 workers, and its margin with respect to UGT was least in those with more than 250.[36] Compared to comisiones, the UGT just did not have the necessary cadres: its policy of non-participation in syndical elections under Franco hurt it, and the harm was only partially obviated by the training programme it ran with some of its

Western European counterparts. Although the UGT did not do badly (particularly if we keep in mind that in the early part of this decade the socialist-led union had nuclei active primarily in Asturias and the Basque country only), CCOO was on balance the victor. Since the socialists had more or less counted on duplicating their June 1977 showing, the fact that the Communists held their own dealt a serious, although not necessarily fatal, blow to PSOE hopes of cementing a bi-polar system in Spain.

Our consideration of Communist strategy and politics in the post-June 1977 period would not be complete without an analysis of what for want of a better term we might call the ideological/propagandistic offensive which the PCE undertook to improve its popular standing. Because of space restrictions, we shall limit our consideration of this, focusing first on the polemics with the Soviet Union sparked off by publication of Santiago Carrillo's book *'Eurocomunismo' y Estado ('Euro-communism' and the State)* and by Carrillo's visits to the USSR and the United States in the autumn of 1977, and then turning to a discussion of the ninth Congress of the PCE in April 1978 and its decision to abandon the term Leninism. Although all these initiatives had a serious and substantive side, we should not overlook the fact they were also public relations gambits undertaken by Carrillo and others in the PCE in an effort to make up the ground the Communists had lost to the PSOE in June 1977.

'Eurocomunismo' y Estado, published shortly after the tripartite summit of Spanish, French and Italian Communist leaders in Madrid in March 1977, will not be remembered for the originality or depth of its analysis. The political importance of the document derives from the fact that for the first time a Secretary-General of a Western European Communist Party put his name to a book which so bluntly assailed the Soviet Union, coming very close to denying the socialist nature of the USSR and declaring that profound structural transformations were necessary there before the Soviet state could be considered a 'democratic workers' state'.[37]

The Soviet reaction to this polemical blast did not come right away: for whatever reasons, only in late June, after the Spanish elections, did the Soviet journal *New Times* publish a vitriolic personal attack on Carrillo. (Had it come before, he only half-jokingly suggested, the PCE might have done better in the elections.) The article accused him of propounding ideas which 'accord[ed] solely with the interests of imperialism, the forces of aggression and reaction'.[38] Some saw in the attack an effort by the Soviets to force Carrillo out, but the Communist Party of the Soviet Union (CPSU) more probably was primarily interested in trying to isolate Carrillo and his party from their Western European counterparts. In this effort, the Soviets were at least partially successful. Although the PCF and PCI expressed a general solidarity with the beleaguered Secretary-General of the PCE, they were also at pains to dissociate themselves from what they perceived to be his desire for confrontation with the Soviet Union.[39]

In the summer of 1977, then, relations between the PCE and CPSU stood at an all-time low, worse even than when the Soviets had encouraged Enrique García and Enrique Líster to split from the Spanish party in 1969–70. With many observers wondering what the next step in the conflict might be, the Spanish Communists announced in early September that a V. Pertsov, attached to the CPSU Central Committee and in Spain ostensibly to attend the San Sebastian film festival, had met with Carrillo and other Spanish Communist leaders in an effort to lessen existing tension. One formula the two sides discussed included possible PCE attendance at the sixtieth anniversary celebrations of the October Revolution in Moscow. Both sides had an interest in tempering the dispute at least temporarily. For the Soviets, having as heterodox a party as the PCE come to Moscow would help to reinforce the much-worn idea that Moscow was still the Mecca of the international Communist movement. The Spanish also had an interest in attending: Carrillo planned to visit the United States in late November, and a trip to Moscow would give his foreign initiatives a sense of balance and, perhaps, help undercut criticism within the PCE and among some Western European Communist parties that he liked to grandstand and was too extreme in his criticism of the CPSU.

Negotiations between the PCE and CPSU continued into the autumn, and the two parties finally came to agreement during the October visit to Madrid of *Pravda* editor and CPSU Central Committee member V. Afanas'yev. Carrillo and the Spanish delegation arrived in the capital of the USSR a few weeks later;

then, in a move which made the PCE leader an international *cause célèbre*, the Soviets did not permit him to speak.

Press accounts of the incident generally placed responsibility on the CPSU or on some faction in its leadership, but there is evidence which suggests that Carrillo was not quite an innocent victim and that the affair was really more a public relations effort worked out in anticipation of the Carrillo visit to the United States and designed to reinforce the impression, domestically and internationally, that the Spanish leader was the most anti-Soviet and thus the most Eurocommunist personality in Western Europe. What is the nature of this evidence?

For one thing, all accounts of the affair agree that during Afanas'yev's visit to Madrid in mid-October, both sides came to terms on the general guidelines for the Carrillo speech and on the date of his arrival in Moscow. Approximately one week before his scheduled arrival, Carrillo notified the organisers of the event that he could not reach Moscow in time for Leonid Brezhnev's inaugural speech since he had in the meantime promised to attend the closing session of the Fourth Congress of the Catalan Communist Party.[40] There can be little doubt that with nearly 20 per cent of the regional vote in June 1977, eight deputies in the Cortes, and some 40,000 members, the Partit Socialista Unificat de Catalunya (PSUC), as the Catalan filial body of the PCE is known, is the most important component of the Spanish Communist Party. But Carrillo could easily have chosen not to go to Barcelona, and he undoubtedly expected the CPSU would interpret his absence for the snub that it was.

Aside from this provocation, there is the question of the Carrillo speech. According to the official PCE version, Carrillo turned it over for translation upon arrival.[41] However, no text of the speech has been published anywhere. Some people have speculated as to whether there ever was a speech (or just vague notes which Carrillo jotted down as an outline and which Soviet leaders would not accept), or whether the speech was so weak compared to that of Enrico Berlinguer that Carrillo, to many the *enfant terrible* of the Communist movement, might have opted not to deliver it. Indeed, what better way to start a trip to the United States than to have been rejected so publicly by the Soviets? This aspect of the incident becomes particularly relevant if we remember that Carrillo and others in the PCE expected, incorrectly as it turned out, that Carrillo would have direct contacts with the Carter administration once he arrived in the United States.

It was during Carrillo's trip to the United States (he spoke at several major universities and at the Council on Foreign Relations in New York) that he first mentioned the possibility that during the Ninth PCE Congress scheduled for early 1978 the party would drop the appellation Leninist and define itself simply as a 'Marxist, democratic and revolutionary' organisation. The proposal, like the foreign policy initiatives undertaken by the PCE with the publication of *'Eurocomunismo' y Estado* and the visits to the USSR and the United States by Carrillo, had as its principal objective a quest for votes and democratic credibility.

In the weeks and months preceding the Congress – the first legal one held since 1932, when the PCE had had some 5,000 members – party leaders sought to make sure that the debate on dropping Leninism did not get out of hand and particularly that it did not catalyse too great a debate on the content of Communist policies since 1956, when Carrillo had assumed a dominant position within the party. To that end, Carrillo – who one former member of the Executive Committee said behaves within the PCE 'like Juan Carlos in the country'[42] – only presented the 15 theses of the new party programme to the Central Committee the day before that body met to convene the national congress. Approval of all theses was virtually unanimous. Carrillo also had the Central Committee adopt a one-third rule: a minority thesis had to collect at least one-third of the delegate votes at any assembly in order for it to be raised at the next higher meeting.

Provincial and regional organisations did not stand idly by either. In as important a province as Madrid, the provincial leadership originally wanted a full half of the delegates from the region to be chosen from above. Although the leadership eventually gave in on this score, it successfully opposed counter-proposals that delegates to the Congress be elected directly by the party base and adopted the rule that the participation of any party member from the provincial conference could be prevented if 20 per cent of those in his neighbourhood *agrupación* voted against him.

These efforts to confine debate had their intended effect with respect to the Congress, but they did not really work at the various provincial and regional conferences preceding the Congress. One reason for this was that many of the new members who had joined the party in the last decade (the PCE claimed 45 per cent of its 200,000 members had entered after 1970) took party leaders at their word when they promised the democratisation of party structures. Party leaders could try to channel dissent, but they could not afford to suppress it altogether.

Also Carrillo and others in the leadership, it is fair to say, underestimated the emotive power of the Leninism issue within the party. It was one thing to abandon Leninism in practice, as the party had increasingly done in the years after 1956; it was quite another to recognise that rejection formally and to develop a substitute doctrine. Some of those who opposed thesis 15 (the proposal to drop Leninism) wanted the PCE to uphold as still valid such fundamental Leninist notions as the armed seizure of power and the dictatorship of the proletariat. Others who were less nostalgic and recognised how much the world had changed since 1917 saw no necessary contradiction between Eurocommunism and Leninism properly understood. However, they wanted the party to be clear about its objective of eventual working-class hegemony and desired a full-fledged debate on Leninism and its implications to promote the development of a coherent 'Eurocommunist'alternative. Those who thought in this fashion (they were to be found primarily in the PSUC and in Asturias, Andalucía and Madrid) feared that electoral avarice would lead the party quietly to drop some fundamental principles. Still others in the party would have liked to abandon Leninism entirely, but voted with those who opposed thesis 15 (and Carrillo) because they felt only a thorough airing of this issue would permit the PCE to rid itself of the scars of forty years of Stalinism.

Ideological, personal and generational cleavages – all of which combined to create a serious PCE identity crisis – helped make the pre-Congress discussion rich and lively. The situation became particularly volatile in three zones: Asturias, Madrid and Cataluña.

In Asturias, a region where the PCE had expected to do well in June 1977 but had not, disaffection had been growing for quite some time. The heavy-handedness of the central party organisation in imposing the legendary Dolores Ibárruri as the head of the Communist list in the general elections had generated a good deal of resentment. The various opponents of thesis 15 drew on this sentiment. Indeed, tension within the party in Asturias reached such a point by late March 1978 that on the opening day of the regional conference nearly one-third of the delegates, including José Ramón Herrero Merediz, a member of the Central Committee, walked out.[43]

In Madrid, the battle over the theses became embroiled in a dispute over control of the provincial organisation.[44] While the conference only approved three of the proposed Central Committee theses without alteration, supporters of the official theses did manage to channel delegate discontent by supporting partial amendments which would 'clarify but not contradict' the official proposals. As in Asturias, none of the rival theses received the one-third of the votes necessary to place it before the Congress as a minority position. The closest vote came on a motion to postpone the decision on thesis 15 until an extraordinary congress had been convened to debate the issue. This motion failed only after Simón Sánchez Montero of the national Executive Committee made a forceful speech against the proposal.

The pre-Congress debates reached their zenith in Cataluña. The PSUC had convened its Fourth Congress in early November 1977, at which time the delegates had included in the programme an allusion to the PSUC as heir to 'Marxism, Leninism, and other contributions to revolutionary thought and practice.'[45] This had been done before Carrillo announced that the PCE would probably drop Leninism, and the failure to co-ordinate matters on this score had serious consequences.

Those who argued for the retention of Leninism – and their base was above all in the labour movement in Cataluña – were able to wrap themselves in the mantle of Catalan nationalism and to take advantage of the concern many militants felt about the loss of definition suffered by the party.[46] A further complication for Carrillo and thesis 15 arose because those who sided with the Central Committee theses from the beginning came from a faction derisively known as *bandera blanca*, which had for a long time been the object of bitter attack within the PSUC for its alleged 'social democratic' orientation.

By the time the PSUC national conference met in early April, the lines had been firmly drawn. Carrillo emerged the victor, but he did not go unscathed. Thesis 15 was approved by a narrow margin of 97 to 81, and the favourable vote came only after eight members of the PSUC Executive, who had up to that point been bound by the rule of democratic centralism, threatened to resign if they were obliged once again to vote with the Executive Committe majority. Amidst talk of a split in the party, the others in the Catalan leadership relaxed the rules on internal discipline. As a result of that decision, a motion to have Leninism mentioned in the statutes won by the same margin as thesis 15.

After all this commotion, the PCE Congress was in a way anticlimatic. Only in Cataluña had the minority theses prospered, and by the time the Congress came around, everyone knew what the outcome of the voting would be. As expected, the delegates approved the report Carrillo presented in the name of the Central Committee by a lopsided margin (898 for, 37 against and 51 abstentions, but with 361 votes unaccounted for), although many criticised its excessively personalistic thrust and its lack of clarity about Communist medium- and long-term strategy.[47] Since the official theses – particularly the first, dealing with the characteristics of change in Spanish society (the transition to the post-Franco era had taken place quite differently from what Carrillo had predicted and the thesis had claimed), and the thirteenth, focusing on national defence – had been substantially modified in the various commissions, the plenum approved most by large margins. The only electric moments in an otherwise dull congress came late in the third day when after an at times stirring debate between spokesmen for majority and minority positions, the delegates voted on thesis 15. The verdict: 968 votes in favour of a slightly revised version of the leadership's original proposal, 240 votes against, and 40 abstentions.[48]

Despite its predictability, the Ninth PCE Congress was in many ways important because it signalled the beginning of a renovation of the Spanish party. Of the 160 members of the Central Committee elected there, 56 are new to that body, as are 14 of the 46 on the Executive Committee. One development, whose implications are not yet clear, is the rise in the influence of those active in labour affairs. Nearly a quarter of the new Central Committee is composed of people with Comisiones backgrounds (the proportion of those of working-class origins on the Central Committee is over 50 per cent, and seven CCOO leaders now sit on the Executive Committee). This influx of labour activists into the highest ranks of the PCE is in no small measure due to the fact that in most parts of the country (Cataluña was an exception) those active in the labour movement distinguished themselves as the most dependable supporters Carrillo had outside the *apparat*. Many of them, we can be sure, are less than enthusiastic about some 'Eurocommunist' tenets, but they sided with Carrillo primarily because they felt that doing so was the best way to ensure that the debate within the party did not get out of hand.

In sum, Carrillo came out of the Ninth Congress firmly, if not necessarily comfortably, in control of his party's affairs; however, his victory there, and particularly the success he had in getting approval of the thesis abandoning Leninism, had not been easy. To achieve it, he and others in the Spanish Communist leadership had to endure a debate and criticism which was in many ways unique in the experience of Communist parties.

While the Congress did not turn out to be as open as some had hoped it would be, neither was it as controlled as other might have wished. Indeed, a myth of party unanimity lies shattered in the wake of the Congress. Moreover, debate over the issue of Leninism has set in motion a process of democratisation which the party apparatus will have a difficult time containing. The debates leading up to the Congress were the first salvoes in what promises to be a long drawn-out battle over the heart and mind, the identity and policies of the PCE. It is still too early to tell what the final outcome will be. However, we can be sure that if the renovators succeed in reversing the flow of decision-making within the PCE, Communism in Spain will have been transformed.

In the months since June 1977, the Spanish Communists have found themselves in the rather uncomfortable position of having to explain away the magnitude of the socialist victory and to reassure Communist militants and sympathisers that the situation is not irreversible. Were the PCE a redoubt of radical sectarianism, any optimism on the part of the Communist leaders and followers in this regard would be ill founded. As it is, however, the PCE has undergone a dramatic transformation over the course of the last two decades, a transformation which, although in many ways responsible for the crisis of identity through which the party is now passing, may nevertheless help the Communists overcome some of their disadvantages. Still, a shift in the correlation of forces on the left will depend not only on how shrewdly the Communists conduct themselves in the next few years, but also on the number and magnitude of PSOE mistakes.

For the present, Communist leaders can be buoyed by the PCE performance in senatorial by-elections held in May 1978 in Asturias and Alicante. While PSOE candidates won both seats, the vote for the socialists declined by 92,000 and 70,000 votes respectively in comparison with the party's 1977 showing in the two provinces; the PCE, in contrast, increased its votes by 26,000 and 7,000. In real terms, the Communist improvement was on the order of a modest 2 per cent in Alicante and a heftier 5 per cent in Asturias, but the general results may have betrayed a disenchantment with the UCD and PSOE among voters.[49] Although the situation remains fluid, the Communists could exploit such sentiment in the next general elections.

No date has yet been set for these general elections. Speculation about anticipated elections has been rife in Spain for many months now. There will be a referendum on the new constitution (approved in the Cortes with only minor hassling among the major parties) some time this autumn, and one scenario has municipal elections next spring and general elections shortly thereafter. The present Cortes's term runs until 1981, however, and it will be up to Suárez to decide if he wants to move the date up.

It is conceivable that in municipal elections the left will emerge with a higher national percentage than the centre. Much will depend, of course, on what sort of electoral law is approved by the Cortes; but in any case, the parties of the left will be particularly well placed to challenge the UCD in the cities. Not only is the centre still an embryonic political party, but neighbourhood and housewife associations – there are more than a hundred of the former in Madrid alone – have long been strongholds of the left and highly politicised. With the turnout in these elections likely to fall below the 78 per cent mark registered for the 1977 parliamentary ones, a fairly disciplined vote will have a much greater impact. Indeed, a preliminary assessment would lead one to expect municipal take-overs by the left in some of the largest Spanish cities.

The economy will also affect the outcome of new elections. The Spanish economy has yet to recover from the nadir reached earlier this year. Particularly disturbing is unemployment. Official figures place unemployment at 800,000 but the total rises to nearly 1.3 million people if we include those willing to work who cannot find jobs.[50] The situation is most delicate in Andalucía, where the figure hovers around the 15 per cent mark. Apparently the Pacto de la Moncloa has helped hold down inflation in 1978, but the 19.2 per cent rate expected for this year is still considerably higher than the 8 per cent average for the other OECD countries.[51]

There has been some speculation that with the unification of the various socialist currents taking place under the PSOE banner – the one with the PSP in early May 1978 is the best known, but similar processes have been under way in Cataluña, Aragon, Valencia and to some degree Andalucía – and recent statements by Felipe González to the effect that at the forthcoming Twenty-Eighth PSOE Congress in 1979 he would propose that the term Marxist be dropped from the party programme, the PSOE may be able to broaden its electoral appeal sufficiently to gain a majority (or close to it) of the seats in a new Cortes. This will not be easily accomplished. Not only has there been some resentment within the PSOE as a result of González's declarations, particularly among a portion of the cadres, but it also appears that in the senatorial by-election in Asturias at least a part of the PSP electorate voted Communist. The PSOE has been weakened, moreover, by the inability of the UGT to win the syndical elections.

A recent poll published by the independent daily *El País* shows the PSOE leading in a hypothetical election with 33.6 per cent of the vote (as compared with 29.3 per cent in June 1977), followed by the UCD with 28.5 per cent and the PCE with 9.7 per cent. Some 13.6 per cent of the voters were undecided, according to the survey. More generally, the poll showed a trend towards the left in the country, with 40 per cent of the electorate identifying itself as left or centre-left, 21.7 per cent centre and 10.9 per cent right.[52]

In the event of new elections, however, it is unlikely that either the PSOE or the UCD will record sharp gains or losses in comparison with their showings of June 1977. We should not, in any case, underestimate the political ability of Suárez, who has up to now demonstrated himself to be a consummate politician. As far as the Communists are concerned, a rise of 3 or 4 percentage points nationally is to be expected. In case either the PSOE or UCD achieves a relative Cortes majority, the most probable outcome would be formation of a coalition government between the victorious party and Catalan and/or Basque minority groups. PSOE participation in a UCD government headed by Suárez is problematic, but socialist leaders would like the inclusion of left-wing sectors of the UCD in any government their party headed. Such a government might also have Communist participation at the middle levels of various Ministries in exchange for a commitment of parliamentary support. Much less likely governments would be UCD or PSOE one-party minority Cabinets.

Any government will have a difficult time of it, though. Not only is the economy faltering and industrial discipline slackening, but peripheral nationalist groups, particularly in the Basque country, are unlikely any time soon to tone down their demands for even greater autonomy and in some cases outright independence. The military will also merit special attention in the months immediately ahead, particularly since it is likely to be the target of attacks by extremists interested in destabilising the country.

Some observers saw the Pacto de la Moncloa as the first step on the road to a Spanish version of the Italian 'historic compromise'. Such an interpretation may be proved correct over the long run, but so far the confluence of interests among the various partners seems to be more tactical than strategic. The UCD, for one, has viewed the PCE more as an instrument with which to increase its bargaining leverage on the PSOE than as a long-term ally. As far as the socialists are concerned, they have little interest in such a broad coalition, and if their party consolidates its hegemony on the left, it will be in a strong position to frustrate efforts in that direction. For their part, some Communist leaders and particularly Santiago Carrillo may well be convinced of the viability and necessity of a 'historic compromise' in Spain; none the less, the situation there differs substantially from that in Italy, and we must be careful about drawing too quick an analogy.

To avoid being locked into a marginal role, the PCE will

pursue a dual-pronged policy of, on the one hand, supporting Suárez (this will help consolidate democratic institutions and underscore the moderation of the PCE) and, on the other hand, keeping the door open to the socialists. At some point, the Communists will have to make a choice between alliance partners, but there is no reason why the PCE should not be able to employ both levers simultaneously for some time to come.

Certainly, it is too early yet to tell what the prospects for a shift in the 'correlation of forces' within the left are in the short to medium term, although the PCE does have an important ace in the hole with its strength in the labour movement. Whatever the outcome of the next general elections, though, competition between the PSOE and PCE will probably continue to be a fixture of the Spanish political scene. At the same time, we should not lose sight of the fact that, even now and however reluctantly, each side perceives the other to be a natural ally on the road to socialism. The socialists would like to reach power alone, but if they fail in this effort – and the next two or three years will be decisive in this respect – it in all likelihood will only be a matter of time before the two parties work out some sort of common platform or programme. The principal obstacles which have impeded such a development up to now – the fact that an *entente*, by conjuring up visions of a 'popular front', would encourage the extreme right, and the socialist desire to reach power without the Communists and, otherwise, to delineate with some precision the areas and limits of Communist influence – are largely conjectural in nature and will probably diminish over time.

Any assessment of Communist prospects for the longer term must emphasise the unlikelihood that the PCE will acquire a role in the Spanish left comparable, for example, to that of the Italian Communist Party in its local left. Nevertheless, precisely because of Communist efforts to reach parity with the PSOE, we can probably expect a deepening of the evolutionary process (which, it should be stressed, is not necessarily equivalent to 'social democratisation') already under way in Spanish Communism. We should be wary of minimising the obstacles involved, but we must not forget that the peculiar constellation of the Spanish left in 1978 does favour such an evolution.

Notes

1. The phrase appears in the principal report approved at the Third Conference of the Madrid Provincial Conference in April 1976 (mimeograph), p. 18.
2. For an assessment of these changes, see the author's chapter entitled 'The Domestic and International Evolution of the Spanish Communist Party' in Rudolph L. Tökés (ed.), *Eurocommunism in the Age of Détente* (New York University Press, New York, 1978).
3. Ramón Chao, *Después de Franco, España* (After Franco, Spain) (Ediciones Felmar, Madrid, 1976), pp. 215–17. For the international aspects of the struggle, see the section entitled 'Relaciones Internacionales' in the report of the Executive Committee to the delegates at the Thirteenth PSOE Congress in 1974. *XIII Memoria de la Gestión que Presenta la Comisión Ejecutiva* (13th Report of Activities Presented by the Executive Committee) (October 1974), pp. 4–9.
4. For a useful overview of these groups, see Xavier Raufer's article in *Est et Ouest* (Paris), 16–31 Mar 1976, pp. 12–20.
5. The PSOE had some difficulty enforcing the decision to abstain once this Junta Democrática took shape. In places like the Canary Islands, the party federation initially joined the Junta and left only after intense pressure from the national organisation.
6. See the text of the declaration in *Mundo Obrero* (published in Paris until the spring of 1977 and then in Madrid), 29 July 1974.
7. The Communists recognised the difference in the situations of the Spanish and Portuguese military quite early on, and they argued that the Spanish armed forces should remain neutral and not become actively involved in politics. See, for example, Santiago Alvarez in *Nuestra Bandera* (published in Brussels until issue no. 87 and thereafter in Madrid), no. 75 (May–June 1974), p. 33.
8. The text of their manifesto was published in the version of *Mundo Obrero* put out by a pro-Soviet faction challenging Carrillo. See the issue of 15–30 June 1973.
9. Carrillo first used the expression in his report to the delegates at the Eighth PCE Congress in 1972. See *Octavo Congreso del PCE (Eighth Congress of the PCE)*, (Bucharest, 1972), p. 7. However, Luis Ramírez may have come up with the appellation initially. See *Horizonte Español*, 1972 (Spanish Horizon, 1972) (Paris), vol. 1, p. 1.
10. The most important issues separating the Junta and the Plataforma had to do with the Communists' rejection of Juan Carlos as a 'slightly disguised continuity'. Interview with Carrillo in *L'Humanité* (Paris), 25 October 1976. The PCE, moreover, had been instrumental in having the Junta adopt as an article of faith the view, clearly expressed in the *Manifesto de Reconcillación Nacional (Manifesto of National Reconciliation)* that 'the democratic evolution of the state by way of legal reforms [is] objectively and subjectively impossible.' *Mundo Obrero*, 3rd week of April 1975.
11. See Victor Díaz Cardiel *et al.*, *Madrid en Huelga (Madrid on Strike)* (Editorial Ayuso, Madrid, 1976).
12. *Mundo Obrero*, 9 April 1976.
13. See *La Democracia Cristiana Afronta el Futuro (Christian Democracy Confronts the Future)*, a report presented to the first ID Congress in early April 1976 (mimeograph), pp. 5–8.
14. *Newsweek* (New York), 26 April 1976.
15. The first reference may be found in *Cuadernos para el Dialogo* (Madrid), 10 July 1976; the second, in *Mundo Obrero*, 14 July 1976.
16. See Eugenio Nasarre's *Ponencia Sobre Estrategia Política (Report on*

Political Strategy), delivered 12 Oct. 1976, at a meeting of the top Christian Democratic leadership at Miraflores (mimeograph).

17. Earlier, at a Central Committee meeting in Rome in late July 1976, the PCE had demanded that Suárez (1) grant a complete and general amnesty for all political crimes; (2) declare inoperative the law on political associations submitted by Arias; (3) resign and submit to the formation of a provisional government; (4) accept quick elections to a Constituent Assembly; and (5) grant full autonomy to the Catalan, Basque and Galician regions. See Santiago Carrillo's report to the plenum *De la Clandestinidad a La Legalidad (From Clandestinity to Legality)* (July 1976), pp. 9–11.

18. *Mundo Obrero*, 15 Sept. 1976.

19. General statements of the party's position may be found in Dolores Ibárruri, *España, Estado Multinacional (Spain, Multinational State)* (Éditions Sociales, Paris, 1971) and in Santiago Alvarez, 'Note on the National Problem in Spain', *Nuestra Bandera*, no. 84 (March-April 1976), pp. 13–25.

20. *Mundo Obrero*, 7 July 1976, carried an article by Ernest Martí (Joaquim Sempere) of the Catalan party making this point.

21. Ibid., 11 June and 26 July 1976.

22. For an exhaustive analysis of the evolution of the labour movement in Spain, see Jon Amsden, *Collective Bargaining and Class Struggle in Spain* (Weidenfeld and Nicolson, London, 1972).

23. *Cuadernos para el Dialogo*, 19 June 1976. The *Manifiesto de la Unidad Sindical (Manifesto of the Unified Trade Union)* issued in January 1976 can be found in *CCOO en Sus Documentos, 1958–1976 (The Workers' Commissions in their Documents, 1958–1976)* (Ediciones HOAC, Madrid, 1977), Appendix, pp. 5–30.

24. Santiago Carrillo, *Informe Presentado al CC (Speech to the CC)* (mimeograph, April 1977).

25. The shift on the monarchy issue had been under discussion in the Executive Committee for several months and had been prefigured by a Carrillo statement to an April 1976 press conference in Paris that his party would not be an obstacle if 'through some miracle' the Crown brought democracy. See *Nuestra Bandera*, no. 84 (March–April 1976). The move, in any case, was not without its historical ironies. In December 1967, in one of the first public signs of disagreement with the Soviet Union, Carrillo had taken the Soviets to task for publishing an article in *Izvestiya* suggesting that a monarch-led transition might be a viable path to the post-Franco era. *Mundo Obrero*, 31 December 1967.

26. See the Carrillo interview/article in *Mundo Obrero*, 16 June 1977.

27. See *Diario 16* (Madrid), 1 September 1977, and *Mundo Obrero*, 16 August 1977, for the statement by Camacho, and *Mundo Obrero*, 8–14 September 1977 for that of Carrillo.

28. A good idea of how the PSOE views its role in Spanish politics can be gained from Antonio Guerra, *Felipe González: Socialismo es Libertad (Felipe González: Socialism is Liberty)*, (Galba Edicions, Barcelona, 1978), pp. 129–265.

29. Carrillo at one point remarked that González and the PSOE were behaving like amateurs in politics. González answered back in an interview with *Le Monde* (Paris), October 1977, declaring that he wondered how Carrillo could emit such a judgment given his track record: 'When I am his age, have his experience and his degree of professionalism, I would not want to be at the head of a party which collected 9 per cent of the vote.'

30. See the Santiago Carrillo speech at the Festival of the PCE, as reported in *Mundo Obrero*, 20–26 October, 1977.

31. At the outset, the Communists were full of bravado. 'The party will control the fulfilment of the accords,' declared *Mundo Obrero* in its 20–26 October 1977 issue.

110   *The PCE in Spanish Politics*

32. *Cambio 16* (Madrid) 6 September 1977, p. 7.
33. *Mundo Obrero*, 10–16 November 1977.
34. For the text of the electoral norms, see ibid., 29 December 1977–4 January 1978.
35. *El País* (Madrid), 28 March 1978, reported the percentages as CCOO 38 and UGT 31. Julian Ariza of the Comisiones National Secretariat, writing in *Nuestra Bandera*, no. 94, p. 47, claimed 44–6 per cent for the CCOO and 27–38 per cent for the UGT. Several weeks later, an article in *Mundo Obrero* (10–16 August 1978) indicated that out of 178,540 delegates chosen and verified so far, 36.9 per cent belonged to CCOO, 23.2 per cent to UGT, 19.5 per cent had no affiliation, and 13.2 per cent were classifiable as independents.
36. See *Saida* (Barcelona), 21 March 1978, p. 18.
37. Santiago Carrillo, '*Eurocommunismo*' *y Estado*, (Editorial Grijalbo, Barcelona, 1977), p. 212.
38. See 'Contrary to the Interests of Peace and Socialism in Europe – Concerning the Book "Eurocommunism and the State" by Santiago Carrillo, General Secretary of the Communist Party of Spain', *New Times* (Moscow), no. 26 (June 1977), p. 11.
39. See, for example, 'Eurocommunism, *Novoye Vremya* and Us', *l'Unità* (Rome), 28 June 1977, and the text of the press conference of Santiago Carrillo and Enrico Berlinguer a few months later, in *Mundo Obrero*, 17–23 November 1977.
40. *Mundo Obrero*, 10–16 November 1977.
41. Ibid. The PCE has been very unclear about what Carrillo was to have said. In remarks reported by *Corriere della Sera*, the Secretary-General of the PCE was quoted as saying that his speech contained 'more or less the same ideas as Berlinguer's' *Corriere della Sera* (Milan), 4 November 1977. Some people in the Italian party have been uneasy about what they perceive as Carrillo's tendency to grandstand. Giancarlo Pajetta, for example, has made some disparaging remarks about Carrillo's having 'an Iberian temperament' (*El País*, 4 November 1977); and in an interview a few days after the uproar in Moscow (*Corriere della Sera*, 8 November 1977) Pajetta, wanting to distinguish between PCE and PCI attitudes, remarked that '[the Italian Communist] verdict, even when it is critical, and . . . our stances, even when they are different, are never connected to propagandistic motives or concessions to this or that adversary.' During his trip to the United States, Carrillo, when asked about possible differences with the PCI, was cautious. Talking about differences of style between himself and PCI leaders, Carrillo often declared that he knew of a word ('sfumaturra') which captured as did no other the Italian Communist tendency. He also speculated on the impact operating next to the Vatican has been on Italian political parties.
42. *La Stampa* (Turin), 26 February 1978.
43. *Diario 16*, 27 March 1978, and *El País*, 28 March 1978.
44. *Diario 16*, 17 March 1978. See also the article by Fernando Lopez. Agudin in *Triunfo* (Madrid), 18 March 1978, pp. 24–6.
45. *IV Congress del Partit Socialista Unificat de Catalunya (Recull de Materials i d'intervencións) (Fourth Congress of the Unified Socialist Party of Cataluña (A Compilation of Materials and Interventions))* (Editorial Laia, Barcelona, 1978), p. 51.
46. See the excellent article by Enrique Sopena in *Informacions* (Madrid), 6 April 1978).
47. The text is carried in *Mundo Obrero*, 20 April 1978.
48. Eurocommunistologists might argue about the underlying significance of the ordering of the words Marxism, revolution and democracy in the final version. The original proposal was for the programme to say that the PCE is a 'Marxist, democratic, and revolutionary party'. The final version, after lengthy debates in the

commission, read slightly differently: 'The PCE is a Marxist, revolutionary, and democratic party.'

49. For a perceptive analysis, see *Triunfo*, 27 May 1978, pp. 20–1. For other discussion, see *La Calle* (Madrid), 23–29 May 1978, pp. 4–50.

50. *El Socialista* (Madrid), 7 May 1978.

51. Dee *Cambio 16*, 4 June 1978, p. 87.

52. *El País*, 15 June 1978.

4 THE ITALIAN COMMUNIST PARTY: BETWEEN LENINISM AND SOCIAL DEMOCRACY?

Martin Clark and David Hine

1 Party Structure and Mass Support

It is an article of faith among Italian Communists that their party, the Partito Comunista Italiano is a 'mass' rather than a purely 'opinion' party. In Italian political jargon this distinction is important. A 'party of opinion' is merely a machine for electing individuals to Parliament on a party label, but a mass party is supported to be a living and working organisation with entrenched and unbreakable roots in society — capable of turning voters into 'sympathisers' and 'sympathisers' into members on a mass scale. Only a well organised mass party ensures permanent links between leaders and supporters, and enables the leaders to change course as occasion arises without having to worry too much about their followers' loyalty. In theory at least, a mass party is less a prey to the whims of its electorate than are 'opinion' parties like, for example, the social democratic parties of northern Europe.

Moreover, the mass party helps the PCI to be effective in a host of other bodies — in local government, in welfare organisations, on planning boards and factory councils, in trade unions and so forth. Thus party organisation is not just an end in itself, but an essential instrument in the Communists' long-term strategy of 'presence' throughout Italian society. It can turn short-term popularity into long-term success. It enables the party's supporters to be kept busy and enthusiastic, to be trained in practical work and to be reconciled to mundane realities; but it also means that new opportunities will be seized and new initiatives taken, and that the party will acquire a reputation for efficiency and responsibility.

Ever since 1944, when Togliatti proclaimed that the elitist, conspiratorial model of the Communist Party had been superseded by the new 'mass' party, the PCI has been striving towards this ideal. Like its Christian democrat rivals, it started with the advantage of a strongly entrenched regional subculture working in its favour. The 'Red Belt' — the area of north

112

central Italy between the Po Valley and the Abruzzi, including the regions of Emilia-Romagna, Tuscany and Umbria — represents the heartland of Italian Communism, with the show-case city of Bologna as its citadel. In this area the strongly anti-clerical radicalism of the nineteenth century spawned a powerful socialist tradition which has regularly benefited the left, and since 1945 the PCI has inherited and capitalised on this tradition.

In this area the social 'presence' of the party is very real. The various organisations which the party now controls — partisans' associations, recreation organisations, women's groups, co-operatives and so on — have all found fertile terrain in the Red Belt. The PCI is much the largest party in electoral terms — it dominates local and regional government, and has managed to convert between 1 in every 3 and 1 in every 4 Communist voters into party members. Here, in the Red Belt, the PCI is the establishment; *here* it is already on the way to achieving something akin to what Gramsci called 'hegemony' (see below, p. 126). But of course the Red Belt is not Italy. It represents only a part of Italian society. In most areas pre-existing cultural and political conditions do not provide a naturally favourable environment and so the party's successes in building up an organisational 'presence' have been correspond-ingly more modest.

Most of the PCI's efforts at national level are devoted to the party organisation itself. With an official annual budget of some £25 million in 1977 (and a real annual expenditure probably substantially in excess of this)[1] the PCI has an army of some 2,100 paid officials, and this excludes others — journalists, and officials employed by associated organisations — who do a great deal of work for the party. It has a large and generally efficient national office, which houses the inner cabinet of the party — the secretariat — and the various departments into which the office is divided (organisation, elections, trade union matters, foreign policy, aspects of domestic policy, etc.).

It is still a highly centralised party. There is a close relationship between the secretariat, the central *apparat* and — through the organisation department — the provincial offices ('federations') of the party. This hierarchy forms the main power structure. There are no independent sources of power: Communist deputies and senators have no special clienteles of their own, nor any access to their own financial or political resources. They have, consequently, far less influence on policy than their colleagues in other parties. In the PCI it is the men at the top of the *party* organisation, a fairly restricted group of professional politicians, who decide all important matters. These men may of course be members of Parliament as well as of the party hierarchy, but it is their *party* status that counts.[2]

None of this means, however, that the grass-roots organisation is ignored. On the contrary, below the 108 provincial 'federations' there are some 12,000 ward or commune-based 'sections' — the basic units of the party — giving the PCI by far the best managed and most extensive local organisational network among Italian parties. Moreover, the party makes strenuous efforts to ensure that grass-roots activists do more than just collect dues and recruit new members. It constantly experiments with new forms of organisation, and is in the process of transferring a large part of its resources to a new regional tier, between the provinces and the centre.[3] But while it is anxious to turn as many members as possible into active militants, and while it encourages a whole range of policy committees of a *consultative* variety at different levels — where ordinary members can and do speak their minds — this activism is kept on a tight rein. It mainly occurs in bodies which are ancillary to the main decision-making structure: committees established to 'stimulate' local councils, or to act as party watchdogs in a particular sector of industry; provincial conferences for policy elaboration in the sphere of social services or local industry; national conferences of provincial party secretaries and so on. It does not occur on the same scale, however, in the main decision-making structure of the party, and it is this structure — 'section' assembly, provincial executive and national secretariat — which really matters.[4] Within it, or more precisely at the top of it, major decisions of party strategy are taken; and the structure remains a strict hierarchy, where the principles of co-optation from above and vertical dependence still operate.

This combination of 'controlled spontaneity' and a high degree of centralisation is vital. It gives the rank and file the illusion of participation and even of control, and it also provides an essential channel of communication by which the leadership can sense the humours of its masses. And while it provides feedback, it pre-empts factionalism. Above all else, the leadership fears that the PCI might ultimately fall victim to the disruption and paralysis of factionalism if any real democracy were introduced into party life. As a result, it is unwilling to transform internal elections of delegates to party congresses, or of the Central Committee, directorate or secretariat, into genuine elections based upon alternative conceptions of party strategy. If real competition were allowed and openly dissenting minorities permitted, factions would rapidly become institutionalised, or so the argument goes.[5]

The principle of unanimity thus ensures that the PCI has neither majorities nor minorities, and that responsibility for decisions is collegiate. This is not to say that decisions are not discussed, both centrally and locally. Naturally, divisions exist, but they are kept behind closed doors, and more importantly the selection of office-holders is kept separate from such discussion. Personnel is thus effectively selected through co-optation, not election, and party leaders command a formidable armoury — both in the norms of the party constitution which forbid activities which 'destroy party unity and discipline', and in the more tangible rewards and penalties at their disposal — to keep it this way. The fact, furthermore, that most party politicians from provincial level upwards are *career* politicians, with no alternative professions to fall back on, persuades all but the most adventurous to keep strictly in line with the leadership.

The internal organisation of the PCI thus still bears the hallmarks of democratic centralism. And while the formal justification for this is the need to prevent factionalism, it nevertheless reflects, as we shall see later in examining party ideology, a deeper ideological predisposition which stems from the PCI's belief in its historic right to lead the working class, and from what is in effect a substantial antipathy to any real social pluralism not guided and regulated by the party itself.

Ideology and organisation are also bound up in another way. Because maintaining the commitment of the activists and preserving the ideological character of the party as a whole is much the most cost-effective method of containing internal pressures, a further substantial part of the party's organisational resources is devoted to the ideological *apparat*. Thus, in addition to the internationally famous Gramsci Institute, there are no less than five permanent training centres where party cadres and local government representatives attend courses of varying length on policy, ideology or organisation matters, and less formal courses are arranged by individual provincial federations. The party also has a vast range of publishing ventures. It produces a daily newspaper, *L'Unità*, and a weekly, *Rinascita*, as well as the theoretical heavyweight *Critica Marxista* and a number of specialist reviews and periodicals — and of course there is the extremely successful publishing house, Editori Riuniti.

Apart from the official party organisation, the most important arena of Communist organisational activity is in the trade union movement. Since the war the PCI has dominated the main trade union confederation, the Italian General Confederation of Labour (CGIL). Although this dominance early on gave rise to breakaway Catholic and social democrat confederations, the CGIL itself has always remained much the most important part of the labour movement, and today has approximately four million members. In recent years it has seemed to act rather more independently of the Communist Party, and has even formed a 'federation' with the other two major confederations, which were traditionally linked to the Christian democrat and social democrat parties. But all the 'official' unions are worried by the militant so-called 'autonomous' unions, free of any links with political parties or national confederations, which are increasingly setting the pace in private, and especially public sector, bargaining. Despite this tendency, however, Communist influence over the unions remains strong, and has been a major factor in helping the party to the strategically important position it occupies in the Italian party system in the seventies.

In other areas its influence has been less significant. Although the largest co-operative movement, the National League of Co-operatives, is controlled by an alliance of Communists and Socialists, the bulk of the agricultural world remains squarely under Christian democratic influence, in the shape of the Coltivatori Diretti, or Farmers' Association. The PCI-controlled sharecroppers' federation has lost importance as the land tenure system·upon which it was based has been phased out, and the new Communist-controlled Farmers' Confederation, combining the former sharecroppers' and peasant organisations, is no match for its Catholic rival. Similarly, in dealing with what the party calls 'women's questions', the PCI has the predominant interest in the UDI, the Union of Italian Women, even though the latter is at times embarrassingly radical for the Communists. In any case it has a difficult task to compete with the social influence of its powerful Catholic rival, the Italian Women's Centre.[6]

In addition to these traditional interest associations, the PCI has had some success in recent years in influencing new movements and groups which have developed since the 'participation explosion' of the late sixties. SUNIA, the vociferous and influential tenants' rights association, is largely under Communist control. The PCI has also taken very seriously the statutory school and university councils and even the parent-teacher associations, and has won a dominant position at this level. It has made similar progress among many environmental and community action groups.

The success of all these efforts to expand Communist influence is of course ultimately measurable in terms of party membership and the party electorate. By comparison with any other party of the left in Western Europe, the PCI's membership record must be counted a success. Neither the SPD, nor the French Communists, nor the Labour Party's direct membership can match the 1.5–2 million members of the PCI (the unconscious millions of Labour's affiliated membership clearly cannot count for comparative purposes).

None the less, there have been some substantial variations in the nature of this membership. First, its size has changed over time. Having risen to a peak of over 2 million in the late forties, membership gradually fell off to about 1.5 million in the long years of the party's isolation in the fifties and sixties. From 1972 to 1977, however, it grew significantly and steadily, and if official figures are to be believed, it had risen to approximately 1.8 million by 1977.[7]

This growth has naturally been the result of a favourable net balance between recruitment and defection. At the base of the party there is a surprisingly large turnover; probably half the present members have joined since 1970. This fairly high rate of defection suggests that the mass party has not become an altogether loyal and committed one. In the south especially, individuals tend to remain in the party for only a short period and in 1978 more people seem to have left the party than have joined it.[8] As one party militant put it, the PCI has 'lost the prestige of a party of opposition without having gained the glamour of a party of government',[9] and it is now facing some real organisational problems at the grass-roots level. One of its main difficulties is simply a lack of competent people, now that its militants and local leaders have much wider responsibilities in local government. In this respect the Communists are following in the footsteps of the Socialists, who encountered the same problem when they too were transformed into a part of the ruling majority in the early sixties.

As for the social composition of the membership, official figures suggest that the class alliance strategy of the PCI has borne some limited fruit. The ubiquitous 'middle strata' of Italian society (small farmers, artisans, shopkeepers and other self-employed categories) are reasonably well represented in the party. Fifteen per cent of the membership is composed of this group, and a further 7 per cent consists of white-collar and professional groups, compared with approximately 47% drawn from the agricultural and industrial working classes.[10] The remaining third is composed of 'inactive' or marginal groups, such as housewives, pensioners and home-workers, and this reflects the increasing tendency to recruit entire families into the party, rather than just the male head of household. Indeed, this practice probably prevented an overall decline in membership in the sixties.

The official figures therefore suggest that the much vaunted alliance between industrial workers (the backbone of the party) and the 'middle strata' bears some relationship to reality. But what the official figures for middle-strata members do not tell us is precisely how successful the PCI is at distinguishing between what it calls the 'productive' and the 'parasitic' elements, and at recruiting only the former. There is indeed some evidence that in the Red Belt the PCI has always tended to attract a fair number of the parasites as well as the 'useful people', and indeed that its expansion in the south in recent years has also associated it with such groups.

If this is the case it may prove a substantial barrier, in the long run, to the so-called 'structural reforms' that the party is always demanding, since such reforms are aimed not just at the 'great monopoly concentrations', but also at the parasitic groups who are alleged to impede the efficient development of the economy. A cynic might of course reply that in an Italian economy increasingly based on a mountain of publicly subsidised credit, and in which the boundary between the public and private sectors of the economy is fast disappearing, the distinction between the productive and the parasitic is becoming irrelevant. This might indeed be the view of many Communists already, but it has not yet become public.

Passing from party membership to the base of the pyramid of support — the Communist electorate — the pattern is of a slow but continuous build-up. In the forties the party overtook the Socialists as the main party of the left, and from an initial 18.9 per cent of the voters in 1946 gradually expanded to 27.2 per cent in 1972 — an expansion which occurred mostly at the expense of the Socialists. In the mid-seventies the party experienced something of an electoral take-off, and made almost as much progress in 4 years as in the previous 25. Its support rose to 34.4 per cent in the 1976 elections: an increase far in excess of the parallel rise in membership.

This success was registered in all parts of the country, although it was noticeable that the Communist vote increased more in parts of the north-west and the south than in the Red Belt, where it was already very high. The causes of the increase were complex. They are in part attributable to increasing respectability, as the party made many loud protestations of moderation and democratic fidelity in the seventies. This tended to improve the public image of the Communists, as successive opinion polls suggested.[11] Moreover, the Christian democrats clearly passed through a desperately difficult phase between 1974 and 1976. A series of public scandals involving party leaders, the defeat in the divorce referendum of 1974 and in the regional elections of 1975, and the country's serious economic problems all damaged their standing and added to the sense of immobilisation and crisis which has been a semi-permanent feature of Italian public life in the seventies.

Without doubt these factors worked to the electoral advantage of the PCI, but in a rather paradoxical way, for while the Communists gained substantial ground, the Christian democrats' electoral support, in aggregate terms, held firm. In fact, what appears to have occurred was a slight shift of working-class voters from the Christian democrats (henceforth referred to as the DC) to the PCI, but a compensating move of middle-class voters from the smaller conservative parties to the

DC.[12] Such a shift, if it continues in the future, would in the long run make it more difficult for the two main parties to collaborate with each other. It would also undermine the official PCI view of Christian democracy as the representative of the 'Catholic masses', with whom its own social constituency has much in common.

A rather more welcome feature of the 1976 vote, from the Communist standpoint, was the clear evidence that electoral turnover was benefiting the party, and that it was getting an increasing share of the younger vote[13] (1976 was in fact the first general election at which 18-year-olds had the vote). This process has been linked by some to the waning influence of the Catholic Church in modern Italy, and it has been argued that the Church's social network can no longer channel the vote towards the Christian democrats. The Marxist subculture is said to be taking over the primacy enjoyed by the Catholic subculture, and in the long run the PCI may become the 'naturally' dominant party.[14]

Unfortunately for the party, however, events since the 1976 election suggest an alternative prognosis. It may be that the two subcultures themselves are breaking down to some degree, and that the Italian electorate — like that of some other industrial nations — is becoming more volatile. This is certainly the inference to be drawn from the two sets of local elections held during the course of 1978, which marked heavy defeats for the PCI.[15] In one case there was a substantial victory for the DC, and in another case for local parties. It must be admitted that these elections were only held in limited areas, and one of them took place in exceptional circumstances immediately after the murder of Aldo Moro. Even so, in the general election of June 1979 the Communist vote dropped to 30.4 per cent, 4 per cent less than in 1976. It looks as if the former trend of a slow and steady increase in Communist support has ended. If new voters, who are better educated and given to greater expectations than their forefathers, also display this volatility, then the PCI may have to rethink at least the electoral dimension of its advance towards 'hegemony'.

2 Strategy and Ideology: the 'Historic Compromise' and the Debate on 'Hegemony'

The PCI's long-term strategy and ideology reflect its

organisational strengths. The party's aim has always been *presenza*, an active 'presence', or permeation, throughout all sectors of Italian society. Ultimately, *presenza* is designed to establish a kind of 'hegemony', i.e. unquestioned acceptance of Communist values and leadership. Clearly both *presenza* and 'hegemony' presuppose an effective and well disciplined permanent organisation. This section discusses the party's strategic aims. It examines first how the PCI has adapted these aims to its circumstances and to the need for alliance with other groups, and second, how the concept of 'hegemony' has in recent years sparked off some intense ideological and political disputes.

The PCI's strategy of 'presence' leading to 'hegemony' was glorified in 1947 with the name of 'The Italian Road to Socialism', and after 1956 party debate concentrated on the details of this road. It was supposed to provide a gradual and peaceful transition from capitalism to socialism. However, it was never very clear how exactly the transition was supposed to occur. Even violence could not be ruled out entirely, for the capitalists might resort to armed reaction, as they had done in the 1920s, and in that case Fascism would have to be fought. The party noticeably failed to debate institutional matters, apart from claiming that the existing constitution — which the PCI had helped to draw up in 1947 — was 'an important conquest on the Italian Road to Socialism'.[16] Vague references to 'popular unity' and to the 'collaboration of all democratic forces' did not contribute much enlightenment. Certainly the 'Italian Road' did not rely heavily on Parliament. The PCI has always been sceptical of the value of parliamentary majorities, and has seen Parliament more as a reflection of the balance of power in the country, as merely one of a number of useful institutions, rather than as the engine of social and political change.

Yet despite the PCI's vagueness about the Road (was it a one-way street?) some things were clear. There was to be no violent revolution and no 'dictatorship of the proletariat', or at least none comparable to that in the USSR. Instead, the Communists had to work through all existing institutions, make themselves indispensable, train a new ruling class, and transform the economy by a series of 'structural reforms' which would also boost the political power of the working class.

The 'Italian Road' was not, however, *solely* a matter of

peaceful infiltration and *presenza*. It also included a 'strategy of alliance'. The PCI has constantly proffered the hand of friendship to other groups in Italy — to the Socialists, to the 'Catholic masses', to the industrial managers, to the independent small farmers, to the artisans and small shopkeepers, to the mysterious 'middle strata' (*ceti medi*). Usually its courtship has been unheeded, but it keeps trying; alliances and coalition-building have been a permanent aim.[17]

In the 1970s this policy of peaceful penetration and alliance has been much more successful than it was earlier, mainly because of the 'participation explosion' that many sectors of Italian society have undergone since 1968. Sometimes the party has taken the lead in stimulating and leading 'grass-roots' movements, for example in city wards or secondary schools; sometimes it has climbed hastily on to a rapidly rolling bandwagon, for example in the 'factory delegates' shop-floor movement after 1969. In both cases the talk has been of *istanze democratiche*, of allegedly irresistible democratic pressures for radical change. The party assigned itself the duty of organising and channelling — and sometimes moderating — these commendable but chaotic demands, of providing leadership and order to a society in rapid transit. Here was a whole new range of opportunities for a well disciplined, efficient bureaucratic *apparat*, scenting real power after nearly thirty years in the wilderness. And there was not much competition. The 'centre-left' government coalition (Christian Democrat–Socialist–Social Democrat–Republican) was visibly collapsing, leaving a virtual power vacuum in Italy by 1974–5; and both the Christian democrats and the Socialists were split into warring factions.

Moreover, regional governments were set up throughout the country in 1970, and during the 1970s they were given greater powers. They organised welfare services and public works, they provided nursery schools and sporting facilities, they issued licences and drew up development plans.[18] Here, too, was a fruitful new source of power and patronage, not just in the regional governments themselves, but also in the host of regional or local specialist agencies that they created or absorbed. The new institutions were, in fact, ideally suited to a well organised party pursuing a strategy of *presenza*. Thus by 1976 the Communist Party had become indisputably the second power in the land, and many people expected it to 'overtake' the Christian democrats. It won over a third of the popular vote, it helped run five regional governments and most of the major cities, it dominated the most important trade unions, and it could hope to place its men into top jobs throughout the very extensive (and rapidly growing) public sector. No wonder intellectuals and place-seekers flooded into the PCI in 1974–6. It all looked like a novel kind of Communist take-over — revolution by quango.

Yet the party's leadership was still cautious. Many institutions — the police, the army, the judiciary, the senior civil service — were still beyond the party's grasp, indeed were subject to considerable neo-Fascist influence; and Chile provided a dreadful warning of what might happen if the left came to power too soon. In any case, Italy's allies were not likely to sit back passively and watch the Communists gain control of the government. The party was just not respectable enough, and Italy's economy was just not strong enough, to make any *sole* exercise of power a feasible proposition. So, the party leaders argued, power-sharing was the most that could be hoped for; the Communists would continue to be 'present', but they would also need to seek more allies wherever they could be found.

In September 1973, therefore, the party Secretary, Berlinguer, put forward his famous plea for a 'historic compromise' with the Christian democrats. The Communists, he claimed, were ready to act responsibly. They were anxious to restore economic stability and public order, and they were willing to guarantee the position of the Church and to respect all the usual 'Western' civil liberties; in return they would expect to influence policy and secure reforms. In other words, the PCI was 'available' as a partner. It was willing to be 'co-involved' in managing the machinery of government, and it could offer a prospect of stable long-term government to a Christian democratic party that was torn by factions and bereft of other allies.

This strategy sounded novel, but in fact only the phrase 'historic compromise' was new. For many years Communist leaders have stressed that the Christian democratic party is 'popular' and anti-Fascist, and have tried to woo the more left-wing DC factions away from the right. Communist and Catholic trade unionists have worked closely together, at least since 1969. In any case, by 1974–5 the Christian democrats were in no position to resist enticing offers, and since the 1976 elections a kind of 'historic compromise' has been gradually implemented. The PCI has not only left the ghetto, it has entered the 'government arena' at national level. In August 1976 Giulio Andreotti formed a new Christian democrat government, which could count on PCI abstention on votes of confidence (the so-called 'policy of no no-confidence'); in 1977 the PCI helped draw up the government programme; by March 1978 the PCI was part of the government majority, and so voted *for* the government. This was a real milestone. The party has apparently achieved full legitimacy: only the final step, Communist Ministers in the Cabinet, remains to be taken. Zaccagnini, the DC Secretary, may have insisted that all this was *not* the 'historic compromise', but it looked uncommonly like it.

Yet the moderate Christian democrats — Andreotti, Forlani and, until his death, Moro — who have favoured alliance with the PCI, have done so with caution. They have envisaged a strictly political, strictly short-term alliance, to cope with a pressing economic crisis; and they have rejected the term 'historic compromise'.[19] Essentially they have seen the alliance as the only way to 'tame', 'absorb', 'co-responsibilities' — and perhaps discredit — the Communist Party. Berlinguer should therefore be given a little encouragement, and above all he should be given plenty of time. The PCI could not be transformed overnight, but it might become more responsible as it became more involved in local and national politics. Moreover, trade union support for economic austerity measures was vital, and here was an added reason to set up a 'national government'. The alliance was, therefore, accepted as an unwelcome necessity, until the economy and the Christian democrat party revived; but that did not mean surrender. Indeed, the DC *must* maintain its strength and self-confidence, and it *must* remain the senior partner in government.

Even this line of argument is far from popular within the Christian democrat party, which is still profoundly mistrustful of Communism. All the right-wing Christian democrats feel that to collaborate with the PCI is a betrayal of everything the party has ever stood for; and many left-wingers (e.g. Carlo Donat-Cattin) warn constantly that the PCI intends to establish a Marxist 'hegemony' over the whole country. Moreover, it should never be forgotten that Italian politics is based on patronage. The DC has no intention of sharing out the jobs with anybody else if it can help it. There have been some unseemly rows over the PCI's claims for posts in state industries, banks, television and the like; by the end of 1978 the Communists were so exasperated that they boycotted the committee set up to distribute these jobs. Some crumbs will no doubt be thrown in their direction, but it seems highly unlikely that the PCI will get its hands on the worthwhile spoils. And given the economic crisis, there is no hope of creating many *new* posts. There is a real conflict of interest here, a matter of passionate concern to many Christian democrats; whatever the senior party politicians might think in Rome, harsh economic necessity elsewhere indicates 'No surrender'.

Moreover, many *Communist* militants are also opposed to any 'compromise'. The PCI rank and file were very restive by the winter of 1977–8, party membership was falling for the first time in years, and the Communist vote declined at the local elections of May 1978. If the party stayed committed to the DC alliance, it risked losing working-class support. Wage restraint is a particularly important aspect of this problem. Leading Communist trade unionists like Luciano Lama preached the need for austerity, but his words were not well received by the party faithful.[20] In fact, during 1978 socialist and independent trade unionists continued to press for higher wages, and there were many strikes in the public sector. By the autumn it was clear that the PCI could not guarantee to 'deliver' peaceful labour relations. Arguably the Communists' 'historic compromise' is not so much with the Christian democrats as with the technocrats and industrial managers of northern Italy; it is on the shop floor that the strategy will succeed or fail – and by the autumn of 1978 it looked as if it were failing.

In any case, it is clear that neither the ordinary Christian democrats nor the rank-and-file Communists have much liking for their alliance; it has been, and remains, an arrangement among party leaders only, undertaken for strictly political ends. The same can probably be said of the PCI's willingness to collaborate with the Church, which has a much longer history than the party's overtures to the DC. In 1947, at the

Constituent Assembly, the Communists voted in favour of recognising the 1929 Concordat between Italy and the Holy See, and thus helped guarantee the Church's influence in the post-war world. Throughout the 1970s there have been continuous, if secret, negotiations for a new Concordat, and thus the PCI has once again had much room for manoeuvre — holding out an olive branch to the Church, making occasional threatening noises, but generally offering its services as a guarantor of future religious harmony.[21] Moreover, the PCI has firmly supported the Vatican's *Ostpolitik*, which aims at better relations with the East European states; and naturally Berlinguer attended the major reception given by Paul VI to the Polish party leader Gierek in December 1977.

In October 1977 the Communists' wooing of the Church became more ardent. The party journal *Rinascita* published an open letter from Berlinguer to the Bishop of Ivrea, explaining that the PCI admits members of all races, faiths and convictions. The PCI was not going to renounce its Marxist heritage, but it did not profess any doctrine as such, not did it seek to give special status to any doctrines in state-run bodies, for example in schools. 'Does the Italian Communist Party as such, i.e. as a party, a political organisation, profess explicitly the Marxist ideology as a materialist and atheist philosophy? I would answer no.'[22]

This letter naturally caused quite a stir. The Communist veteran Gian Carlo Pajetta remarked caustically that the PCI was in danger of becoming 'the second Catholic party'. Various commentators pointed out that while Article Two of the PCI's Statute said anybody, of any belief, could join the party, none the less Article Five laid down that all members had 'a duty to study and apply the teachings of Marxism–Leninism' (This clause was, in fact, altered at the next party Congress in 1979). The Vatican's response was immediate, and positive. It noted that Berlinguer had reaffirmed the PCI's Marxist heritage, and it stressed that Marxism was indeed incompatible with Christianity. Even so, the Church welcomed Berlinguer's statement, as a first step. 'No one could rejoice more sincerely than we, if a great mass party, so rich in strength and activities (*fermenti*!) as the PCI, were really to succeed in overcoming, both in theory and practice, its Marxist–Leninist, materialist and atheist prejudice.'[23]

Yet it would be wrong to stress the harmony and agreements too much. Like the PCI and the DC, the PCI and the Church may have something to offer each other on certain issues, but they remain profoundly suspicious of each other's long-term intentions. They are often in conflict with each other on concrete local issues like nursery education or welfare provision, to say nothing of major 'ideological' issues like abortion. In 1977 a major row blew up over new laws on the powers of regional governments, which in the Church's view brought social welfare under political control. Bishops proclaimed that the laws were a direct attack on private (i.e. Church) activities, and even a proof of totalitarian tendencies. Cardinal Benelli of Florence – where Catholic ambulance and hospital services are particularly old-established – warned that

> a State that wishes to do everything by itself, and considers welfare as its own exclusive function, and thus thinks it has a duty to suffocate any private initiative, is a collectivist, totalitarian, Marxist State. A State whose installation in Italy is beginning to be regarded as inevitable.[24]

Thus the 1977 dispute was not about the fairly trivial question of regional powers, but about the whole issue of uniformity and state control *v.* private enterprise and 'pluralism'. Essentially the Communists and the Church are competing in the ideological market-place. Berlinguer may have told the Bishop of Ivrea that the PCI was not an ideological party, but no sensible cleric believed him,[25] and indeed by 1978 Berlinguer was defending Lenin and the Marxist heritage once again. In fact, the PCI takes ideology very seriously indeed. Like the Church, it too has its saints and martyrs, its old Testament (Marx) and its New (Lenin, or rather Gramsci), its processions and its feast-days (1 May, Festival of L'Unità). It, too, has its prevailing norms of good conduct, laid down in handbooks for the faithful – duty, discipline, obligation. It, too, is always anxious to restrain its fanatics, to curb any excess of millenarian enthusiasm; and it, too, is essentially a didactic organisation, preaching its official Word to the City and to the World. Even its basic strategy, of presence and hegemony, has largely been taken over from nineteenth-century Catholic social thought. Above all, the party, too, offers its faithful the prospect of Heaven. If there are going to be few material rewards from the historic compromise, the PCI can hardly afford to annoy its ordinary members by ditching its ideology as well. As for the Church, it is quite happy to accept the ideological challenge openly and publicly: after all, that is what it is for. From the Church's point of view, the situation has some similarities with that in Eastern Europe; the election of Cardinal Wojtyla to the papacy in October 1978 will no doubt strengthen the Vatican's resolve to continue the struggle.

The *de facto* 'historic compromise' thus provided an added stimulus for the major ideological debates of 1975–8, which we will now consider. Much of the debate focused on the PCI's martyred theorist, Antonio Gramsci, whose writings can certainly be used to support a policy of infiltration and gradual take-over (if not of alliance, once the potential allies have read him). Gramsci was a brilliant Marxist intellectual who had been the leader of the PCI between 1924 and 1926, and had been imprisoned by the Fascists from 1926 until near his death in 1937. His main theme was the importance of 'hegemony', the process by which the values of the dominant class were transmitted throughout the rest of society. Here, thought Gramsci, was the real foundation of bourgeois rule. Ordinary people obeyed capitalist regimes because they had been 'socialised' to do so. All states rested on 'consensus' as well as on force. But 'consensus' was not spontaneous, it was engineered by the culture industry and by intellectuals through a series of 'private' or semi-private bodies – schools, churches, publishers, advertising, the mass media, etc. Obviously the key problem for a revolutionary party then became: how to erode 'bourgeois' values, how to undermine 'bourgeois hegemony'? And the answer, too, was obvious: infiltrate existing institutions, and set up a 'counter-culture' wherever possible. A network of Communist journals, publishers, festivals, etc., would end the bourgeois monopoly of ideas, and would instil 'socialist consciousness'. It would all take time, but it had to be done, for no socialist society could survive unless men were already imbued with socialist ideals. New 'socialist' institutions could also help the process of conversion. Factory committees, workers' and peasants' councils, trade unions and the like would all enable workers to learn about socialism. Thus Gramsci was not merely advocating a *Kulturkampf*. Practical experience was probably a better teacher than any amount of propaganda, and in his writings 'ideology' and 'institutions' were never fully separated. Institutions embodied and affected modes of thought; ideas, in turn, might undermine or transform institutions. 'Hegemony' meant a dominant system of ideas, but it also meant a dominant series of institutions.

These theories are clearly designed for complex, industrial, democratic countries with a free press and a literate population, especially if such countries are familiar with the idea of a clerisy and with a permanent organisation that preaches an all-embracing ideology. Gramsci's views stress the role of intellectuals and the media, and are therefore welcome to them; and they promise harmony, consensus and a peaceful, if slow, transition to socialism. His writings have thus been immensely influential in post-war Italy. The PCI has used them to attract intellectual support, to justify its highly intellectual leadership, to rebut charges of 'reformism' or of having become a pragmatic 'social-democratic' party. Above all, it has used them to educate its members and to persuade them to study historical, philosophical and cultural themes. Gramsci's works have become canonical, not only in Italy. They give the PCI its cultural credentials; they have themselves become virtually 'hegemonic'. To criticise Gramsci has been on a par with 'speaking ill of Garibaldi' – just not done in polite society.

Yet Gramsci himself, in his later prison years , was an isolated figure, condemned and shunned by his fellow Communists in prison for opposing the Comintern's leftward turn in 1930; and, in any case, his writings are not so liberal as has often been claimed. Gramsci was a Communist revolutionary first and foremost. His 'hegemony' means simply that society is always permeated by a dominant set of values. Quite apart from the question of whether this is a plausible view or not, it is worth noting that Gramsci had no belief in (or desire for) 'pluralism', no time for the clash of rival political ideas, no faith in a multi-party democracy. His heroes were Machiavelli's Prince, the Jacobins, Lenin and the Bolsheviks – i.e. men who dreamed of, or succeeded in, imposing new values on the whole of society. In his view, a disciplined Communist Party was needed in Italy to do the same thing, and it would naturally aim at as complete a cultural monopoly as it could achieve. In other words, Gramsci was a Leninist too – not perhaps as authoritarian as his mentor, but just as convinced of the need for party discipline and intellectual leadership, and just as ambitious for 'totalitarian' control of society.

And so the PCI's adoption of Gramsci as its patron saint had its dangers. During the crucial years of Communist advance in 1975–7, the unthinkable happened. There was a furious debate about Gramsci, about 'hegemony' and 'pluralism'.[26] The attack was led by socialist intellectuals, for the most part university teachers of philosophy, who pointed out various inconvenient aspects of Gramsci's thought, and went even further. They argued that Gramsci was a 'post-Catholic' thinker, more clerical than the Pope. Not only did he wish to install a new Rule of the Saints (thinly disguised as 'organic intellectuals', to use Gramsci's term, or more familiarly, the radical intelligentsia) and give them a monopoly over education and cultural life, but he also wished to abolish the market.[27] Texts in hand, the socialist critics waged their campaign in the Gramscian heartland, among the left-wing intellectuals, spreading dismay and irritation where they went. 'Hegemony', they claimed, was incompatible with 'pluralism'.[28] How could a 'hegemonic' party tolerate an independent judiciary, or a free press or opposition parties? How could it refrain from seeking to regulate the whole of society, including the trade unions, the business firms, the churches and the welfare organisations? If Gramsci was indeed the father figure of the Italian Road to Socialism, as the PCI claimed, then that road began to look a good deal less attractive to other would-be travellers. In 1977 the PCI celebrated the fortieth anniversary of Gramsci's death in noticeably low-key fashion, compared with the thirtieth anniversary ten years earlier.[29]

All these arguments were directed, of course, not just against Gramsci, but against the PCI's whole strategy. Even if the Communists were willing to observe a genuine 'historic compromise' with the Church, that was hardly reassuring to socialists or liberals, who were 'laicists' to a man: they might be faced by a new massive power bloc, hegemony *à deux*, which would be even more likely to crush liberties and suppress social change. Moreover, the critics argued, the PCI had been very silent about which social or political institutions would administer a socialist Italy. Although on good terms with Tito, the PCI had never advocated the 'Yugoslav model' as applicable to Italy, and there was nothing much else in Communist literature about how a distinctively socialist state might be run. Where were the guarantees?

Moreover, the debate did not remain an esoteric academic discussion. Socialist *politicians*, especially the new party Secretary, Bettino Craxi, began adopting very similar arguments, although he normally preferred to attack the PCI's 'Leninism' and its lack of democratic credibility, with only passing reference to Gramsci. Leninism was, in Craxi's view, 'dominated by the ideal of a homogeneous, compact, classless society'. It was a 'religion disguised as science, which claims to have found the answer to all problems of human life'; it was necessarily totalitarian; it meant 'the State as father of everything – economic resources, institutions, men and ideas', and it meant all this *inevitably* and deliberately. It would necessarily result in the bureaucratisation of everything, and in the ruthless persecution of dissidents. It was all anathema to any decent democrat. Socialism, for Craxi, had to be 'democratic, lay and pluralist'; the private sector would therefore, have to flourish even in a socialist society, and so would the market, although some 'regulation' would no doubt be necessary. Craxi was obviously influenced by Yugoslavia, and by some recent French socialist writers on 'autogestion'. His hero, it seemed, was Pierre-Joseph Proudhon, which led to an unexpected rush to the bookshops to find out what Proudhon had actually written.[30]

The Communist reaction to these attacks was a predictable mixture of irritation, defensiveness and assertiveness. There was nothing to be ashamed of, they proclaimed. Gramsci had been a true Leninist; so was the PCI and proud of it. The PCI had fought Fascism, had helped found the Republic, and had helped to cope with the grave economic and political crisis of recent years. Its democratic credentials were beyond question, and it was not going to take irresponsible criticism from renegade 'Atlanticists' like Craxi. Biagio de Giovanni, for example, declared that 'pluralism' meant many centres of economic power, and that was undemocratic. Flavio Colonna wrote that bourgeois democracy was a sham anyway, because of the unjust electoral laws in Britain, France and West Germany – 'we must take great care not to think too highly of the empty phrases of the bourgeoisie's deceptive ideological luggage – the bourgeoisie has used it to *hinder* the development of democracy whenever it did not coincide with its own interests.'[31]

Berlinguer attempted to mediate, as usual. He spoke of 'pluralism' in Moscow itself, in November 1977, in an attempt to show that the term was acceptable even at headquarters; and he recognised the need for institutional safeguards against abuses of power in a socialist state. But Berlinguer's hands were tied. He could not propose anything very detailed without implicitly criticising the USSR; nor, of course, could he criticise Leninism unless he was willing to transform the party's organisation. So Craxi's offensive had its predictable consequences. It forced Berlinguer back to defending the glorious Marxist heritage against impudent socialist critics. In August 1978, in a newspaper interview, he praised democratic centralism and Leninism – not as a dogma, of course, but as a 'living and valid lesson' – and expressed the aim of 'liquidating capitalism'.[32] In September, in a major speech at Genoa, he returned to the theme. Neither the Russian experience nor the 'social democratic model' was valid for Italy. The social democrats had accepted the capitalist system, which the PCI was pledged to overthrow. The party aimed at achieving 'socialism', but would do so by a 'third way', within the framework of the democratic Italian constitution. It was capitalism, not socialism, that was now in crisis, and hence was incompatible with democracy:

> the defence and development of democracy today can only happen via the struggle to overcome capitalism; in this sense the workers' struggle for democracy has also a precise class content. Here is the difference between us and liberal or social-democratic views.[33]

As for democratic centralism, it was a healthy safeguard against indiscipline and factional struggle: 'we shall never wish to be a party of factions or *clienteles*' (ibid.).

In practice, of course, the PCI leaders act first and look in the sacred texts later, like any other sensible politicians. Yet ideology matters to them, especially at a time when the PCI is undergoing a serious identity crisis. It is significant that Berlinguer has been forced to appear 'Leninist', and that Gramsci's image is looking a little tarnished. Gramsci is the Communists' last line of defence: they have to rally to him. Yet they cannot propose a Communist 'hegemony' too loudly, and they are trying hard to build up a 'pluralist' reputation. It is not surprising if party ideologists sound unconvincing, or if many militants are confused. Berlinguer's much-quoted remark that the PCI is 'both conservative and revolutionary'[34] is not a great help either.

The Socialists, too, have other reasons besides ideology for attacking the PCI at this time, including quarrels in regional and local government and a fear of being squeezed out of any influence in affairs. Even so, it seems to us that some of them are genuinely concerned about ideological matters. They do not want the PCI to be accepted into the political establishment too soon, before it has changed enough; and they are also worried at the prospect of individual liberties being suffocated by some long-term Catholic–Communist 'national government'. Craxi speaks of, and perhaps dreams of, a 'left-wing alternative' to DC rule, but this prospect is only feasible if the PCI becomes genuinely social democratic and 'Western'. No doubt he also dreams of the PSI becoming the dominant party of the Italian left. In any case, the Socialists' ideological arguments are the first move in a campaign to 'delegitimise' the PCI among the intellectuals. The debate has been Italy's equivalent of President Carter's 'human rights' campaign of 1977 – partly just good propaganda, partly a necessary device to revive morale and self-confidence among non-Communists, and partly an attempt to encourage change in the Communist camp – and this last aspect backfired in Italy, as it did elsewhere.

Perhaps the final word should lie with the speaker of the Chamber of Deputies, the veteran Communist Pietro Ingrao. He proclaimed, with his customary obscurity, that the PCI wanted 'hegemony of the working class within pluralism';[35] but what he really worried about was that 'pluralism' might infect the major trade union confederation, the CGIL. The unions should, of course, be independent centres of power ('pluralism'), but on the other hand there was a real danger of 'corporatism' if they acted only for their members, and an even bigger danger that trade union militancy might frighten voters away from the party.[36] This was a major issue in 1978, as 'autonomous' trade unions, without any links to political parties, led unofficial disputes throughout the public sector. If these small unions could bring about such chaos, what might happen if the big official unions started acting more independently? So the Communists had a sound argument here, if they dared use it. 'Pluralism' looked a good deal less attractive if it meant simply undisciplined disruption; 'hegemony' looked less frightening if it offered 'social peace'. Ugo La Malfa, the very influential leader of the Republican Party, has consistently supported the PCI's admission into government on these grounds. The outcome of the 'hegemony' *v.* 'pluralism' debate, like that of the 'historic compromise', is likely to be settled on the shop floor.

3 The PCI and 'Polycentrism'

Much of the debate about the PCI and Eurocommunism revolves, of course, around the party's links with the USSR and with the Eastern European regimes. The party was founded, after all, to be a branch of the Communist International, and it has remained an honoured member of the 'international working-class movement' ever since. Party leaders confer in Moscow and the Eastern European capitals regularly; much Italian trade with Eastern Europe passes through Communist-controlled import/export firms, or is arranged through Communist good offices. So, too, is tourism to Eastern Europe or to Cuba; indeed, PCI branch offices are sometimes mistaken for travel agencies. Many of the older party leaders have spent years in Russia: in December 1977 the party's President, Luigi Longo, spoke proudly of his 'links of affection' with the USSR, and of the fact that his two sons were brought up there.[37] The party's newspaper, *L'Unità*, inveighs constantly against American imperialism, and firmly supports Cuban or Soviet intervention in Africa and elsewhere; and it is the PCI's official view that the 'crisis of capitalism' is fundamentally caused by the successful fight against imperialism.

The Socialist's offensive of 1975–8 naturally concentrated on all these concrete issues, as well as on the nature of 'hegemony' and 'democratic centralism'. They stressed the lack of civil rights in Russia, and this had immediate political repercussions in Italy. In Emilia-Romagna, for example, there was a significant squabble about whether a regional delegation should attend the Moscow agricultural fair – only the PCI thought it should go, and the issue nearly brought down the regional government. 'Eurocommunism' did not mean much, argued Craxi, so long as the Communist parties maintained their solidarity with the USSR.[38] And Claudio Signorile wanted to know whether the PCI thought the USSR was a socialist society.[39]

Berlinguer's answer was characteristically firm and characteristically evasive. He wisely ignored the question of socialism, but equally wisely spoke warmly of the USSR:

> Let us make it quite clear, we do not regard as of equal importance from the historical point of view, the experience of the October Revolution and of the U.S.S.R., and the experience of Social-Democracy. In fact, however much we criticise Soviet experience – and certainly we do not regard it as a model – we recognise that the October Revolution, and the later construction of a new society in that part of the world, have the value of a historic breach which has had important consequences for the whole later development of human society, providng the impetus for a process of liberation of the masses and of the oppressed peoples . . . We will never deny or lose sight of the value for the whole world of Lenin's work and of the October Revolution and its developments, the most important historic event of this century. If others want to deny it, let them; certainly we, from intimate conviction, will never do so.[40]

Clearly the PCI does not intend to give up its international links. Nor does it intend to 'excommunicate' anybody, least of all the Russians.

Yet it would be wrong to conclude that the party is subservient to Moscow. It is, rather, continuing Togliatti's policy of 'polycentrism'. It aims at the maximum possible independence for each party, each pursuing its own road to socialism, but maintaining friendly contacts with each other and joining up to fight 'imperialism'. The party leadership is well aware of what goes on in the East, but prefers – like some of the Eastern European leaders – to work for gradual change. It regrets the more blatant dissident trials, but it is careful never to be too critical, and it noticeably failed to support Carrillo in his disputes with the Russians in 1977. It defended – and still defends, even today – the invasion of Hungary in 1956 on the grounds that 'the forces of reaction were attempting to detach the country from the Soviet bloc.'[41] On the other hand, it condemned the invasion of Dubcek's Czechoslovakia, for the Czechs had never attempted to leave the Warsaw Pact. The 1968 invasion was simply a case of a national road to socialism being destroyed and clearly the PCI could never be expected to approve of that.[42]

Thus the PCI's policy is nothing if not diplomatic. It gives tacit encouragement to the less strident dissidents, but it also holds lengthy talks with Suslov and Zamyatin, and certainly it does not denounce the USSR on the human rights issue.[43] The PCI thinks it is much wiser to stay friendly with Moscow and seek to influence events from the inside.

Above all, there is trade. The PCI's influence and prestige within Italy rest heavily on its ability to smooth the path of Italian trade with the USSR and Eastern Europe; so obviously the PCI is not going to annoy the USSR unnecessarily. Eurocommunism, like *détente*, is 90 per cent trade. Italy is the USSR's fourth-largest Western trading partner (after West Germany, Japan and Finland); Italian exports to the Soviet Union, mainly machinery and pipelines, were worth £700 million in 1977.[44] As for Eastern Europe, new trading links are being forged very rapidly. In one typical week, in early October 1978, the Hungarian Industry Minister visited Italy; the head of Italian TV visited Poland, to conclude a 'cultural exchange' of programmes; an Italian economic delegation visited Hungary (since 1977 there has been a joint Italo–Hungarian committee for industrial and technical co-operation); a group of Italian trade unionists visited Rumania, as did the Italian Defence Minister; and virtually all Italy's top businessmen – including Giovanni Agnelli of Fiat, Guido Carli of the Industrialists' Confederation, Giuseppe Medici of Montedison, Pietro Sette in ENI and Alberto Boyer of IRI – were in Poland, for a meeting of another joint economic committee. This is quite apart from the even closer links with Yugoslavia, which an official PCI delegation led by G.C. Pajetta visited a week earlier, and which Berlinguer visited a week later. The point is that 'official' Italian industry is often too inefficient to compete in Western markets, and it desperately needs its (traditional) export outlets in Eastern Europe. The PCI helps provide them. It is good business, and good politics; and it naturally makes Italian business leaders rather more enthusiastic about Italian Communism.

Thus there has been, and will be, no breach with the East. But

Berlinguer would like to go further. Ideally the PCI would like to face both ways, to be able to play off East and West against each other, to be – like Tito – respected and courted on both sides. When Berlinguer met Tito in October 1978, Zagreb radio reported that the two parties 'take identical or very similar stands on all questions of co-operation and relations in the Communist and workers' movement' – including non-alignment and friendly relations with China.[45] The wish was father to the thought; the PCI does not 'take identical stands' to the Yugoslavs yet. If this is its aim, it needs to become far more 'legitimate' in Western eyes than it is now.

And so the PCI has, in recent years, tried to reassure the West. It formally voted for Italy's current foreign and defence policies in December 1977.[46] Its leaders – Segre, Pajetta, Napolitano – journey tirelessly to Ivy League universities and Labour Party conferences. They proclaim that Italy should remain a member of NATO, in order not to upset the balance of power or endanger *détente*, and even in order to prevent Russian interference while democratic socialism is being built.[47] Above all, the Italian Communists are 'good Europeans'. The PCI is firmly committed to the EEC and to Western integration. It supports direct elections, it favours 'enlargement', and it has always played its full part in Community institutions. Supporting the EEC helps to make the PCI more respectable and 'legitimate' on the European stage, just as supporting the Church does within Italy.[48]

These diplomatic overtures had some success, especially in 1975–7, but nothing like as much as the PCI had hoped. The Americans remained unimpressed about NATO, and Kissinger in 1977 issued a series of warnings about the international dangers involved if the Communists entered the government. The Carter administration, after some initial hesitancy and some 'liberal' concessions,[49] followed suit: on 12 January 1978 President Carter expressed the hope that Communist influence in Western Europe would diminish, and declared roundly that the USA did not want Communists to enter any government coalition. NATO was obviously a major consideration, but the American policy-makers were not just concerned with defence. They worried about the broader, less tangible issues of 'security' and 'influence'. It was not solely a matter of Mediterranean naval bases or the 'southern flank', or even the Nuclear

Planning Committee, but of the *morale* of the Alliance, the willingness of American public opinion to devote resources and men to defending a 'Communist' country, and the impact on West Germany.

There were, of course, other reasons why Berlinguer's initiatives foundered. It is all very well favouring Western European integration, but what if the other major Western European Communist Party stays hostile to the whole idea? Relations between the PCI and the PCF grew very cool in 1978, as direct elections grew nearer. The two parties failed to agree on a common electoral platform; and the PCF remained opposed to any enlargement of the Community. As for the PCE, it was too outspoken: more of an embarrassment than a support. Moreover, the PCI failed to convince either the British or the West German governments of its good intentions. West German public opinion, in particular, is deeply suspicious of Communism in any form, and it is difficult to see what the PCI can do to make itself more 'legitimate' there.

One other reason for the failure of Berlinguer's overtures in the West was the Socialist revival. Craxi set out to remind the social democratic parties of Western Europe that the PSI still existed; by 1977 he was a familiar visitor in Lisbon, Madrid, Paris and Bonn, and he was certainly present at the mysterious meeting of the Socialist International on Crete in the summer of that year — as was Carrillo.[50] Here was a counter-voice to the PCI's, a voice that stressed the Communists' continuing links to the USSR, and that also promised to commit the PSI more deeply to the Western alliance. If the Western social democratic parties had to choose, they were bound to choose Craxi rather than Berlinguer. Arguably the PSI was playing a foolish and dangerous game here, in delaying the Western European left's willingness to accept (and perhaps absorb) the PCI into its ranks; but no doubt the temptation was irresistible.

In any case, Carrillo's presence on Crete pointed the lesson out clearly. The PCI can come to be accepted by the West, as the PCE has been, but it must first break with the East. No wonder the Russians were suspicious. Berlinguer could not go too far without being disowned in Moscow. Longo's remarks in 1977 were a warning to the party's Secretary; and the Russians themselves joined in with scarcely veiled threats. *New Times* thundered that 'to speak of ideological pluralism as a characteristic of socialist society means in practice to concern oneself with maintaining anti-socialist ideological positions.'[51] Moscow's attacks on Carrillo and Azcárate were not meant exclusively for the PCE. There was even an unwelcome re-use of the term 'proletarian internationalism', and Zagladin claimed that the 1976 Berlin conference had been 'proof of the monolithism of Communists'.[52] The days are probably over when Moscow could decide a change of PCI leadership, but even so the Russians could cause much unpleasantness for Berlinguer if they wished. They could appeal to some members of the directorate (Chiaromonte? Cervetti? Cossutta?) as well as to the rank and file, and they could certainly put the economic pressure on. They could even support terrorism.[53] Thus Berlinguer's public praise of the October Revolution in August–September 1978 was prudent. It soon brought its reward. In October the Russians publicly accepted the PCI's strategy, and Berlinguer could face his forthcoming party congress with a good deal more confidence.

To summarise, the PCI remains less 'independent' than it would like. Much of its influence in business circles at home depends on its maintaining its Eastern European connections. Its attempts to establish its 'Western' credentials have aroused only scepticism in the West and suspicion in the East. Its closest friends are in Yugoslavia, Poland and Hungary, but that is hardly reassuring. *Détente* has certainly given the party more room for manoeuvre, but that room is still strictly limited. In 1978 all this became clearer, and the PCI became more fulsome about Russian achievements. Even so, while the PCI may not have many close friends, at least it does not have any implacable enemies (except perhaps Helmut Schmidt). Craxi himself claims only to be 'stimulating' it along the path to virtue. With the Chinese reappearing on the international scene, there may be more room in future for the PCI's ambiguous manoeuvres. And with a Polish Pope, the PCI may yet forge its own peculiar brand of an international 'historic compromise'.

4 Conclusion

The PCI, like Eurocommunism itself, gives an overwhelming impression of duplicity. It aims at *presenza* and infiltration, yet tries to secure 'alliances'; it has sanctified Gramsci, but proclaims 'pluralism'; it remains within the 'international Communist movement', while praising both NATO and non-alignment. It denounces capitalism, but works closely with capitalists, and promises no extension of public ownership. It refuses to be 'social democratic', yet it has integrated much of the Italian working class into a democratic political system. The one thing that is undeniable about it is its diplomatic skill. A great deal of juggling ability is needed to keep all the balls in the air at the same time, and so far Berlinguer and his colleagues have put on an admirable performance. Even so, the audience has grown restive of late, and it seems unlikely that the PCI's luck will last for ever.

Yet perhaps it is too easy to be sceptical. Let us imagine how things look from party headquarters in Via delle Botteghe Oscure. Undoubtedly the PCI leaders feel they are much misunderstood and much maligned. They are doing their best to control the unions; they are trying their utmost to preserve law and order; they are very anxious about the South and the young unemployed, and are seeking desperately for ways to help them. After all, they probably reason, they did not lead Italy into this mess; on the contrary, they are taking great political risks in trying to pull the country out of it. Their patriotism and sense of responsibility deserve a greater reward. Many thoughtful people, including Giulio Andreotti and Ugo La Malfa, clearly agree with them.[54]

Nor is Italy alone in being virtually ungovernable: the rest of Europe is in the same state. As Berlinguer and his colleagues sit in Rome, they foresee the Collapse of Western Civilisation. They genuinely believe that the present crisis is very profound. It is not just economic or political but, above all, moral and ideological. Western Man, they rather grandiloquently proclaim, has to evolve a New Civilisation; otherwise there is a real danger of a new Dark Age, of a 'modern barbarism' — a phrase that recurs surprisingly frequently in Communist literature.[55] The party leaders are intelligent, pessimistic and perhaps even rather religious men. They wish to preserve everything of value in the past, for it is certainly going to be needed in the future; and that applies particularly to the Church. But they see no point in trying to return to capitalism. That would simply lead to much more violence, and possibly to a complete collapse of law

and order and to a right-wing dictatorship.[56] The party is deeply
scarred by the experience of Fascism; anything likely to upset
stability must be avoided at all costs. Somehow, it believes, an
acceptable 'socialist' society will have to be worked out, one
which has some chance of popular acceptance and is not too
inefficient economically. No one can tell in advance what such a
society would be like: there are no models, and it is fatuous to
pretend that there are. And somehow the workers and
peasants — or rather the unemployed, the school-leavers and
the recent graduates — must be 'integrated' into the existing
political and economic system. These are all European
problems, and they can only be tackled effectively on a
European basis. But they are perhaps most acute in Italy, and
there the PCI has a great contribution to make, provided it
retains its discipline and its organisation.

The PCI's insistence on keeping its party machine intact, its
ambiguity on many strategic issues, its anxiety to cool down
international tensions, its deep conservatism on social issues, its
infuriating patience, are all understandable in these terms. The
PCI is *worried*, deeply worried, about the long-term prospects.
It does not believe that any party, or any part of Europe, has a
monopoly of the truth; and it believes that the problems of
Western and Eastern Europe are more similar than either side
cares to admit. So it advocates 'compromise' and 'co-respon-
sibilisation', not just for itself but for everyone else. This mess is
one we are all in together.

Assessment of the PCI must, therefore, depend on one's
assessment of the 'crisis of industrial democracies' in general,
and of the depths of the Italian crisis in particular. If it is true
that all hands are now needed on deck, then Socialist attacks on
the Communists' credentials are thoroughly irresponsible, for
what might happen if the PCI were forced back into opposition?
On the other hand, if one sees the present economic, political
and spiritual situation as reasonably tolerable, or at least as no
worse than usual, then the PCI's assistance will be thought
irrelevant or even harmful. However, even many who accept the
first assessment in principle are not necessarily going to welcome
the PCI's help in practice, for it means sharing out the influence
and the patronage. The Communist Party may be as responsible
and high-minded as it claims, but it will not get far if it does not
reward its supporters. In Italy, where people are used to

142   *The Italian Communist Party*

political rhetoric, the PCI's ideological and international ambiguities are relatively insignificant; what matters is jobs. It may seem a frivolous conclusion, but it is true none the less: the PCI's most important immediate task is to persuade the Christian Democrats that it takes two to quango.

Notes

1. See G. Arè, 'La struttura politica del P.C.I. dal 1968 al 1978' in A. Lombardo, *Le trasformazioni del comunismo Italiano* (Rizzoli, Milan, 1978), pp. 125–6, and E. Auci, 'Verità e preblemi dei bilanci dei partiti' in *Il Mulino*, vol. XXVII, no. 255 (March 1978), pp. 65–73. The figure for officials is taken from M. Barbagli and P. Corbetta, 'Partito e Movimento: Aspetti del Rinnovamento del P.C.I.' in *Inchiesta*, no. 31 (January–February 1978), pp. 3–46, at p. 21. This article, which is the best available study of PCI organisation, will shortly appear in book form: M. Barbagli, P. Corbetta and S. Sechi, *Dentro il P.C.I.* (Il Mulino, Bologna 1979).
2. See Salvatore Sechi, 'L'austero fascino del centralismo democratico', in *Il Mulino*, vol XXVII, no. 257 (May–June 1978), pp. 426–38. This is an important point. It is often mistakenly assumed that the advent of 'Eurocommunism' has involved some major change in the *internal* practices and structures of Western Communist parties, but at least in the Italian case this is not so. There have indeed been changes within both the national and provincial level leaderships of the PCI (see, for example, Fulco Lanchester, 'I dirigenti del P.C.I.: continuità e cambiamenti' in *Il Mulino*, vol. XXVII, no. 257 (May–June 1978), pp. 454–66), but these changes have occurred gradually through co-optation.
3. Sechi, 'L'auster fascino', pp. 427–30.
4. Ibid., pp. 446–7.
5. This fear of factionalism, especially at a moment when the party is on the verge of power, is not perhaps entirely unfounded. Factionalism is rife in the two main parties of government, the Christian democrats and the Socialists, and is encouraged by a number of features of the Italian political environment such as the institution of the preference vote in virtually all elections (which transforms elections into battles between candidates of the same party as well as between parties) and the widespread powers of patronage available to politicians in office. The experience of the Socialist Party is chastening in this respect. Formerly organised along the lines of democratic centralism, it immediately fell victim to rampant factionalism when genuine democracy was introduced into party life at the end of the fifties. See David Hine, 'Social Democracy in Italy' in W. E. Paterson and A. H. Thomas (eds.), *The Social Democratic Parties of Western Europe* (Croom Helm, London, 1977), pp. 67–87.
6. For an excellent, if now slightly dated, account of Communist presence in these groups see G. Galli and A. Prandi, *Patterns of Political Participation in Italy* (Yale University Press, New Haven, 1970), pp. 166–226.
7. See Arè, 'La struttura politica del P.C.I.', p. 115, and Barbagli and Corbetta, 'Partito e Movimento', p. 11.
8. See 'I vertici del P.C.I. chiedono consigli ai segretari di sezioni', *Corriere della Sera*, 24 October 1978.
9. Ibid.
10. The data on social composition is drawn from *Rinascita*, 5 March 1975, and refers to 1973. No more up-to-date estimates are available.

11. For an excellent illustration of the changes in public perceptions of the PCI between 1967 and 1974–6, and likewise the changes in an opposite direction of the PSI and the DC, see *Bollettino della Doxa*, vol. XXX, nos. 17–18 (1 September 1976), pp. 140–9.

12. On this question see S. Hellman, 'The Longest Campaign: Communist Party Strategy and the Elections of 1976', in H. R. Penniman (ed.), *Italy at the Polls* (American Enterprise Institute for Public Policy Research, Washington DC, 1977), pp. 175–8.

13. See G. Sani, 'The Italian Electorate in the Mid–1970s: Beyond Tradition?' in H. R. Penniman (ed.), *Italy at the Polls*, pp. 105–12.

14. Ibid., pp. 116–22.

15. In the local elections held on 14 May 1978, which involved approximately 2 million voters, the PCI lost one-third of those who voted for it in 1976, falling from 35.6 per cent in the relevant provinces to 26.7 per cent: see *Corriere della Sera*, 16 May 1978. In the regional elections of 20 November held in Trentino Alto-Adige only, the PCI again lost one-third of its 1976 vote: see *Corriere della Sera*, 21 November 1978. There are of course certain dangers in any strict comparison of local or regional results with those of general elections, but the overall trend is unmistakable.

16. 'Elements for a Policy Declaration' presented to the Eighth Congress of the PCI, 1956. In 1966 Luigi Longo defined the 'Italian Road' as 'a road of popular mass struggles, in which all the progressive forces in the country, both lay and Catholic, collaborate and unite to achieve profound transformations of the political, economic and social structures of Italy, so as to move towards Socialism, and with Socialism as their objective and final outcome' (*L'Unità*, 22 January 1966; cf. also *Tesi per il XI Congresso del P.C.I.* (1966), para. V, section 8).

17. For an excellent study of this policy, see S. Hellman, 'The P.C.I.'s Alliance Strategy and the Case of the Middle Classes', in D. Blackmer and S. Tarrow (eds.), *Communism in Italy and France* (Princeton University Press, Princeton, 1975), pp. 373–419. Cf. also R. Seidelman, 'P.C.I., Decentramento e Politica delle Alleanze', in *Il Mulino*, vol. XXVII, no. 257 (May–June 1978), pp. 467–98.

18. On Italian regionalism, see Martin Clark, 'Italy: Regionalism and Bureaucratic Reform' in J. P. Cornford (ed.), *The Failure of the State* (Croom Helm, London, 1975), pp. 44–81; and David Hine, 'Italy' in F. F. Ridley (ed.), *Government and Administration in Western Europe* (Martin Robertson, London, 1979).

19. Cf. Aldo Moro, interview in *La Repubblica*, 4 February 1978. He envisaged a temporary 'Grand Coalition', after which each party would resume its own strategy.

20. For Lama's view, see his interviews or speeches in *La Repubblica*, 24 January 1978, *L'Unità*, 5 March 1978, and *La Stampa*, 27 May 1978. Cf. also S. Bevacqua and G. Turani, *La Svolta del '78* (Feltrinelli, Milan, 1978) for documents on the relations between the PCI and the unions in 1977–8.

21. Many of Berlinguer's closest advisers (e.g. Franco Rodano) are practising Catholics, as is his wife. In March 1976 the PCI set up a high-powered 'work-group', including Ingrao, Bufalini, Natta, Jotti and Rodano, to examine Church-state relations and suggest amendments to the 1929 Concordat (*L'Unità*, 26 March 1976).

22. *Rinascita*, 14 October 1977; also in *The Italian Communists: Foreign Bulletin of the P.C.I.* (October–December 1977), pp. 23–34.

23. *L'Osservatore Romano*, 18 October 1977.

24. Speech to Federazione Italiana per la Scuola Materna, reported in *Corriere della Sera*, 17 October 1977; *The Times*, 18 October 1977. Similar

views were expressed by Cardinal Albino Luciani, Patriarch of Venice (the future Pope John Paul I) and by the Permanent Council of the Italian Bishops' Conference on 27 January 1978:

> A hegemonic and totalitarian planning of education, schools, of culture and its expressions, of leisure, of social security, of health, and of the economy, can only tend to reduce people's sense of responsibility and create the dangerous preconditions for a collectivist society that destroys Man, suppressing his fundamental rights and his capacity for free self-expression.

25. Some non-sensible ones did. Cf. G. Baget Bozzo, *I Cattolici e la Lettera di Berlinguer* (Vallecchi, Florence, 1978).

26. See, in particular, F. Coen (ed.), *Egemonia e Democrazia: Gramsci e la questione comunista* (Quaderno di Mondoperaio, Rome, 1977); L. Pellicani, *Gramsci e la questione comunista* (Vallecchi, Florence, 1976); M. L. Salvadori, *Eurocomunismo e Socialismo Sovietico* (Einaudi, Turin, 1978); B. de Giovanni, V. Gerratana and L. Poggi, *Egemonia, Stato e Partito in Gramsci* (Riuniti, Rome, 1977); L. Pellicani, 'La cultura politica del P.C.I. — leninismo e gramscismo' in A. Lombardo (ed.), *Le Trasformazioni del Comunismo Italiano* (Rizzoli, Milan, 1978) pp. 145–68.

27. Cf. Pellicani, *Gramsci e la questione comunista*, pp. 41–5; and his 'La cultura politica del P.C.I. — leninismo e gramscismo', pp. 156 ff., where he quotes Gramsci on the role of the Communist Party (the 'modern Prince'):

> 'the modern Prince, as it develops, overthrows the whole system of intellectual and moral relationships, for its development means precisely that every act comes to be perceived as useful or harmful, as virtuous or evil, only insofar as it has the modern Prince itself as its point of reference, and serves to increase its power or diminish it. The Prince takes the place in men's consciences of God or of the categorical imperative, it becomes the basis of a modern lay viewpoint and of a complete secularisation of all life and of all customary relationships'. (A. Gramsci, *Quaderni del Carcere* (Einaudi, Turin, 1975), p. 1561).

28. To be precise, not all of them said quite this. Norberto Bobbio argued there was no *necessary* incompatibility — the hegemonic class may firmly believe in pluralism and liberty, preach it constantly, and even permit it in practice, as nineteenth century liberals did. But there was no sign of the PCI doing anything of the kind: it did not even accept dissension within its own ranks. See interview with Bobbio, in *Corriere della Sera*, 10 March 1978.

29. A *party* seminar was held in Rome in May, later published as a book: de Giovanni, Gerratana and Paggi, *Egemonia, Stato e Partito in Gramsci*. A more general conference was also held in Bologna in December.

30. Craxi's 'Il Vangelo Socialista' was published in *L'Espresso*, 27 August 1978. Craxi's essay was a reply to an interview Berlinguer had given to *La Repubblica* on 2 August. Cf. also L. Colletti in *Paese Sera*, 27 August 1978; G. Napolitano in *L'Unità*, 27 August; U. La Malfa in *Voce Repubblicana*, 30 August; N. Bobbio in *La Stampa*, 1 September; P. Spriano in *Rinascita*, 1 September; A. Cossutta in *L'Unità*, 3 September; and F. De Martino in *Epoca*, 9 September 1978. There is a collection of articles from this debate in B. Craxi, *Pluralismo o Leninismo*, a cura di C. Accardi (Sugarco, Milan, 1978).

31. F. Colonna, 'La regola della maggioranza' in *Critica Marxista*, vol. XIV, nos. 3–4 (May–August 1976), p. 100. De Giovanni's views are quoted from his essay in E. Altvater *et al.*, *Egemonia, Democrazia e Transizione al Socialismo* (Angeli, Milan, 1977), p. 207. Cf. also A. Tortorella, 'E Democratico solo chi

accetta il Capitalismo?', *L'Unità*, 22 September 1978. The party's intellectual journal, *Critica Marxista*, was full of articles like Colonna's in 1976–8.

32. *La Repubblica*, 2 August 1978. He even quoted Machiavelli's dictum that parties have to renew themselves in order to survive; the way they do so is to return to their original principles.

33. *L'Unità*, 18 September 1978.

34. Speech at Turin, 26 February 1978.

35. In de Giovanni, Gerratana and Paggi, *Egemonia, Stato e Partito in Gramsci*, p. 241.

36. *Ibid.*, p. 254.

37. Interview with Walter Tobagi, in *Corriere della Sera*, 30 December 1977. Longo insisted that the Russian Revolution 'constitutes, whatever anyone may say, a strong democratic and progressive force not only for the country of the Soviets, but for the whole world situation'. Cf. also his interview in *Pravda*, 27 July 1977. Similar sentiments were expressed by Paolo Bufalini in his speech at Modena, September 1977: see 'Value and Meaning of the October Revolution Today' in *The Italian Communists*, no. 4 (October–December 1977), pp. 3–22.

38. Interview in *Le Monde*, 4–5 September 1977.

39. *Mondoperaio* (June 1978); *La Repubblica*, 28 July 1978.

40. Speech at Genoa, in *L'Unità*, 18 September 1978.

41. Cf. R. Fontana, 'Che cosa ha significato la primavera di Praga?' *L'Unità*, 15 September 1978.

42. Relations between the PCI and the Husak regime have remained very bad. The most overt and apparently incautious pro-dissident move the PCI has yet made, its support for Charter 77, should be seen in this context; as also should the persistent rumours in Italy about Czech training camps for the Red Brigade terrorists.

43. J. F. Revel in *Foreign Affairs* (January 1978), p. 300, claims it was Berlinguer who insisted, at the Madrid meeting of Western Communist leaders in March 1977, that the final communiqué should contain no mention of human rights in the USSR.

44. *Financial Times*, 26 April 1978.

45. On 10 October 1978 (Caversham Monitoring Service, Eastern Europe, 12 October). The final communiqué of this meeting made no mention of the USSR, but did praise the non-aligned countries and also included an 'invitation to greater dialogue in the international workers' movement' — i.e. with China.

46. Natta, of the PCI, signed a joint motion with other party leaders in Parliament. It included the statement that membership of the Atlantic Alliance was a 'fundamental term of reference'; cf. *Corriere della Sera*, 2 December 1977.

47. Cf. Berlinguer's famous interview in *Corriere della Sera*, 15 June 1976, just before the 1976 parliamentary elections. Just *after* them, in East Berlin at the end of June, he said precisely the opposite — 'a Marxist cannot consider NATO as a shield in the struggle for socialism' (E. Bettiza, *Il Comunismo Europeo* (Rizzoli, Milan, 1978), p. 17). But Berlinguer is a subtle fellow, and the sentence is open to another interpretation.

48. Cf. R.E.M. Irving, 'The European Policy of the French and Italian Communists', *International Affairs* (July 1977), pp. 405–21; and G. Amendola, *I Comuniste l'Europá* (Riuniti, Rome, 1971).

49. In 1977 Italian Communists were granted visas to visit the USA far more readily; and *L'Unità* opened an office in Washington. For the American reaction to the PCI in 1976–8, see R. Leonardi, 'Gli Stati Uniti e il compromesso storico', in *Il Mulino*, vol. XXVII, no. 257 (May–June 1978), pp. 370–90; and P. Lange and M. Vannicelli, 'L'America e il P.C.I.: i principi della politica estera americana e la "questione comunista" ', ibid., pp. 343–69.

146 *The Italian Communist Party*

50. See E. Bettiza, *Il Comunismo Europeo* (Rizzoli, Milan, 1978), p. 139.

51. *Novoye Vremya* (January 1978) (reported in *Corriere della Sera*, 12 January 1978).

52. *For a Europe of Peace and Progress* (Moscow, 1978).

53. This may appear unlikely, but see footnote 42. And it is very noticeable how the PCI insists on including a condemnation of terrorism in the final communiqué of its meetings with Eastern European leaders. In October 1978, for example, the communiqué after Berlinguer's meeting with Brezhnev included the following: 'The P.C.I. delegation provided information about the adventurist activity of criminal groups, with the aid of which reactionary forces seek, by organising terrorist acts, to hinder the development of the democratic victories of the Italian people and workers.' One wonders whether Berlinguer really believes the Red Brigades are 'right-wing' reactionaries.

54. See interviews with Andreotti in *Quotidiano dei Lavoratori*, 23 September 1978, and with Ugo La Malfa in *L'Espresso*, 17 September 1978. La Malfa said, 'The country is on the brink of civil war.'

55. See, for example, G. Chiaromonte, '3 Domande a 60 Anni dalla Rivoluzione d'Ottobre', *Critica Marxista*, vol. XV, no. 3 (1977), p. 71.

56. Cf. R. Minucci, 'Ma è possibile una soluzione moderata alla crisi?', *Rinascita*, 15 September 1978.

5 THE FRENCH COMMUNIST PARTY AND EUROCOMMUNISM

Peter Morris

Definitions of the word Eurocommunism lay emphasis on two linked themes. The first is the autonomy that each Communist party must enjoy in the formulation of a strategy to achieve political power and the consequent rejection of a universal model for that strategy; the second is the need to preserve both in the achieving and in the working of a socialist society those political and civil liberties that are associated with the Western democratic tradition. These two theories are linked by a refusal on the part of Eurocommunist parties to see the Soviet Union as providing a model of how to achieve and how to exercise power. Communist parties, both inside and outside Europe, have accepted the validity of the word Eurocommunism. What gives the prefix 'Euro' its justification is the fact that the leaders of three of the most influential Communist parties in Western Europe (those of Italy, Spain and France) have, in a series of meetings and communiqués, stressed their commitment to national autonomy and political pluralism.

Signs of the French Communist Party's (PCF) apparent acceptance of Eurocommunism are easy to find. The party leadership no longer rejects the word as meaningless. Criticism of certain aspects of Soviet government repression (abuses of judicial procedure, the existence of labour camps, the use of psychiatric hospitals to silence dissent) culminated in September 1978 in the appearance of *l'U.R.S.S. et Nous*.[1] This book has been criticised for not going far enough in its condemnation of Soviet party practice but it nevertheless marks a new stage in the PCF's analysis of the Soviet Union and it received the unusual honour of a special recommendation by the party's governing body, the Bureau Politique.[2] The PCF has refused to follow all the initiatives of the Soviet party (CPSU) in the international Communist movement, notably in the final stages of the preparations for the 1976 Berlin conference of European Communist parties. It has also moved away from a position of total opposition to the institutions of the West (the Atlantic

147

Alliance, the European Economic Community) to one of partial acceptance. The PCF claims to have abandoned any strategy for obtaining power other than the peaceful one of the ballot box, and to be willing to respect the verdict of the ballot box after a period of Communist government, even if that verdict is unfavourable. This acceptance of bourgeois democratic practice was symbolised by the party's decision at its 1976 congress to remove from its statutes a reference to the dictatorship of the proletariat.

The importance for the notion of Eurocommunism of these policy changes lies partly in the fact that the PCF is an extremely strong political organisation. In Western Europe it is second only to the Italian party in the size of its electorate and membership. The party's share of the French vote has declined slightly over the last four parliamentary elections from 22.51 per cent to 20.55 per cent but, even so, has remained more stable than that of any other political formation.[3] With some 500,000 members (the figure claimed is higher) the PCF is far and away the largest political party in France and it is well implanted in the French local government system. It is also exceedingly rich, possessing magnificent new headquarters in Paris, a large amount of property and many commercial undertakings (publishing houses, supermarkets, other wholesale and retail outlets, import-export firms dealing notably with Eastern Europe).[4] Although the circulation of its daily newspaper *l'Humanité* and (more recently) the weekly *l'Humanité Dimanche* are in steady decline, the PCF remains the only political organisation in France to have a party press of any importance. It has too tight a grip over the leadership of France's largest trade union movement, the Confédération Générale du Travail, whose Secretary-General is a member of the Bureau Politique.

Yet it is not merely the size of the PCF that makes it important in any discussion of Eurocommunism. Of all the Communist parties who have accepted the new ideas, the PCF is the one which has had to change most to be able to do so. The PCF has never produced a Gramsci, able to give its Marxism a human face. Its organisational structure has long appeared to be dully and rigidly authoritarian. Above all, it has seemed in the past to be at both inter-state and inter-movement levels a servile executant of Soviet wishes. If this party could suddenly adopt ideas more readily associated with a Berlinguer and a Carrillo, then the Communist world indeed had changed. It might require little for Jean Elleinstein, Deputy Director of the Centre of Marxist Studies and a party candidate in the 1978 elections, to question the nature of the Soviet achievement and attack the absence of freedom in the USSR. It took much more profound change for similar questions and attacks to be publicly voiced by more senior members of the party like Jean Kanapa, Charles Fiterman and the General Secretary, George Marchais. Kanapa's earlier uncritical praise of the USSR led him to indulge in a vicious public polemic with J.P. Sartre;[5] Fiterman denied in 1973 that abuses of psychiatry had occurred or could occur in the Soviet Union; Marchais in 1975 backed the Leninist intransigence of the Portuguese Communist leader Cunhal against criticism from the Italian and Spanish parties.

Thus it was the apparent willingness of the PCF to change that gave plausibility to the idea of Eurocommunism – Edgar Faure, a leading French politician, called the abandonment of the dictatorship of the proletariat by the Twenty-Second Congress the most important political event of 1976. More recently, however, the disrepute into which the term Eurocommunism has fallen stems directly from the behaviour of the PCF in the months spanning the French parliamentary elections of March 1978. In 1972 the PCF and the Socialist Party (PS) transformed an already existing electoral alliance into a governmental one by signing the Common Programme of the left, a statement of policy to be carried out if the left were successful at the polls. By 1977 it looked very likely that the left would indeed be successful at the parliamentary elections which were to take place in March 1978. Then in September the PCF suddenly turned on its allies, accusing them of a betrayal of the Common Programme and making demands on policy and the composition of a left government which it knew the socialists could not accept.[6] Marchais even threatened to abandon 'republican discipline', the venerable electoral agreement between the two parties, and campaigned with rolling-eyed truculence on the simple slogan 'Les riches peuvent payer' ('The rich can pay'). As a result of all this, the dynamic of the left was broken and the elections were lost. Thereafter the PCF leadership simply declared that it was all the fault of the socialists and that the party was in any case not interested in 'alternance' on the English or German model, which is the only model on which the term makes sense.[7] Pictures showing a party leader shaking hands with a Soviet dissident suddenly disappeared from party literature. It is hardly surprising that the British Communist Party criticised the PCF's behaviour and that a prominent Spanish Marxist saw it as sounding the 'death knell' of Eurocommunism.[8]

Yet the party leadership has vigorously denied that it has gone back on decisions made at the Twenty-Second Congress; and we have seen that *l'U.R.S.S. et Nous* came out after the March elections. At the Twenty-Third PCF Congress (May 1979) George Marchais stressed the continuing vitality and usefulness of the concept of Eurocommunism.

So the problem of assessing the policy goals of the PCF is a complex one and this complexity is mirrored in the contrasting analysis of the party given by two of its most prominent students, Annie Kriegel and Ronald Tiersky. Kriegel stresses the international dimension of the PCF and its distance from purely domestic politics, whereas Tiersky sees the primary goal of the PCF as the search for national power.[9]

1 The PCF, the Soviet Union and International Communism

There is nothing new in the PCF asserting the necessity of the independence of the nation-state of France and of itself as a policy-making organisation. This has been said throughout the party's history. One General Secretary described the relationship between socialist parties and countries as based on 'complete equality; integrity of territory; sovereignty of their policies and non-interference in each others' internal policies'.[10] The vehemence with which the PCF proclaims its independence is often justified by reference to the party's heroic role after 1941 in the French resistance to Hitler; it is probably better explained by the need to efface the memory of earlier political choices made by the party. In the past, the French Communists were always seen as the most faithful defenders in the West of the strategic interests of the Soviet Union and of the right of the CPSU to determine the policy of all other Communist parties. It is very easy to find examples of this subservience. The decision to create the 'popular front' in 1934 was taken as part of Stalin's defensive strategy against Hitler, just as the decision to oppose the war in 1939 followed (albeit at a short distance) the signing of the Nazi-Soviet Pact and was imposed on the party leadership by Moscow. Hitler's invasion of Russia in 1941 led to a long period of PCF co-operation with other parties that culminated in the Communists' participation in the governments formed by de Gaulle and his successors. This period came to an abrupt end with the freezing of the Cold War in 1947 when, at a secret meeting in Poland, the French and Italian parties were severely criticised for their 'right deviationism'. The PCF leader, Maurice Thorez, who had not originally opposed Marshall Aid, led the party into a semi-insurrectionist posture, marked by the declaration that 'the French people will never go to war against the Soviet Union.'[11] In 1956 the party whole-heartedly supported the Soviet intervention in Hungary. The primacy of Soviet interests did not necessarily involve radicalism in domestic politics – the policy moderation of the popular front and post-war periods is matched by the caution over decolonisation in the 1950s – but on other occasions, notably the early 1930s and late 1940s, it did.

Now this subservience to Soviet foreign policy was obviously not limited to the French party; it was the essence of international Communism. The Italian party also changed its policy after the 1947 Poland meeting and it too welcomed the Hungarian intervention. Moreover, there were in the immediate post-war period two occasions on which the PCF did take its distances from Moscow. The first was the unanimous decision of the Bidault government, in which Communists were represented, to demand the Saar for France (a demand which Molotov categorically rejected), and the second was the famous Thorez interview in *The Times* in 1946 in which he spoke of political strategies for the PCF not modelled on the Soviet Union.[12] Nevertheless the French party does appear to have been particularly dependent on Moscow. In the 1930s a Comintern official called Arthur Fried was permanently based in Paris and no decision was taken without him. The difficulties and persecutions to which the party was subject after 1939 did not prevent regular contact between Moscow and the clandestine leadership in Paris of a kind which Carrillo says did not take place in the Spanish party.[13] After the war, Thorez was the subject of a personality cult modelled on that of Stalin. In the 1950s occurred 'trials' of various party leaders which differed from those taking place in Eastern Europe only in that the party was unable to turn its political death sentences into physical ones.

The French Communists' Moscow fixation is sometimes explained by the inexperience and the then neurotic dogmatism of the party's most famous leader, Maurice Thorez, Secretary-General from 1930 until 1964, when, just before his death, he became President. Philippe Robrieux has written an important study of Thorez which suggests that he was a weak character, able to be dominated by Stalin (who possessed incriminating evidence of his youthful Trotskyite sympathies) and by his second wife, the formidable Jeanette Vermeersch. Thorez's intellectual mediocrity and his obsession with Stalinist control over the party are contrasted with the greater intelligence and flexibility of the Italian leader, Togliatti. Whereas the Italian welcomed the 'de-Stalinisation' associated with the Twentieth Congress of the CPSU, Thorez condemned the Moscow leadership for turning against the memory of Stalin and attempted to suppress Khrushchev's speech. This explanation of PCF behaviour in terms of Thorez alone is too simple. It is true that Thorez was immensely popular within the party, but the prestige of the Soviet Union cannot just be reduced to the actions (and failings) of one man. The 'liberalisation' of the party did not follow immediately on his death in 1964 and his replacement by Waldeck-Rochet; for a long time after the PCF remained the most 'loyalist' of the Western parties.

The re-integration of the PCF into the French national community was initially facilitated by General de Gaulle's own hostility to American hegemony in Western Europe. De Gaulle returned to power in 1958 and Thorez, who was willing to cite F.D. Roosevelt as a witness on the General's dictatorial ambitions, saw him as even more dependent on the State Department than his Fourth Republic predecessors.[14] Thorez was wrong, as Moscow had realised earlier. France withdrew from NATO and de Gaulle strongly criticised both the American intervention in South-East Asia and the Israeli action in the Six Day War. At the same time he sought good relations with the countries of Eastern Europe, notably the USSR, thereby re-establishing a tradition of co-operation between governments of France and Russia that has few parallels

elsewhere in Western Europe. The PCF was bound to support
these Gaullist initiatives which had the twin advantages of
pleasing the Soviet Union and identifying French Communism
with French nationalism. After Thorez's death in 1964, de
Gaulle wrote a letter of condolence to his widow.[15] Gaullists and
Communists together voted against the censure motion which
was introduced into the National Assembly in April 1966 on the
French withdrawal from NATO. In 1974, Marchais spoke
warmly of the heroic periods of co-operation between Gaullists
and Communists in a notably unsuccessful attempt to persuade
the former to vote for the latter's candidate (the socialist
Mitterand) in the second round of the presidential election.

It was internal politics that appeared to produce the first
conflict between Moscow and the PCF. In 1965 the PCF
supported Mitterrand's first bid for the presidency while the
Soviet Union made plain its preference for de Gaulle's
re-election. Nine years later occurred the famous occasion when
the Soviet ambassador ostentatiously visited Mitterrand's
presidential opponent, Giscard d'Estaing, between the two
rounds of the 1974 election and received an indignant protest
from the PCF. Yet between these two elections occurred the
events of 1968 in which the deeply ambiguous role played by
the PCF convinced some of its left-wing critics that it was
underwriting Moscow's interest in de Gaulle's survival. In the
1969 presidential election to succeed de Gaulle the Communists
refused to vote for the Atlanticist Opposition candidate Poher
against the Gaullist Pompidou. Thus it still appeared to be the
case that where the foreign policy goals of the Soviet Union
(good relations with a France that asserted its independence of
the USA) conflicted with the domestic strategy of replacing
Gaullist-led government, the PCF leadership preferred the
former. One commentator has claimed that this preference
explains the abrupt change in the party's tactic before the 1978
election – J. Baulin argues that the socialist proposal to submit
the issue of France's independent deterrent to a referendum
raised the possibility that France would once again be forced
right under the American nuclear umbrella and that to the PCF
anything, even electoral defeat, was preferable to such
protection.[16]

It is clear that the Soviet view of what is good and bad in
foreign policy at an inter-state level is still largely accepted by

the PCF. The famous condemnation by the Bureau Politique of the Russian invasion of Czechoslovakia in 1968 was assuredly a landmark, in that it was the first time that the party had publicly condemned Soviet policy. That condemnation has never been withdrawn. It was, however, almost immediately moderated in tone and thereafter the party welcomed the 'normalisation' of Soviet-Czech relations.[17] The PCF was the first Western party to send a delegation to Moscow to renew contacts after Prague. George Marchais, who succeeded Waldeck-Rochet as Secretary-General in 1969 when the latter's health collapsed, expressed his support for the interpretation of 'proletarian internationalism' that had been used by Brezhnev to justify the destruction of the Dubcek experiment. Indeed the appointment of Marchais, whose career owed everything to Thorez, was seen as marking a return to unconditional fidelity to Moscow. The PCF still closely identifies itself with Soviet foreign policy positions. The PCF acceptance of the EEC came after the Russians had realised the benefits to be obtained from it. Like the Russians, the PCF denounced the two interventions in 1977 and 1978 by Giscard in Zaire and in June 1978 organised demonstrations against them; by contrast, there has been until recently little adverse comment on Soviet involvement in East and West Africa. Over the Middle East and over the Sino-Vietnam conflict the Soviet and PCF positions coincide. The French party's criticism of France's disarmament proposals in 1978 exactly mirrored the Russian one – that Giscard was attempting to weaken the Geneva talks of which the Soviet Union is co-chairman. The PCF may accept France's participation in the Atlantic Alliance, but it does so without any of the enthusiasm of Berlinguer, who sees the pact as a guarantor of the possibility of building socialism in Italy. Hostility to West Germany is expressed with a xenophobic intensity that was given full rein in the 1979 campaigns against the Lorraine steel closures and the possible extension of the powers of the European Parliament.

This harmony of foreign policy views between the French party and Russia is not enough for Jean Montaldo, who argues in 'Les Finances du P.C.F.' and *La France Communiste* that nothing has changed in PCF-USSR relations.[18] Montaldo points to the constant two-way traffic between officials of the Soviet and French parties (a traffic that is little reported in the French

Communist press), to the influence exercised on the French party by Russian leaders like Ponomorev and Zagladin, and to the financial benefits which the PCF derives from its privileged links with Moscow.[19] From Montaldo's position it is difficult to know what could constitute adequate proof that the PCF was not still an utterly subservient tool of Soviet foreign policy. Any statement that Marchais might make on the duty to resist Russian aggression must be meaningless because for a French Communist there never could be Russian aggression;[20] the present Communist 'alliance' in the French Parliament with the Gaullists against alleged Giscardian supranationalism (attitudes towards the European Parliament) owes nothing to nationalism, everything to Moscow. One feels that for writers like Montaldo the Russian tank is always waiting to get through and will always be helped on its way by the French Communists.

Yet it is possible to detect changes in the PCF's attitude towards Russian foreign policy. The current foreign policy in the PCF involves an acceptance of French membership of the Atlantic Alliance and the European Economic Community; resistance to all attempts at West European integration (a joint monetary system, strengthening the European Parliament); good relations with the USSR and the USA both of whom are referred to as 'friends'; a refusal to accept the participation of France in either bloc; and support for France's independent nuclear deterrent. There has in recent months been a tendency for the party to take its distances from certain Soviet activities in Africa, and for its leaders to hope that the Cuban interventions there will end.[21] At the same time, the party has rejected hegemonies of whatever sort, thus implying that the USSR as well as the USA exercise one. By stressing the closeness of the PCF's friendship with the Rumanian party, Gaston Plissonnier made clear at a meeting with Ceausescu in December 1978 his party's support for the Rumanian president in his conflicts with Moscow over the Warsaw Pact.

At the inter-movement level, the PCF's rejection of Soviet hegemony is now explicit. When in 1973 the CPSU originally conceived the idea of a conference of European Communist parties, most commentators assumed that the PCF would, as in the past, go along with whatever Moscow proposed. This assumption appeared correct in that the PCF allied with the CPSU in desiring for the conference an ideological as well as a political content and in opposing the 'autonomist' position of the southern parties. Suddenly, in November 1975, the PCF joined with the autonomists in rejecting a Soviet-inspired draft document for the conference on the grounds that it demanded a unified strategy.[22] At the same time the PCF signed bilateral communiqués with the autonomist Italian and Spanish parties and early in 1976 Marchais made the unprecedented decision not to attend the (twenty-fifth) congress of the CPSU. The French delegation to that conference was led by Plissonnier, who told a Kremlin press conference that if 'proletarian internationalism' meant nothing more than an identity of views between Communist parties, then the term had better be dropped. The PCF does not agree with those Spanish and Italian Communists who argue that internationalism is a historical relic, doomed to disappear; it appears to want a return to a traditional (pre-Stalin) internationalism based on 'genuine equality and solidarity'. Yet when the Berlin conference finally occurred (June 1976), Marchais said it probably ought to be the last one of its kind. More recently the French party leadership has reacted strongly to the pro-Moscow (and anti-Eurocommunist) criticism of its activities voiced by Thorez's widow and has once again repeated its condemnation of the 1968 invasion of Czechoslovakia.[23]

That there has been a change in the tone of CPSU-PCF relations appears indisputable; but whether an altered tone means an altered substance is much less clear. For Roy Macridis the only proof of a changed relationship would be a total break with Moscow. The fact that this has not occurred makes the independence thesis invalid and differences over, say, Czechoslovakia or the Berlin conference irrelevant in that they are purely doctrinal, not followed by any concrete disengagement.[24] The recent PCF support for Hanoi against Peking is simply the latest example of a complete alignment of French Communism on Moscow's foreign policy. On the other hand, at least one of Macridis's criteria of disengagement – criticism of the Cuban presence in Africa – has been fulfilled. We have noted the PCF's support for Rumania and the tension that exists between the domestic political stability which Moscow's *détente* policy implies and the political change demanded by the PCF. More generally, it is plainly the case that the PCF, like most Western and some Eastern parties, has undergone the liberating effect of the breakdown of Moscow-centred internationalism. Yet national liberation is not a synonym for political liberty, as the examples of Rumania and Yugoslavia demonstrate. Eurocommunism must imply the latter as well as the former, and so we must turn to the question of the PCF and democracy.

2 The PCF and the Pursuit of Power in France

The historical uncertainty as to the PCF's ultimate loyalty – international Communism versus the nation-state of France – has more recently been supplemented by a new area of doubt, the precise role of the party within the French political system. Is the PCF interested, as it says it is, in achieving partial political power for a limited period through the democratic process in alliance with other political parties? Or is it still determined to exercise a monopoly of power by whatever means possible for the purpose of revolutionising France? Is the PCF above all determined to maintain its organisational and numerical superiority on the French left even if this means sacrificing the chance of exercising power? Or has it been integrated into the existing political system of which it has become an objective supporter? Answers to these questions depend at one level on differing political positions. Thus the far left sees the PCF's integration into capitalist France and its obsession with its organisational control as explaining the party's 'betrayal' in 1968 when it 'stopped the revolution' because the revolution had started without it. Many socialists see the party's actions in breaking the unity of the left as explicable only in terms of its monopolistic demands in the exercise (though not necessarily the use) of power. Most conservatives (but also some socialists) still see the PCF as aiming at the immediate revolutionary transformation of France.

These answers depend, as has been said, on political beliefs. Yet the questions to which they form replies have also led to an academic interest in explaining the complexity of PCF behaviour. In his influential study, *French Communism*, Ronald Tiersky has postulated four basic roles of the PCF: a revolutionary vanguard party, uniquely capable of working out the Marxist laws of social development; a counter-community, for those who reject and seek shelter from the prevailing values of French society (here the comparison would be with the German social democrats before 1914); a tribune for and defender of those most disfavoured by the distribution of power in France; a governmental party, seeking to implement precise policies in alliance, if necessary with other groups. These four roles, according to Tiersky, develop simultaneously; they are not necessarily in contradiction with each other, though one or other will be stressed depending on particular circumstances. Any analysis of the PCF and its behaviour must keep them all in mind, though the concentration here will be on the tension between the vanguard and the governmental roles.

It has long been the case that the PCF has sought alliances with other political forces in France in order to promote social change. Thus the party leadership vaunts the popular front period as evidence of its desire to work with all democratic forces and it points with pride to the period of Communist participation in government after 1945.[25] This alliance policy has been called by party intellectuals the 'historic tendency' of the party, but we have already seen that in the early days both the nature and extent of the strategy were imposed on the party by Stalin. Moscow decided, against Thorez's wishes, that the PCF should not participate in Blum's Popular Front government and determined the moderation of the party's policy both in 1936 and 1945. The alliance strategy disappeared in the ice of the Cold War in 1947. Although the PCF occasionally voted in Parliament for particular governments and policies of the Fourth Republic, its support was explicitly rejected by politicians of the non-Communist left – notably by Pierre Mendès-France in 1954. The socialist leader Guy Mollet summed up the exclusion of the PCF from the French political community in a phrase which became famous: 'The PCF is neither on the Right nor the Left. It is in the East.' Mollet was here echoing the Gaullist view of the Communists 'as separatists'. It is worth remembering just how virulent was the anti-Communism that gripped many sections of French political opinion in the Fourth Republic.

The return to power of General de Gaulle marked the post-war nadir of the PCF as a mass political force in France. In the parliamentary elections of 1958 it obtained 18.9% of the votes cast – a respectable percentage, certainly, but far lower than the 25.7% it had won in 1956. Its vote was down from 5.7 million to 3.9 million. The party's campaign against the 1961 referendum on Algerian self-determination failed to stop many of its supporters voting for de Gaulle's proposals; at the same time party membership fell to around 200,000, compared with 900,000 at the time of the Liberation. In the 1962 elections the Communist vote barely moved above its 1958 level. Nevertheless in that election occurred the first signs of a revival of the alliance strategy as Socialists and Communists remade the electoral pact known as 'republican discipline' (whereby the least favoured of the two parties' candidates stands down in the second round of an election on behalf of the other one to maximise the chances of defeating the right). Thus the socialists with fewer votes than in 1958 gained 24 seats in the new National Assembly (from 41 to 65) while the Communist representation rose from 10 to 41. Similar electoral pacts have operated in all parliamentary elections since 1962, though in 1978 the party leadership for a while questioned their worth. In 1965 the PCF, as we have seen, supported Mitterrand's bid for the presidency.

These early agreements between the PCF and other left groups opposed to de Gaulle were never likely to lead to the defeat of the Gaullist forces and thus were not displeasing to Moscow. They had the advantage of maximising the PCF's electoral presence and of underlining its 'democratic' credentials; republican discipline fits firmly into the French democratic tradition of political unity against a common right-wing enemy. Yet the agreements did not mean that the party had abandoned its Leninist strategy for achieving and exercising power. Waldeck-Rochet, the Secretary-General whose 'liberalism' led him to being compared with Pope John XXIII, described in 1966 what a left-wing government would need to do once it achieved power:

> While fully guaranteeing the development of the largest possible democracy for the immense mass of the people it will be necessary that the new socialist régime adopt laws tending to protect and defend the new social organisation and take measures in order to ensure respect of the law.

Statements of the sort have an ominous ring to them. They help to explain the deep suspicion with which other anti-Gaullist parties (notably the socialists) continued to view the PCF, a

suspicion demonstrated by the difficulty in transforming an
electoral agreement into a political strategy. In December 1966,
in February 1968 and again in December 1970 Communists and
Socialists drew up a statement of their agreements and
disagreements. On all three occasions the areas of agreement
were very general (both parties agreed on the need to 'control
the key sectors of the economy'), while those of disagreement
were very precise (for or against the Atlantic Alliance and the
EEC. Moreover, Communists and Socialists continued to have
divergent appreciations of what constitutes a political
democracy; thus in 1971, the former saw *alternance* as possible
between socialist parties but not between socialist and capitalist
parties. This was not encouraging for believers in democracy
Western-style, and neither was a statement by George Marchais
to the effect that 'out of the 14 socialist countries single parties
exist in only six, while there are two or more parties in the
other eight'.

The next stage in the development of the alliance strategy
came in 1972 with the Common Programme of government.
This was signed by the PCF, the Parti Socialiste and the Left
Radicals, and was a statement of the policy that a left-wing
government, once elected to power, would carry out over a
five-year period. Never before had the left-wing parties publicly
agreed on a policy programme which they would attempt to
implement; never before had the PCF gone so far in its
concessions to the French democratic left. Thus the Communists
formally accepted the principle of the plurality of parties and
the obligation for a left government to hand over power to its
opponents if defeated in an election. At the same time, they
dropped their demands that France quit henceforth the Atlantic
Alliance and accepted instead the simultaneous dissolution of
both military pacts. What they got in return was an acceptance
by their partners of the need for an extensive nationalisation
programme to cover the key sectors of the French economy.

The Common Programme could be, and was, much criticised
for its inconsistencies and incoherences in both domestic and
foreign policy. Yet even if these are left aside, problems
remained about the nature of the alliance which the
Communists had concluded and their attitude towards political
democracy. The Common Programme was specifically limited to
the period of one legislature; it did not claim to introduce

socialism but rather 'advanced democracy', it stressed that each of the contracting parties remained faithful to the principles on which it had been founded. What this could mean for the PCF became clear in 1974 when a speech made three years earlier by George Marchais to the Central Committee was released. In this speech, Marchais was extremely critical of the Socialist Party (with which he had first signed the agreement) and spoke of the Programme as if it had a purely tactical value – 'We consider it as a step forward which allows the creation of the most favourable conditions for the mass acceptance of *our* ideas, *our* solutions, *our* objectives.'[26] Also in 1975 the PCF strongly supported the insurrectionist, consciously anti-'democratic' strategy of the Portuguese Communists under their leader Cunhal, and in so doing clashed not only with the French Socialists but with the Italian and Spanish Communists.

Yet it was in 1975 that the PCF finally came to adopt the commitments to political and civil liberties that are central to any definition of Eurocommunism and that parallel the changed attitude towards international Communism described above. A year which had begun with noisy support for Cunhal's Leninist intransigence ended with the important assertion that 'advanced democracy is incompatible with the idea of scholastic distinctions between political and arithmetical majorities.'[27] George Marchais made what Tiersky had called 'very serious and in some ways stupefying remarks' to the effect that Communists could not be for liberty in Paris and against it in Lisbon:

> Liberty is unitary, this is fundamentally correct. There is no democracy and liberty if there is no pluralism of political parties, if there is no freedom of speech . . . there will be no socialism in France without political democracy. We consider that the principles which we enunciate concerning socialist democracy are of universal value.[28]

Above all, the PCF signed with the PCI a joint communiqué in which both parties asserted that, since socialism is a higher stage of democracy and liberty, the liberties won by bourgeois-popular revolutions must be protected and developed.

This is so for freedom of thought and expression, publication,

meeting, association and demonstration, free circulation of
people at home and abroad, religious liberty, absolute liberty
of expression of philosophical, cultural and artistic opinions.
French and Italian Communists favour the plurality of
political parties – including the right to existence and activity
of opposition parties – the freedom of the formation and the
possibility of democratic *alternance* of majorities and
minorities, the secular and democratic functioning of the
State, the independence of justice. They are also in favour of
the free activity and independence of the unions. They attach
an essential importance to the development of democracy in
factories so that the workers can participate with real rights in
management and have real powers of decision.

In 1976, as we have seen, the party dropped from its statutes
any reference to the dictatorship of the proletariat.

For Communists it is not enough just to assert a commitment
to a political principle, the principle must be explained in terms
of social reality. The PCF justifies its abandonment of the
Leninist strategy for achieving and exercising power essentially
on the grounds that the social and cultural conditions of Russia
in 1917 are not those of France in 1977 and that therefore the
Bolshevik model is inappropriate. The State can be changed, it
no longer has to be violently overthrown. This is the thesis of
The Communists and the State, written by three party
intellectuals in 1977.[29] Another book, *Social Classes and the
Union of the French People*, argues that the nature of capitalism
in contemporary France means that almost the whole population
is now on the side of progress because almost all are
wage-earners. The working class is still the largest – relatively
and absolutely – part of the workers' population but its goals are
now in harmony with those of employees, technicians, cadres
and the peasantry. Only the monopolists stand outside the union
of the French people.[30] Political democracy is not only good in
itself, it is also the surest way of achieving social change.

Thus the PCF claims to have a policy for France that, if
implemented, would at once guarantee and develop political
democracy while at the same time producing social justice. Yet,
as was suggested in the introduction, the behaviour of the
Communist leadership in the last two years has led even those
who do not reject out of hand the idea of Eurocommunism to

question the extent to which the PCF has actually shaken off its Stalinist past. The doubts concern three areas in particular – the PCF's assessment of the USSR as a socialist society; the decision-making process within the party itself; and, most important, the role that the party demands for itself in alliance with other political organisations.

In the past, the USSR was always worshipped not only as the inspiration of all Communist parties but as the model of what a socialist society should look like. Any criticism of the Soviet Union was by definition an attack on the most perfect society on earth and, therefore, sacrilegious. Opponents of the PCF draw much attention to the fact that its leaders still refer to the USSR as socialist and talk of the immense progress accomplished there. It was only recently that readers of *L'Humanité* learned the shock news that Trotsky had been murdered on Stalin's orders. The clear implication is that the Communists' proclaimed 'socialism in the colours of France' would, if it ever materialised, produce the Gulag as surely as Soviet socialism did. There is no way to test the truth or falsehood of this implication. French Communists deny it, their enemies deny the value of this denial. What can be said is that many French Communists from the leadership down continue to admire the Soviet experience with an enthusiasm not shown elsewhere; the 1979 congress insisted that the record of the socialist societies of Eastern Europe was 'globally positive'. On the other hand, some Communist intellectuals, notably Elleinstein, have indeed asserted that the USSR constitutes an anti-model rather than a model of socialism.[31] They have not yet been expelled from the party for so doing. Some party members have sent an open letter to Marchais asking him to propose the rehabilitation of Bukharin. The party leadership's 'hardening' of its position has not led to an end of criticism of the political practices of Soviet Russia. In his post-1978 election report to the Central Committee, Marchais said things had got worse rather than better in the Soviet Union. The PCF protested against the circumstances of the dissident trials in Russia in the summer of 1978 and took part in demonstrations against them. Jeanette Vermeersch was attacked by the party leadership in July 1978 for calling the USSR a socialist democracy. That Moscow took these criticisms seriously is demonstrated by the widespread diffusion in Russia of a strong attack on *l'U.R.S.S.*

et Nous, which appeared in December 1978 in the theoretical journal of the CPSU.

The second area of doubt about the PCF's commitment to democracy relates to its internal organisational structure. How can the party be in favour of democracy at a national level when its own decision-making procedures are so authoritarian, when democratic centralism has everything to do with centralism, nothing to do with democratic participation? French Communist congresses are a byword for manipulated unanimity. In recent years two major policy shifts have been thrust on the membership without any forewarning; the decision to drop the dictatorship of the proletariat was first announced by Marchais in the course of a television programme, and the party's acceptance of the French nuclear deterrent came overnight after years of strenuous opposition. The leadership's analysis of the 1978 election – in which it absolved itself of any responsibility for the defeat of the left – was made without any effort at all to consult the membership. A number of permanent officials and journalists resigned their jobs after the elections in protest against the way the leadership had behaved. That this protest was not linked to the 'liberals' was demonstrated by a series of articles in *Le Monde* written by the Marxist philosopher and party member Louis Althusser. Althusser had opposed Elleinstein-type liberalism and in particular the abandonment of the dictatorship of the proletariat. Yet in his articles he bitterly criticised the absence of horizontal discussion in the party and the leadership's refusal to allow party members freely to express their opinions in the party press. He implied that the leadership was paranoiac about its right to control policy.[32]

The extent to which political parties are or are not democratic in their procedures is a complex question and one certainly not limited to analyses of Communist parties. Moreover, it is plainly wrong to assume that a monolithic party structure is necessarily a united one. The PCF elite, like other Communist elites, has frequently been internally divided – as recently as 1974 Marchais's position was challenged by hard-liners like E. Fajon and R. Leroy, and his aggressiveness after the 1978 elections suggested defensiveness rather than authority. At a non-elite level, official party policy has at various times in the past come under attack from sections of the membership, notably intellectuals and students. After the 1978 elections, the criticisms were more numerous (and certainly more widely publicised) than before. Yet such attacks have never before shaken the leadership's grip on the mass of the party membership and they failed to do so in 1978. A petition which originated after the elections in a party cell in Aix en Provence and which criticised certain aspects of the leadership's behaviour was widely published in the non-Communist press. It attracted no more than a couple of thousand signatures (including that of the historian Albert Soboul). The plain fact is that for the bulk of the committed membership of the party (though not for the mass of sympathisers and floating voters), the Communist organisational structure is not controversial. Elleinstein himself has referred, since the election, to the popularity amongst the membership of the party's permanent officials.

The leadership is today prepared to be less brutal in its treatment of its own dissidents than in the past – the fate of Roger Garaudy, who was expelled in 1970, has not yet befallen his successor dissidents. There was even in December 1978 an uneasy meeting at Vitry between the leadership and the intellectuals. At the 1978 Fête de l'Humanité, Paul Laurent, generally seen as the party's number two, and as a liberal in organisational terms, said that the PCF was not yet democratic enough. Such internal liberalisation as there is, however, is wholly at the discretion of the leadership, which will censure and prevent discussion of that of which it does not approve. Marchais could speak benignly in September 1978 of Elleinstein and others as 'des camarades qui discutent' ('comrades engaged in discussion'), but earlier in the year he had been much more harsh. Dissidents were systematically excluded from active participation in the 1979 congress. Though there has been more open criticism of the party line in the last year, it has been so far limited to a small section of the membership; as already suggested, the majority of Communist members do not resent the nature of the leadership's control. Indeed it contributes to the average member's awareness of his or her participation in a unique political organisation.

The third question-mark over the PCF is also the most important – what place does the party demand for itself in French politics? This question is at the heart of the debate over the PCF and the alliance strategy implied both by Eurocommunism and by the Common Programme. It is crucial because it raises the contradiction between the limitation on political power inherent in liberal democracy and alliance with other parties and the pretension of Communist parties to play a determining, and therefore limitless, role in political choice. The failure to resolve this contradiction led directly to the failure of the French left in the parliamentary elections of March 1978.

At first the issue at stake was economic policy, in particular the extent of the nationalisations which a left-wing government would introduce. When the Communists and Socialists attempted to renegotiate the Common Programme in 1977, the PCF delegation demanded an extension of the nationalisation programme to include both new companies and also all the subsidiaries of the firms concerned. This the socialists refused to accept. It is important to remember that this refusal was not simply the result of a social democratic dislike of nationalisation. The PS had accepted in 1972, and would accept again in 1977, a nationalisation programme much more extensive than that advocated by the 'managed capitalism' social democratic parties of northern Europe. This is evidence of the intransigence with which the whole of the French left views the socio-economic system in which it operates. It is not only the French Communists who reject the 'responsible', supportive economic policy of the PCI. What the French non-Communist left feared in the extended nationalisation programme was that the PCF would be able to control both the heights of the economy (through its occupation of a new Ministry of Economic Planning) and its foundations (through its strong links with the CGT, which is particularly powerful in the nationalised sector). The PCF was known to be lukewarm to what Althusser has called the 'detestable notion' of autogestion (a form of workers' control), though it had formally – and opportunistically – accepted the idea. Many Socialists feared that the Communists' economic proposals would enable them to determine on their own French economic strategy. And then where would be those autonomous centres of power so essential to democracy?

The controversy over economic control became part of a larger crisis, that of the effects of the alliance strategy on the Communists' own strength. When the Common Programme was signed, the PCF was a manifestly stronger organisation than the PS, and this continued to be the case in the 1973 parliamentary elections. After the 1974 presidential election, however,

Mitterrand's party started to overtake the PCF – it did very well in by-elections, local elections and polls, while the PCF vote stagnated and in many cases fell. Some opinion polls suggested that in the 1978 elections the PS might get up to 30 per cent of the vote while the PCF could fall to under 18 per cent, its lowest share since the Second World War. If this percentage were to be realised nationally and if the electoral pact were to operate, then a left victory at the polls would actually mean a sharp drop in the number of Communist deputies elected. There were those like Giscard d'Estaing who saw in this clear evidence of the 'historic decline of the PCF'; political sociologists noted that the structure of French society, and in particular the declining relative importance of the working class, had ominous consequences for the PCF vote. Such speculation and analysis could be – and was – rejected by the PCF as mere political propaganda. What could not be ignored was the real danger that the party risked of being reduced, in sharp contrast to the Italian Communists, to the role of mere auxiliary to a triumphant Socialist Party. And where then, given that the PCF had formally accepted the parliamentary road, would be the party's fundamental insistence that it must play the vanguard role?

For whatever else has changed in the PCF, that insistence has not. Marchais' definition of the vanguard role quoted in Kanapa's *Foreign Affairs* article does not exactly glow with clarity: 'We do not aspire to exercise a monopoly in the democratic movement today – nor in the Socialist society tomorrow but – and this is quite different – to play a vanguard role in soviet and human progress.' Yet it was absolutely clear after 1974 that the party would resist any tendency towards its own marginalisation and by 1977 it became clear that the best way to remain powerful was to weaken the Socialist Party. In other words, the primacy of the PCF had to take precedence over the union of the left. There is evidence – relating to the timing of the printing of *L'Humanité* – that the PCF had decided even before the Common Programme renegotiations collapsed on 22 September 1977 that no agreement would be reached with the PS. Therefore, the Communist strategy was continually to attack the socialists, and in particular Mitterrand, for their 'shift to the right' and at the same time to make ever more lavish promises over pay benefits and to insist that no ministerial portfolio should be barred to the PCF. This, it was hoped, would convince the workers that only the Communists were their allies; but at the same time it would expose the fragility of the socialist position. If the PS accepted the Communist demands over higher pay and benefits, it would alarm its more moderate supporters, while if it rejected them as unrealistic it would be seen to be defending a policy of capitalist austerity. The right, of course, stressed the risk of governmental crisis that would follow the victory of such quarrelling partners.

The PCF strategy failed to prevent the Communist share of the vote on the first round declining slightly from 21.4 per cent to 20.5 per cent (though because of the lowering of the voting age to 18 its poll rose from 5.1 million to 5.9 million). It was, however, completely successful in demonstrating the heterogeneity and instability of a crucial section of the socialist vote, which deserted in the last week of the campaign. Instead of the 28–30 per cent which had been confidently expected, the socialists and Left Radicals obtained 25 per cent – and the socialists on their own under 23 per cent. There followed a farcical reconciliation which fooled no one. Few would have predicted at the beginning of the campaign that the PCF would gain in metropolitan France more seats than the socialists and Left Radicals, but so it turned out. The PCF had a net gain of 13 seats (96 against 73 in the old legislature), the PS and Left Radicals one of only 10 (112 against 102). The Giscardian–Gaullist coalition had a comfortable, though unstable, majority in the new Chamber.

It was reported that after the election, socialist supporters went up to Communist workers selling *L'Humanité* and said bitterly, 'Congratulations, Marchais, you've won, the Left has been defeated.' Mitterrand said publicly that the Communists had aimed to destroy him ('Ils ont voulu m'abattre'). There can be little doubt that the breakdown of the PCF-PS alliance caused the defeat of the left and that the Communist leadership caused the breakdown. This was not done, however, just to gain a few more seats in the Chamber of Deputies. It was the result of a determination to preserve at all costs the centrality of Communist influence in French left-wing politics even if that meant sacrificing governmental power. The vanguard must not be reduced to an auxiliary.

It can be argued that the PCF's behaviour and the sociology

of the French electorate do indeed condemn French Communism, if not to decline, then at any rate to stagnation. The party has failed to expand its electorate, or membership, beyond its traditional strata; its strident, almost Maurrasian, nationalism has not made it a 'national' party if such was the aim of the 'union of the French people'. This is serious for a party pledged to take the parliamentary road to advanced democracy. By-election results since March 1978 have been bad, there is increasing disaffection in the CGT with its Communist leadership, the 1978 Fête de l'Humanité was not a success. The chorus of dissatisfaction with the party leadership and its methods may be limited, but it is nevertheless unprecedented; the seriousness with which the leadership regarded it can be shown by the replacement, ostensibly on health grounds, of the Secretary of the Paris federation, H. Fizbin. This occurred in February 1979. It was the result of Fizbin's failure to control dissent in the Paris federation, a failure which demonstrated that he could not be relied on to ensure that 'troublemakers' would be excluded from the Paris delegation to the Twenty-Third Congress of the PCF.

Such events could lead to the twin conclusions that the drawbridge is once again being drawn up into the fortress, but that the fortress is fast disintegrating. These conclusions would be wrong. The 1979 congress showed that Marchais's supporters are in control of the party (his leading opponent among the hard-liners, Leroy, lost his membership of the highly influential Secretariat) and that the post-1975 changes have not been repudiated. The PCF remains, as was said at the beginning, an extremely strong political organisation and has survived greater crises that it is currently enduring. It is not going to go away – in recent elections to the European Parliament it managed to increase slightly its percentage of the total vote. The problem for the PCF is not primarily one of membership, internal democracy or even votes. It is one of strategy and resides in the contradiction within Eurocommunism between the limited use of power that a commitment to alliances and liberal democracy implies and the continuing insistence on the unlimited right to determine policy that the Communist view of the party demands. This does not mean that policy will be dictated by the Soviet Union. Nor does it necessarily imply that the French Communists are patiently planning changes that will involve the destruction of those democratic liberties, that 'autonomy of the political', in Elleinstein's words, which they now claim to uphold (though critics of the Eurocommunism like Macridis see the upholding as a dialectical response to a particular situation which will change when the situation does). What the French Communists will not give up is an insistence on the supremacy of the party. This insistence, Leninist in inspiration, makes the other aims of Eurocommunism exceedingly difficult to achieve. The Soviet Union may no longer dictate French Communist policy or provide a model of a socialist society. But the French Communists are still wedded to the theory of politics of the Communist Party in the Soviet Union. That is the dilemma of the PCF – and also of Eurocommunism.

Notes

1. *L'U.R.S.S. et Nous*, A. Adler, F. Cohen, M. Décaillot, C. Frioux and L. Robel, (Editions Sociales, Paris, 1978).
2. See the criticism of the book's insufficiencies by J. Amalric in *Le Monde*, 14 September 1978.
3. In 1967 the PCF obtained 22.51 per cent of the votes cast, in 1968 20.02 per cent, in 1973 21.25 per cent and in 1978 20.55 per cent.
4. J. Montaldo, '*Les Finances du Parti Communiste* (Paris, 1978).
5. Jean Kanapa, whom Sartre called a cretin, was head of the foreign policy section of the PCF until his death in September 1978.
6. See below, p. 164–5.
7. Marchais's speech to the Central Committee of the PCF, 29 April 1978.
8. *Marxism Today* (August 1978); Jorge Semprun, 'Le Glas de l'Euro-communisme', *Le Monde*, 30 April/1 May 1978.
9. R. Tiersky, *The French Communists 1920–72* (New York, 1976) and 'French Communism', *Problems of Communism* (January–February 1976); A. Kriegel and D. Blackner, 'The International Role of the Communist Parties of Italy and France', Harvard Studies in International Affairs, no. 33 (1975).
10. M. Thorez, *Fils du Peuple* (1971 edition), p. 244.
11. Communiqué of the Bureau Politique, 1 October 1948.
12. P. Robrieux, *Maurice Thorez. Vie Secrète et Vie Publique* (Paris, 1975), p. 299.
13. S. Carrillo, '*Eurocommunism' and the State* (London, 1977).
14. Thorez, *Fils du Peuple*, p. 231.
15. Robrieux, *Maurice Thorez*, p. 623.
16. J. Baulin in *Le Monde* 2/3 April 1978.
17. Kriegel and Blacker, 'The International Role of the Communist Parties', pp. 50–1. It is worth pointing out that the French government's response to August 1968 was muted and that in 1978 a French Minister, Olivier Stirn, said in Prague that people should not be obsessed by the events of ten years ago (*Le Monde* 11/12 June 1978).
18. *Les Finances du Parti Communiste; La France Communiste* (Paris, 1978).
19. *La France Communiste*, p. 336.

20. Ibid, pp. 328–9.
21. *Le Monde*, 28 January 1978 and 18 February 1978.
22. K. Devlin, 'The Inter Party Drama, *Problems of Communism* (July–August 1975) and 'Eurocommunism', ibid. (January–February 1977); Tiersky, 'French Communism', ibid. (January–February 1976).
23. *Le Monde*, 28 June 1978; 30 June 1978.
24. R. Macridis, 'Eurocommunism', *Yale Review* (Spring 1978), pp. 328–35.
25. J. Kanapa, 'A New Policy of the French Communists?' *Foreign Affairs*, vol. 55 (January 1977), p. 283; J. Fabre, L. Sève and F. Hinker, *Les Communistes et l'Etat* (Paris, 1977), pp. 26–7.
26. Quoted in R. Verdier, *Le PC-PS Une Lutte Pour l'Entente* (Paris, 1976), p. 276.
27. J. Chambraz in *L'Humanité*, 4 September 1975, quoted in Devlin, *Problems of Communism* (January/February 1977).
28. Quoted in Tiersky, 'French Communism', p. 42.
29. See note 25.
30. C. Quin, *Classes Sociales et Union du Peuple de France* (Paris, 1976). Few non-Communist sociologists would accept this analysis of the character of French society.
31. Elleinstein wrote a series of articles in *Le Monde* after the 1978 elections attacking the party leadership for, among other things, not sufficiently criticising Soviet society.
32. *Le Monde* articles, 25–28 April 1978.

6

THE FINNISH COMMUNIST PARTY:
TWO PARTIES IN ONE

Seija Spring and D. W. Spring

The Finnish Communist Party (SKP), relative to Finnish society, is one of the most significant in Western Europe in its size, influence and role. In a population of 4.7 million, it currently has 48,000 members. Its share of the national vote in its electoral alliance of the Finnish People's Democratic League (SKDL), of which the SKP is the core, has fluctuated since 1944 from a high of 23.2 per cent in 1958 to a low of 16.6 per cent in 1970. In the most recent elections in 1979, the SKDL obtained over half a million votes, 17.9 per cent of the total. Their representation in Eduskunta, the Finnish Parliament, since 1944 has varied from a high of 50 seats in 1958 to a current low of 35 seats, including 6 allied non-Communist socialists. On local government councils, the SKDL/SKP currently hold 2,050 out of a national total of 12,550 seats. The party has the support of a very significant minority in the Finnish trade union congress (SAK) and holds over a third of the posts in its organisation. Communists control the 100,000-strong construction workers union and the 38,000 strong food industry union as well as two smaller unions. They have 47 per cent support, compared to the Social democrats' 50 per cent majority in the 140,000-strong metal workers' union, the largest in Finland.[1]

The SKP is also currently unique amongst Communist parties in Western Europe, having participated in seven Finnish governments since 1966.

The SKP was founded with a revolutionary programme in August 1918 in Petrograd by the exiled majority of the leadership of the Finnish Social Democratic Party, defeated in the recent civil war of January to April 1918.[2] In December 1918 in Helsinki, V. Tanner refounded the Social Democratic Party (SDP) with a less radical programme, to work as a reformist party within the newly established Finnish Republic. The birth of the Communist Party, therefore, not only followed on from the 'White Terror' and concentration camps with

172

which the civil war culminated, outlawing a generation of the Finnish radical left, but was also accompanied by the splitting of the workers' movement. The SKP suffered an attack of 'left infantilism' in its early months, until Otto Ville Kuusinen secretly visited Finland in 1919 and came to the conclusion that underground work offered only limited prospects and proposed a programme in essence based on the ideas of the peaceful transition and of different roads to socialism in different countries. His principles clearly involved the moving of the party's central direction from exile in Soviet Russia back to Finland. However, on returning to Petrograd, a compromise was reached between the revolutionary and more pragmatic wings of the party, which resulted in the maintenance both of the party in exile and its legal fronts in Finland.[3] In various guises the party managed to play a role in Finnish politics in the 1920s in spite of persecution. They obtained votes of well over 100,000 and a maximum of 27 seats (in 1922) in the 200-seat Parliament. Until 1930 the Communists were also dominant in the Finnish trade union organisation of the time.

In 1930 a right-wing movement in Finnish society resulted in the banning of all Communist organisations and press and for most of the decade work in Finland collapsed. Hundreds of Communists were arrested and tried each year in the first half of the decade. From 1935 repression eased and organisations sympathetic to the Communists resurfaced and even made use of the decade. From 1935 repression eased and organisations representation in Parliament. But at the same time the leadership in exile in the Soviet Union suffered severely in Stalin's attack on foreign Communist parties, losing many of its most experienced and prominent members. When war broke out with the Soviet Union in late November 1939, Kuusinen, the only surviving prominent leader, in a move now embarrassing to Finnish Communists, was persuaded to set up an alternative government in the rear of the Red Army on the Karelian isthmus. But by February 1940 the Soviet government had convinced itself that the existing Finnish republic was not about to collapse from internal disunity. Having achieved significant military progress in its campaign on the isthmus, it made peace in March 1940.

In the months after the peace the rapid rise of the Soviet-Finnish Friendship Society (SNS) for a brief period during 1940 suggested once again that the radical policies of the Finnish Communist Party met a need within Finnish society for those who felt themselves to be outcasts, those whose experience and understanding of the events of 1918 made them irreconcilable to 'White Finland'.[4]

In 1944, after Finland's second unsuccessful war against the Soviet Union, the terms of the armistice required the legalisation of the SKP and other pro-Soviet organisations. The Finnish Communist Party thus surfaced for the first time to work in full legality within the Finnish republic. For the first time it became a mass party with 30,000 members by the end of 1946.

In the post-1944 conditions, the party's practice was to 'recommend democracy on the basis of the bourgeois economic system. It corresponds to the needs of the working people.'[5] But it still retained the revolutionary programme of 1918 and many members and supporters who were impatient with its current gradualist approach. In the parliamentary game, however, the party was outmanoeuvred by the social democrats. In 1948, after a scare over a supposed Communist *coup*, for which there now appear to have been no solid grounds, but which in the general context of the time it was not unreasonable of their opponents to expect, they lost eleven seats in the elections.[6] They failed to come to an agreement with the SDP and the Agarian Party over participation in the government, though in principle they continued to be prepared for it, and remained out of the government for the following 18 years.

Between 1944 and 1948 the SKP and its allies established themselves as a major political force within Finnish society, obtaining nearly 400,000 votes and 49 per cent of the 200 parliamentary seats. They participated in particular in the government of the dissident social democrat, Mauno Pekkala, from 1946–8, holding the largest number of posts, including the Ministry of the Interior. This participation in government was influenced by, but was by no means entirely dependent on, the presence of the Soviet-dominated Allied Control Commission in Helsinki until 1948.

The tactics of the party were those of the 'popular front' exemplified by the 'Big Three' agreement of April 1945 between the Communists, social democrats and Agrarians for a foreign policy based on the United Nations and co-operation with the Soviet Union, elimination of the remnants of Fascism in

Finland and restraints on big business, including nationalisation where appropriate. The party did not appear before the electorate under its own programme, but only as a member of the Finnish People's Democratic League (SKDL) founded in November 1944. The existence of this organisation as the electoral front of the Communist Party was to play an important role in easing the process of reform within the SKP in the 1960s. It was not intended to be a political party and SKP rejected the idea that it should have a socialist programme. It was to be an umbrella organisation, 'a tie between citizens and organisations which are democratic in ideas and act on democratic principles'. It should in particular bring together all those who were committed to a new policy towards the Soviet Union, in order to prevent further conflict. However, the hope that a large part of the Social Democratic Party might be drawn to it proved vain. Its other constituent elements were democratic women's, youth and student organisations. Although some dissident social democrats did join, the SKP by 1950 remained as the only political party in the SKDL and has throughout its existence been its leading force.

The exclusion of the SKP/SKDL from participation in government between 1948 and 1966 resulted from the unwillingness of the other parties to take them into coalition. The withdrawal of the Allied Control Commission reduced outside interference in Finland's internal affairs. The conclusion of the Treaty of Friendship, Co-operation and Mutual Assistance with the Soviet Union in 1948 and the presence of Paasikivi as President until 1956 were adequate assurances to Finland's eastern neighbour. The unfavourable image which the party undoubtedly had amongst the majority of Finnish voters was intensified by the experience of the Cold War, during which the SKP was not backward in its uncritical admiration for Stalin and the Soviet Union and contempt for the achievements of existing Finnish society.

During its 18 years out of government, the party had always been ready in principle to participate in a coalition. From his election in 1956 as President, Urho Kekkonen encouraged the SKDL and the other parties to co-operate in government. The SKDL continued to hold its electoral support, although excluded from the government by the attitudes of the other parties. But in the early 1960s changes in Finnish society and within the

SKP/SKDL enabled the party once again to enter government.

Not surprisingly, the SKP leadership was slow and cautious in responding publicly to the denunciation of Stalin's 'cult of personality' at the Twentieth Congress of the Soviet Communist Party in February 1956.[7] It did, however, provoke the party into revising its pre-Stalinist revolutionary programme of 1918 at its Eleventh Congress in June 1957. Even in 1948 Hertta Kuusinen had shown an awareness of the need for the party to adapt its programme to its actual tactics and to the new situation in which it found itself after 1944.[8] The new programme claimed to be based on Finnish conditions for the democratic road to socialism on the basis of the popular front and the will of the majority. However, the bourgeoisie would be unlikely to give up power without a struggle and parliamentary activity therefore needed to be supplemented by the action of the masses. In the election of 1958 the SKP/SKDL gained 7 seats to reach a total of 50, their highest ever. But it was not significantly more than in 1945 under the old programme and the result probably reflects more the severe economic conditions of the time and the division of the social democrats rather than a response to the change of programme. The party, however, still remained out of government.

In the 1960s the pace of change increased both inside the party and in attitudes towards its aims in Finland. A new generation of the intelligentsia was emerging, which had been educated since the war, had a less nationalistic view of 1918, was less conservative than the previous generation, with many individuals with an ideologically free interest in socialism. Such elements found that the possibility for discussion in the SKP/SKDL newspaper, *Kansan Uutiset*, was very limited. In 1961 Jarno Pennanen, former editor of the *Kansan Uutiset*, set up his own journal, *Tilanne*, to provide a forum for the discussion of socialism. The journal called for a constructive debate on the theories of both social democrats and Communists, and the establishment of the unity of the working class as preparation for the achievement of socialism by democratic means.[9]

Within SKP the old-guard Moscow-trained leaders were reluctant to enter this debate. But there were pressures within the party for change. As early as 1956 Mauri Ryömä, editor of the party's *Työkansan Sanomat* and a member of the Central Committee, had allowed a limited self-criticism of the party's whole-hearted admiration of the Soviet Union and its form of socialism in the paper.[10] In the 1960s these pressures within the party, and an awareness that Finnish society was changing and the party must change with it, became irresistible even to the old leadership.

At the Twelfth Congress in 1960, the Secretary General, Ville Pessi, reasserted the party's well known willingness to co-operate in government with all other genuine representatives of the working class. When the transition to socialism took place, it could definitely occur without violence as long as the working class was united.[11] For the new intelligentsia, however, this missed the real point of the incipient debate – what was the content of that socialism?

In 1962–3 the party undertook a full examination of what its members thought about 'the defence and expansion of democracy' in view of the fact that the party was widely regarded as 'a party of dictatorship, which, they say, is trying to destroy all freedoms and democracy. Once it gains power it will introduce the kolkhoz by force, destroy other parties, suppress religion and close the churches'. The party, it was said, must be aware of the differences between Finland where there was a multi-party system and democracy (*kansanvalta*), while in the Soviet Union there was a one-party dictatorship.[12]

At the Thirteenth Congress in April 1963, Ville Pessi recognised that there had been since 1950 significant changes in Finnish society which they must take into account. Traditional class barriers were breaking down. The numbers of white-collar workers had grown three times as quickly as manual workers. The party must increase its activity in particular amongst the intelligentsia so that its membership would reflect these changes. The proportion of the intelligentsia in the party was still small: 84 per cent of its members were workers.[13] In 1964 and in particular in 1965 the leadership was no longer able to contain the reform movement within the party. Their failure to do more than repeat the Soviet line on the removal of Khrushchev in October 1964 brought criticism not only from sympathisers outside the party, but also from within it. For the first time the SKP/SKDL newspaper, *Kansan Uutiset*, published an article criticising the party leadership. Evidence was accumulating of an emerging reform movement within the party.[14]

In the following February the pressure from sympathetic

critics outside the party and particularly from reformers within resulted in the election for the first time of a non-Communist, Dr Ele Alenius, as Secretary-General of the SKDL, defeating Hertta Kuusinen the SKP's candidate. As the SKP was the most active force in SKDL, this development could only have come about as a result of support for Alenius by 'reformist' elements in SKP.

Alenius had been a member of SKDL since 1948. With a few other educated and like-minded non-Communist socialists, he now sought to rectify SKDL as an umbrella organisation for the socialist left, with more of a balance between its Communist and socialist elements. In a speech in March 1965, which was printed in full in *Kansan Uutiset*, Alenius said that the SKDL had failed to take account of the recent changes in Finnish society. It had not been regarded by the electorate as a genuinely Finnish organisation. The activisation of socialist elements within SKDL would enable it to be a bridge between the social democrats and the Communists, a prerequisite for a socialist Finland.[15] The new mood in SKDL encouraged by the reformers in SKP brought a much fuller public discussion amongst party members, which culminated in the publication by the SKP Central Committee of its 'October manifesto' in October 1965. This signified that the reformist tendency in the party had achieved predominance in the leadership.

In the summer and autumn of 1965, the reformists called for greater inner-party democracy, a new leadership, revision of the rules and programme and acceptance of parliamentary democracy. For the old leadership, Ville Pessi argued that because of the different property relationships democracy in Stalin's Russia had been more extensive than in any capitalist country. But Erkki Salomaa, one of the leaders of the reformers in the party, suggested that Pessi did not know Finland well enough, nor appreciate the extent of its political democracy since 1944. They did not want a Soviet Finland, but a socialist Finland, he argued, and the term 'dictatorship of the proletariat', with its erroneous implications, should perhaps be rejected as the description of one of the party's goals.[16]

On 16 October 1965 the Central Committee approved the publication of what some of the reformers called its 'manifesto', entitled 'Marxist state theory and the Finnish road to socialism'. It had a distinctive blue and white cover to emphasise the national roots of the party. Its most important sections concerned the question of democracy. The party should not criticise in a negative fashion the democratic institutions of bourgeois society, in the establishment of which the working class had also played a role.

> The goal of socialist revolution is not to destroy democratic institutions and freedoms and to create a new socialist democracy out of nothing, it only wants to give a new content to the old forms and to develop them further.[17]

In the change to the new system it was important that there should be a majority in Parliament which would begin to carry out the reforms leading to a socialist system. But it was impossible to deny the importance of non-parliamentary but perfectly legal pressure groups such as the trade unions in this process. The SKP did not claim an exclusive role in this movement towards socialism, but was convinced of the need for relations of complete equality with those other parties which were committed to a change in the economic system. The prospects for a peaceful move towards socialism in Finland were good because of the strong democratic institutions and the relative weakness of monopoly capitalism. As for the nature of the future society, the use of the term 'dictatorship of the proletariat' had become inappropriate. The term 'dictatorship' recalled the Fascist regimes of the 1930s and the negative characteristics of Stalin's rule. It would be more appropriate to say 'workers' power', which would arouse less misunderstanding about the eventual aims of the party. But in any case, both during the change-over and under socialism, the party was committed to the Finnish tradition of a multi-party system, freedom of expression, of organisation, strike and demonstration, and equal rights guaranteed by the law, both for those in government and for those in opposition.[18]

When the Fourteenth Congress of the SKP met in January 1966, however, the debates did not reveal fully the differences within the party. Behind the scenes there was a much fuller discussion but 'some kind of unseen force prevented the disagreements being carried to the meeting hall'.[19] Pessi remained Secretary-General and complacently observed: 'We have no reason to change or revise the views we hold on the basic questions of socialism and on the struggle for it,' although perhaps some clarification was necessary when changing conditions brought new prospects. But this was a rearguard action. Already the Central Committee's document of October 1965 belied Pessi's claim. A clear split within the party was still ahead, but the congress showed that the old leadership was weakening. The Central Committee was instructed to prepare a draft of a new programme to replace that only recently agreed in 1957. Aaltonen, one of the old-guard leaders, was removed as Chairman and was replaced by Aarne Saarinen, a former stonemason and a man of the post-Stalinist generation. The new vice-chairman, Erkki Salomaa, had played a prominent role for the reformers in the press discussions in 1965. The reformist opposition within the SKP had now become the 'majority men'.

In March 1966 the general election provided a test for public reaction in Finland to the new trends in the SKP and SKDL. It proved to be a striking victory for the left parties, which obtained 103 out of 200 seats in Parliament. But the move to the left benefited most of all the reformist Social Democratic Party, which with a total of nearly 650,000 votes (27.2 per cent) and 55 seats became the largest single party in Parliament. The SKDL total vote, however, remained fairly stable at 503,000 (21.1 per cent), compared with 507,000 (22 per cent) in 1962. But the complicated proportional representation system lost them 6 out of their 47 seats. More significant was the fact that, although they strengthened their position in Lapland and Oulu in the north, their vote declined in the more industrialised southern towns.[20]

After the election, at a joint post-mortem meeting of the SKDL and SKP, the non-Communists showed disappointment at their limited success: Rauno Setälä, Cultural Secretary of SKDL, fiercely criticized the 'brakemen of our movement', who prevented the process of reform of the organisation. The movement and particularly the SKP must make a definite choice:

> either you keep clearly and consistently to the Leninist teachings and to the ideas of proletarian dictatorship and the possibility of violent revolution, or else you say clearly, distinctly and unambiguously to the Finnish people that we will not resort to violence in any circumstances.

Taisto Sinisalo, one of the emerging leaders of the 'minority' in the SKP, protested that Setälä was demanding that they should give up Marxist-Leninism. He would choose the Leninist alternative. The representatives of the SKP 'majority', however, made no comment.[21]

In fact, the limited success of the SKDL in the elections probably owed nothing to the struggle within the SKP or the SKDL. Their vote was a distinctly traditional one and has fluctuated over the whole post-war period only between 16 and 23 per cent of the total votes cast. The SKDL failed to draw new elements to its support even at those times when its rivals, the social democrats and the Agrarians (Centre Party) were split. The two elements in the SKDL vote were the northern backwoodsmen in Lapland and north Finland and a share in the working-class votes of the industrial towns of south and west Finland. To a considerable extent it was a protest vote by those who felt they had been left outside the increasing prosperity of Finnish society. But traditional loyalties which owed nothing to social and economic factors and going back to the deep rift created by the civil war can be detected in some areas.[22] The complaint of the SKDL was that, although this traditional vote had been held, there had been no breakthrough in attracting new elements to the party, as the social democrats seemed to have done, since their vote had increased by 200,000 over 1962.

Nevertheless the 1966 election marked a transitional point for the role of SKDL and therefore of the SKP in the Finnish political system with their entry once again into government. The SKDL and SKP had consistently declared their readiness to participate. Kekkonen was in favour of a government not excluding the SKDL, but this idea had been frustrated since 1948 by the hostility of the other parties and particularly of the social democrats. This hostility was founded simply on the premiss that, whatever tactics the SKDL/SKP might temporarily employ, they were still committed to the idea of violent revolution and seizure of power. But it was not so much the incipient changes within the SKDL and SKP which allowed them to enter government, but rather a change of attitude and move to the left in the Social Democratic Party. The removal of Tanner as leader in 1963, with his wartime anti-Soviet associations, and his replacement by Rafael Paasio was a step which made co-operation with the SKDL more possible. Even before the elections there were indications of the social democrats' awareness of the need for the co-operation of the left-wing parties: the social democrats could not reform on their own. In 1965, Leskinen, one of the leaders of the SDP, went to Moscow to assure the Soviet government that there was only one rational foreign policy for Finland to pursue in relation to its eastern neighbour. An alliance of the left would be a means of changing the anti-Soviet label which the Social Democratic Party had acquired under Tanner.

Nevertheless it was still somewhat to the surprise of the SKP leaders that the SDP invited them to participate in forming a government. Neither the result of the elections for the SKDL nor pressure from its members or supporters made such participation an imperative at this time. Three representatives of the SKDL entered the 15-member, four-party government. Their participation continued in the unusually stable administrations of Paasio (1966) and Koivisto (1968) up to 1970. The choice of the three Ministers suggested a unity of approach to participation in the government within the SKDL and SKP. Alenius for the socialists of SKDL became deputy Minister of Finance; Leo Suonpää from the 'minority' of the SKP Minister of Transport, and Matti Koivunen from the 'majority' of the party became Minister of Social Affairs. These were not the central positions in the Cabinet and the caution of the participant groups towards each other was suggested by the careful balancing of the SKP Ministers in Social Affairs and Transport with 'deputies' from the Centre Party. But the SKP/SKDL leaders felt that it was important not to repeat the situation of 1958, to take advantage of the new atmosphere and take a small step towards the co-operation of the left.[23]

Thus for the first time in Western Europe since the Cold War a Communist Party participated in a government coalition. That it occurred in Finland was no coincidence. The party had always been ready to participate in a government coalition with other parties and had a stable and substantial electoral support. President Kekkonen pressed for the inclusion of the SKDL, and the Communists, though they were disliked by the other parties, no longer seemed so frightening. Finally, the SKDL's recommendation of a friendly policy towards the Soviet Union was not an obstacle to their co-operation in government in

Finland as it was in NATO countries.

Participation in government and responsibility for its actions, however, created new problems for the party and its electoral alliance. Up to this point all its strategy and policy had been geared to opposition activities. A substantial part of the party found it difficult to accommodate themselves to the new situation in which their criticisms of government would be muted by participation in it. Even more, they feared the integration of the party into bourgeois Finnish society and the compromising of its revolutionary ideals.

The limitations of the discussion in the Fourteenth Congress in January 1966 meant that the very real problems for the SKP involved in its new direction as shown by the October 1965 'blue and white' Central Committee document had not been resolved. It soon became evident that there was a struggle within the party, although there was extreme reluctance to recognise it.

The split became public knowledge in the autumn of 1967. The discussion of the new programme for the 'Finnish Road to Socialism' which the Fourteenth Congress had instructed the party to prepare had revealed deep and irreconcilable differences on many questions. The opponents of change in the party's attitude found it impossible to accept the way the party was moving. On 22 September the Turku branch of the SKP formed the 'SKP Co-operation Committee' in order to co-ordinate the activities of groups opposed to the majority ('reformist') leadership throughout Finland. This was followed by Vice-Chairman Salomaa's speech at Raisio on 1 October condemning such moves:

> Within the party there exists a group, which I would not call the left, but which from the very beginning has taken a negative view of the decisions taken in the 14th Party Congress. The views it holds are dictated by the power struggle. One cannot explain in any other way its tactics. It tries to ride on Marxism-Leninism and canonises itself as its only defenders. And what is directly provocative, it claims that only this group supports comradely relations with the Soviet Communist Party.

At the end of 1967 the Uusimaa provincial organisation of the party began to publish a new party news-sheet, *Tiedote*, reflecting the views of the organised 'minority'. A total of 6 out of 15 area branches of the party came into the control of opponents of the 'majority' leadership.[24]

The division only deepened in the course of 1968. The entry of Warsaw Pact forces into Czechoslovakia allowed the opposition to show itself as the true friend of the Soviet Union. The SKP Politbureau by a vote of 24 to 9 on 22 August condemned the invasion, stating that they thought that negotiations could have led to a settlement, 'without those actions which the five countries of the Warsaw Pact considered necessary in order to secure the achievements of socialism' and which were 'harmful to the whole international workers' movement'. Such was their disgust that it was immediately decided that it would be inappropriate to carry through the celebrations for the fiftieth anniversary of the Finnish Communist Party at the end of August.[25] The welcoming of a Soviet delegation for such a celebration might cause misunderstanding about the attitude of the party to the Czechoslovak events. It would naturally arouse distrust amongst its SKDL allies and provoke unfavourable press comment. If a socialist Finland was achieved, as the SKP wanted, would its ideological credentials also be in question and under threat of action on the initiative of the Soviet Communist Party in conformity with the 'Brezhnev doctrine'?

For the 'minority' opposition there were no such problems. The Turku and Uusimaa branches published resolutions declaring they were working in support of the Soviet Communist Party and approving its 'courageous defence of workers' internationalism'. Only these local resolutions, and not that of the SKP Politbureau, were published in the Soviet press. Contrary to the party decision in August, the two local centres of opposition in Uusimaa and Turku organised separate celebrations in September for their fiftieth anniversary, at which Soviet party representatives appeared. In the same autumn they began publication of a nationally distributed newspaper, *Tiedonantaja*, to air their views and compete with the SKP/SKDL *Kansan Uutiset*.

The events of the Fifteenth Party Congress (3–6 April 1969) formally registered the split in the party in a drastic manner. The opening was delayed by agitated discussion about the composition of the delegation from Turku. The latter branch demanded also that the 'question of personalities' should be dealt with before the new party programme. The 'minority' were in particular opposed to Vice-Chairman Salomaa, who had publicly declared the split and denounced the opposition in 1967. They failed to obtain satisfaction and in spite of attempts by the visiting Soviet party dignitaries to dissuade them, a substantial body of delegates representing up to 20,000 members left the Congress and called their own meeting in a neighbouring hall. They established a shadow 'National Consultative Committee of Communists' to represent them and defend their views against the party 'majority'. The rump Congress continued its activity without the 'minority' and elected a new Central Committee from those who had remained behind. They approved the new programme, but the discussion of the new party rules was postponed and the chief task set for the new Central Committee was to restore the unity of action of the party.[26]

The draft programme presented to the Congress bore the imprint of the majority wing of the party, but nevertheless, in comparison with the Central Committee document of October 1965, it shows some effort at compromise in order to hold the party together. On the critical issue of the socialist revolution and democracy the programme stated:

> The aim of the SKP is that the socialist revolution in our country will be carried out in a peaceful and democratic way and that the Finnish transition to socialism will take place through reforms which will fundamentally change the structure of our economy, society and property and power relationships. The transition to socialism is only possible in a situation in which the great majority of the Finnish people, and above all the working class, spontaneously feels the necessity for socialism and is ready to conduct a decisive mass struggle for it against the powers of reaction.[27]

Further:

> Socialist democracy guarantees the right to exist and freedom of criticism to all parties which have the support of the working people and to various minorities which function according to the constitution of the socialist state and

prevailing legal system.

But 'in no case can the successful building of a socialist society be carried out without a working-class party guided by the theories of scientific socialism of Marx, Engels and Lenin.'[28] Thus the programme of 1969 emphasised the peaceful 'Finnish road to socialism', which would take into consideration the democratic institutions of bourgeois Finland. But its language was less explicit than the document of October 1965, for instance about the multi-party system. The Central Committee report for the Congress stated that there were now no fundamental differences on the programme and that all sections of the party were agreed on the importance of 'proletarian internationalism' and comradely relations with the Soviet Communist Party. The SKP had never doubted the sincerity of the intentions of the socialist countries in the Czechoslovak events of the previous year and agreed that 'one of the central principles of socialist democracy is preserving the leading role of the Marxist-Leninist party in society.' This principle was also emphasised in the new programme, while at the same time the need for equality of the different parties representing the working class was recognised.[29]

In the view of the Congress the split was essentially a question of party discipline.

> The central reason for the disturbance of the common action of our party, however, has been numerous infringements of our organisational principle of democratic centralism. Some members of the party leadership, after finding themselves in a minority on decisions made, have acted against the decisions of the central organs of the party.[30]

They stated therefore that

> the precondition for the return to unity is that members of the Central Committee and party workers will comply with decisions made by the Central Committee and act to fulfil them irrespective of whether these decisions have been made unanimously or after a vote.[31]

In the minority meeting, however, the Uusimaa District Secretary, Kainulainen, declared that the division within the party was much more than a question of discipline. It was a question of a revisionist deviation, which expressed itself in particular in the acceptance by the leaders of the party of the government's measures of stabilisation in the interests of capital.

> We know that with persecution taken to an extreme and with press propaganda and the aid of the central organs of the party, the will of the membership was suppressed and all the Leninist norms of party life were broken. Those who have amongst other things strayed from our party's main line by adopting a bourgeois incomes policy, accepting and signing agreements on the terms of big business, those who violated the working people's deep feeling of internationalism, fraternalism and friendship and were against the socialist Soviet Union in the August days, those who dishonoured the achievements of our Communist Party and working class over the past fifty years by cancelling the anniversary celebrations, these people managed temporarily to gain a majority in the Fifteenth Party Congress and unscrupulously continued to break the Leninist norms of party life disregarding delegates from local branches representing about 20,000 members in the Fifteenth Party Congress.

> Why was this necessary? It was in order to put our party in line with the reformist parties of the capitalist system. Because the Central Committee elected at the Fifteenth Party Congress does not have the confidence of our membership, it aims to continue with the stabilization policy which is against the interests of the workers. In order to clamp down on class-conscious ideas it was necessary with the help of a right-wing group to disunite our party congress and take the Central Committee under the control of those forces which are ready to serve capitalism by expelling and persecuting our class-conscious members who work for the theory of scientific socialism. These are the reasons and these are the men guilty of wrecking the Fifteenth Party Congress.[32]

This statement of the minority's position showed how difficult it would be to attain a reconciliation. In the months after the Congress the minority in the provinces established shadow branches of the party, opposed to the official leadership. Saarinen recognised that there were in fact two parties. He himself supported the majority view, but was determined to maintain some form of party unity and resist appeals from the right for the expulsion of the opposition. The Soviet Communist Party representatives also advised in favour of unity and reconciliation.[33]

By February 1970 it proved possible to call an Extraordinary Congress to try to restore the unity of the party. This resulted in a novel and unique solution for the SKP.

It was accepted by this time that in fact ideological unity of the party was not possible. Saarinen thought that such differences might be solved in the course of time if the party could hold together. For the present it was important to emphasize what united them. The Extraordinary Congress therefore did not discuss ideology, but only organisational and personnel questions on which some kind of compromise might be reached. It was agreed that the Central Committee and Politbureau elected at the Fifteenth Congress should be re-elected, allotting 20 seats to the 'majority' and 15 to the 'minority'. Saarinen was to remain as Chairman, but there were to be two vice-chairmen – Salomaa for the 'majority' and Sinisalo, the new leader of the 'minority'. In the Politbureau there were to be 9 from the 'majority' and 6 from the 'minority'. The secretariat was divided 5–3 in favour of the 'majority', with A. A. Aalto (majority) as Secretary-General. But the 'Communist National Consultative Committee' and all the separate organs of the 'minority' had to cease functioning within two weeks of the meeting. The newspaper *Tiedonantaja* must also cease publication. Those members who had been expelled from the party or had left because of disagreements should be reinstated if they so wished. The local organisations were in future to conform to the decisions of the Politbureau and Central Committee and conciliation committees were to decide on the local balance of representation of the two wings of the party.[34]

This latter was the weakest point of the agreement. The confirmation of the participation of the 'minority' in the central organs maintained their position there as a minority. But they could not be expected to give up the hope that the balance would change as a result of the struggle for control of the local branches.

Such a papering over of the cracks was doomed to failure and the situation in the party deteriorated. The separate 'minority' organisations were not abolished and in fact two separate party organisations remained in existence. A common front was made for the elections of 1970 but the 'minority' only publicised its own candidates and the results were a severe disappointment. In a general move to the right in this 'protest election', the governing parties, including the social democrats, suffered. The SKDL was left with only 36 of its 41 seats and a reduction in its voting strength by 82,000 compared with 1966 from 21.1 per cent to only 16.6 per cent of the total vote, their worst ever. Of the 36 SKDL representatives, 22 were from the 'majority', 12 from the 'minority', and 2 were SKDL socialists. A five-party coalition was, however, reconstructed under Karjalainen in June 1970, again with 3 SKDL Ministers. For the 'majority' of the SKP Anna-Liisa Tiekso became Minister for Social Affairs and Veikko Saarto again Minister of Transport. But the surprise was the appointment of the 'minority' Communist, Erkki Tuominen, as Minister of Justice, which provoked unfavourable comment from the right-wing press.[35]

While both wings of the party participated in the government, it proved impossible to hold the latter together. The 36 SKDL members of Parliament refused to accept the price control relaxation bill which was proposed by the majority of the government and which was part of the Kekkonen package for stabilisation of the economy, agreed with the majority of the trade unions in December 1970. Extensive strikes followed in February-March 1971. The SKDL members refused to vote for the bill or to withdraw their Ministers from the Cabinet. The result was the reorganisation of the Karjalainen Cabinet in March 1971 with three social democrats replacing the SKDL members. In this crisis, as Saarinen later recognised, the split in the party had played a role. He would not accept the bill unless the parliamentary group could act unanimously. As the 'minority' refused to have anything to do with it, Saarinen felt they must all continue to oppose it even if it resulted in the exclusion of their representatives from the Cabinet.

The withdrawal of the SKP from the government did not, however, heal the breach in the party. On the contrary, the situation deteriorated. In April 1971 the Central Committee by 20 votes to 10 instructed the Politbureau to restore order in the party and stop splitting. At the Sixteenth Congress in April

1972 both Saarinen and Sinisalo recognised for the first time in a full Congress the depth of the split and the deleterious effects it had had on the party. Saarinen accepted that the principles established at the Extraordinary Congress had not been able to be carried out in practice. The basic question was not the party rules but that 'the party is in fact divided into two' and 'the division is still very deep.' The cause was 'certain political and ideological disagreements' reflected from the mid-1960s in both 'right revisionist' and 'left sectarian' views in the party press, according to whether members wanted significant changes in the party or defended its old leadership. This had created very deep distrust, which had been a feature of party life for many years. The conditions did not yet exist for the Central Committee to be able to reconcile the different views. Saarinen called meanwhile for moderation and an understanding attitude towards each other and for self-criticism as well as criticism, because all the past and present leadership bore some responsibility for the dispute.

Sinisalo also tried to place himself on the middle ground between 'right revisionists' and 'left sectarians', but made clearer his attachment to the minority view in the party. There was no question of compromise: 'Marxism believes there is only one solution to any question' and if the party held to Marxist-Leninist theory and proletarian internationalism, this should overcome any divisions. But Sinisalo complained: 'Our party has still not considered the basic causes of our problems and this task is still before us.' He condemned nationalistic tendencies and the denials of the leading role of the Communist Party and of proletarian internationalism 'in areas close to the SKP'. Likewise he now condemned such participation in government as was playing into the hands of the Social Democratic Party, and working according to the 'rules of the game' set by others. There was a need for a full evaluation of the party's experience in government. The Communist Party was a party of class struggle and ought not to serve the cause of stabilisation of the capitalist system, as it would lose its identity, carry out the policies of other parties and be unable to fulfil its own aims. Like Saarinen, he recognised that the decisions of the Extraordinary Congress had been unable to be carried out in organisational matters. In essence he asserted that for the time being 'democratic centralism' could not be applied in the party because of the deep split. This gave the game away: the conflict was essentially, as Saarinen recognised, a power struggle within the leadership, each group seeking to achieve dominance of its own political and ideological concepts.

Saarinen's criticism of the 'minority' was muted: they ought to keep to Marxist–Leninist organisational principles and they should recognise that participation in the government had its positive as well as its negative aspects. Yet the differences in the party were clear, particularly from their attitudes towards the SKDL. Saarinen welcomed the strengthening of SKDL as a separate organisation and noted that many disillusioned members had left the SKP to work in the SKDL organisations. In Saarinen's view the SKP needed an active SKDL with more left socialist allies in it. This would make it resemble more the original concept of a wide umbrella organisation for the democratic forces.

For Sinisalo, however, these had been most disturbing developments. The changes in SKDL, its acceptance of socialism in its programme in 1967 and Alenius's recommendation of a different kind of socialism from that of the SKP were threatening for party unity. The SKDL should not acquire the characteristics of a political party and it was essential that the SKP should continue to play the leading role in it.[36]

The lines of dispute were more clearly drawn at this congress than at any previous one, but there was no fundamental discussion of the issues dividing the two wings for the guidance of the party. Indeed, compromise was hardly possible, as the essential roots of dispute were the attitudes of the party towards the means of achieving socialism and towards the Soviet model.

Even though the SKDL/SKP remained outside the government between 1971 and 1975 the tension within both organisations increased. The conflict in the SKP overflowed into the SKDL organisations. In 1973 the attacks of the 'minority' on the SKDL socialists were so fierce that the SKDL board and the SKP Politbureau had to condemn them. There was a satisfactory working relationship between the SKP 'majority' and the SKDL socialists. But the proportional system agreed for the party was also applied to the party's representatives on the SKDL board on which the 'minority' at the SKDL congress in 1973 secured 22 per cent of the seats. Attacks still continued from *Tiedonantaja* attempting to depict the SKDL leadership as anti-Soviet and petty bourgeois.

In 1974 Alenius, who had been elected chairman of SKDL in 1967, published his thoughts on the Finnish Road to Socialism in his *Suomalainen Ratkaisu* (*The Finnish Solution*), and his views on the SKDL/SKP relationship as a result of nearly thirty years' experience in SKDL. He wanted the SKDL to return to its original conception. It should not be like the popular front organisations of socialist countries where the Communist Party had a leading role. There was nothing in the SKDL rules which institutionalised SKP domination. SKDL was intended to be a league for co-operation between various equal parties based on mutual respect. Alenius recognised that in practice the SKP had dominated the SKDL because of the passivity of its non-Communist members. Only 42,000 out of 170,000 corporate members of the SKDL were in the SKP. Of the 60,000 individual members of SKDL only 10,000 were also members of SKP. However, most of the candidates put forward in local and national elections by SKDL were SKP members. In the SKDL representation in Parliament, 33 out of 37 were SKP members. The Secretary-General of the SKDL and his deputy were both Communists and out of 24 members of the board, 16 were members of SKP. This situation, Alenius complained, did not reflect the real composition of the membership of SKDL. The domination by the Communists and the limited trust of the SKP amongst Finns had restricted the growth of their support and prevented the establishment of a common programme and plan of action towards socialism for the whole left, including SDP, SKP, SKDL and the trade unions.[37]

These ideas did not radically differ from those which the SKP Central Committee majority had already approved in January 1967 and re-emphasised by publishing in their congress report for 1972. Here it was admitted that, apart from bourgeois propaganda, 'the Communists' own clumsiness had restricted the SKDL's possibilities of development into an extensive enough organisation for co-operation' and that SKP members should act in SKDL

to form the decision-making organs at the centre and in the area organisations in such a manner that they will correspond more than in the past to the nature of an organisation for co-operation, and be composed of representatives chosen by SKDL and its member organisations.[38]

The 'majority' in SKP received Alenius's book favourably. In *Kansan Uutiset* it was noted as an open, honest but personal view of a Finnish socialist. Saarinen felt that Alenius saw the Finnish road to socialism as too easy. But he did not question his motives.[39] The 'minority' were not content to leave Alenius's dangerous ideas without comment. In April 1975, two weeks before the SKP's Seventeenth Congress, the Soviet journal *Novoe Vremya* published an unsigned article, 'Whose alternative is this?', reviewing Alenius's book. It condemned Alenius for his denial of the class struggle and as a reformist right-wing social democrat, petty bourgeois sympathiser with NATO, who resented SKP's participation in the international Communist movement, which he claimed harmed the progress of socialism in Finland, and who wanted to bring the SKP under his control. Alenius's book was another of the 'attempts to fob off the Finnish working class with the theories of pseudo-socialism and unceremoniously interfere with the activity of the Finnish Communist Party'. Tass distributed the article to all the Finnish press. *Kansan Uutiset* published in full this attack on the Chairman of one of the bodies responsible for its publication – but entirely without editorial comment! It was left to Alenius to defend himself. This emphasised the weakness of the position of Alenius and the SKDL socialists. The political organisation through which they could present their views was dominated by a party which, while in its majority wishing to maintain co-operation with them, had little inclination to defend their good faith, particularly when attacks came from the Soviet Union.

Alenius and his supporters detected in the unsigned *Novoe Vremya* article the accusations and tone of the SKP 'minority'. In mid-May he replied with a statement distributed to all the papers which had received the Tass report and gave several interviews in which he calmly and rationally tried to answer the charges against him. For Alenius the seriousness of the matter lay not so much in the accusations, many of which seemed absurd to him, but in the lack of good faith and mutual respect for different opinions which they displayed. How could the SKP expect to win the co-operation and trust of forces outside the SKDL and draw them into it, if it made such ludicrous charges as that he was an enemy of the Soviet Union? As Alenius pointed out, he would hardly have been a member of SKDL for nearly thirty years, through a time when it had been and continued to be dominated by the SKP, if he had not felt sympathy and understanding for the Soviet Union. In Alenius's view the matter was so serious that they might even have to consider the formation of a new socialist party 'if the pressure of minority Communists against those who are not members of the Communist Party becomes really too great'.

The affair emphasised the weight of the 'minority' not only in its own circles but also in its influence on the 'majority', who were concerned to prevent the final split of SKP. After many letters to *Kansan Uutiset* from local organisations 'showing their trust and confidence in comrade Alenius', an editorial statement was finally published claiming that there was no need for editorial comment on the attack on Alenius as he had been quite capable of defending himself in his reply which they had already published. But this was merely a tactical step to prevent the deepening of the split in the party by a public statement of sympathy for Alenius, in opposition to the 'minority'. The real views of the 'majority' were suggested rather by the pointedly warm welcome which Alenius received at this time from the majority of the Seventeenth SKP Congress when he presented greetings from the SKDL to them.[40]

On the eve of the Seventeenth Congress in 1975, the party published three of Saarinen's party reports of September 1974 to February 1975 in order to explain the division within the party to the bewildered 40 per cent of members who had joined since the split began. He freely narrated the history of the struggle for hegemony within the party. The decisions of the Extraordinary Congress had still not been carried out on the abolition of parallel organisations. The division in the party had become so rigid that votes even in the Politbureau were always cast the same way and there was no way for the party to make its decisions effective. Of course a complete split could be a solution but no one was prepared for that. For Saarinen 'peaceful coexistence' had acquired a new dimension. The situation on the eve of the Seventeenth Congress was worse than ever. The 'minority' paper *Tiedonantaja*, 'the most important parallel organ', was still being published. It had acquired a substantial readership and tried to make people believe that the leadership of the SKP was revisionist. 'Are these people mentally sick when they claim some people in the party are hostile to the Soviet Union?' Saarinen asked. The split, he admitted, had reached the point where it affected not only the party but also the SKDL and other organisations in which Communists were involved, to such an extent that the 'majority' and 'minority' were opposing each other in the trade unions and even as members of the SKDL faction in Parliament. The personal hostility and spitefulness between the leaders could be felt particularly at the very highest level in discussions of the Politbureau.

The differences could be alleviated by discussion, Saarinen felt, and were not ideologically irreconcilable, as Oivo Lehto a 'minority' member of the Politbureau considered. The 'minority', he continued, found it difficult to adjust itself to the new post-1966 situation when the party had acquired some responsibility in government and had had to consider its attitude towards the practical policies supported by its coalition partners. Wages policy had been a critical issue and had split the SKDL faction in Parliament. The 'minority', Saarinen complained, still looked at such measures in a purely oppositionist spirit. It was stupid not to take part in the discussion on wage levels. The Communists had already done this in the Pekkala government of 1946–8.

The division within the party, however, did not appear to affect its attraction for new members, although it remains open to question which party they thought they were joining. Since the Sixteenth Congress in 1972, 11,000 new members had joined to make a total of 42,000, and the average age was now much younger. But this figure of Saarinen's appears to show that in the same period some 17,000 members had left or died, as the total membership of the party fell between 1972 and 1975 from 48,000 to 42,000. In the trade unions, membership had rapidly increased since the mid-1960s and with the reconciliation in 1969 between the Communist dominated trade union organisation, SAK, and the social democrat SAJ, the influence of the SKP had become greater than at any time since the banning of the Communist trade unions in 1930.[41]

The Seventeenth Congress produced a resolution 'On the principles for strengthening party unity', but the two wings of the party remained estranged. In November 1975, after severe pressure by Kekkonen on the parties to form an 'emergency' left-centre coalition to combat unemployment, the SKDL and

SKP again agreed to participate in the Miettunen government, but only for a limited period. Saarinen and Alenius refused to take posts. Aitio, for the 'majority' of the SKP, took the Ministry of Labour and Kivistö for the socialists became deputy Minister of Education. The 'minority' no longer took part. The vote on the decision to participate showed the lines of division between the 'majority' and 'minority': 16 against 4 in the SKDL Executive Committee; 23 to 10 in the parliamentary group and 20 to 14 in the SKP Central Committee, even though the Seventeenth Congress had decided recently that such decisions must be made unanimously.

The Cabinet stumbled on for ten months trying to maintain its party basis. Agreement was reached on a price freeze and a 3.5 per cent wage increase in January 1976, but the SKP resisted the proposal of the other parties for a 2 per cent increase in turnover tax to pay for expenditure to relieve unemployment. Saarinen found himself under pressure from Sinisalo and unable to compromise. This created a government crisis in May. Miettunen presented the resignation of his Cabinet, but Kekkonen refused to accept it and gave the SKDL members a special dispensation to remain in the government while voting against the 'majority' policy. This breaking of the 'rules of the game' was not at all satisfactory to the SDP, and when a new crisis occurred in September over measures to encourage employment, the Miettunen government was reorganised without either the SDP or SKDL members. This minority government relied on the centre and right for its support and showed the dangers if the SKP by their abstention made a left-centre coalition impossible. Therefore in May 1977 when the SDP seemed prepared to enter the Cabinet again, the SKP and SKDL accepted posts in a five-party Cabinet in order to prevent the continuation of the co-operation of the right and centre. This was in spite of the fact that the period out of office had improved relations between the two wings of the SKP and that SDP Chairman Sorsa insisted that the Communists must accept the 'rules of the game', the unanimity of decision-making in the Cabinet. The SKDL/SKP took three posts: K. Kivistö, deputy Minister of Education for the SKDL socialists with A. A. Aalto, Secretary-General of the party (Labour) and V. Saarto (Transport) for the SKP 'majority'. Once again the 13-strong 'minority' in the SKDL parliamentary group opposed participation.[42]

In these conditions the SKP met for its sixtieth anniversary Eighteenth Congress, 1–3 June 1978. There was a certain impatience evident in Saarinen's criticisms of the 'minority' at the congress. In his view the differences could be settled with a little goodwill. The 'minority' were not opposed in principle to participation in government nor to co-operation with the left and centre. As for the policies of the government, the 'majority' were not satisfied with them either, but they depended on the relative weight of the elements in the government. The only alternative was to stay out, but the party would have to accept the consequences of that.

Care was taken to ensure that the congress did not intensify the division within the party and so no public votes were taken on the critical issues. The political document presented to the congress expressed both 'minority' and 'majority' views as alternatives. On the question of participation in government there was a full session which revealed that 9 out of 17 area organisations with 278 delegates against 215 approved the Central Committee's majority decision to participate in the government, which had strengthened the co-operation of the democratic forces. The strength of the 'minority' was not insignificant. It had since 1975 gained control of two more area organisations and those which it controlled were mainly in the industrial areas of the south, where the SKDL vote had increased in the general election of 1975.[43] According to Sinisalo, these areas included nearly half of all the party's 48,000 members.

Although Sinisalo and the 'minority' did not make it a matter of principle, they clearly do not believe that the conditions exist at present for the SKP to participate in government. The programme is not sufficiently directed against the monopolies. Sinisalo thinks there are more benefits to be obtained from staying in opposition.

> If the party does not take into consideration the alternative of staying in opposition, it is not only a prisoner of the government but it will also cause unforeseen harm to the future development of the party. From experience we also know that to be in opposition does not mean the same as to be outside politics.[44]

For the Communist Party reforms should take a secondary place to the development of the revolutionary movement. In Sinisalo's view, Sorsa's insistence on the SKDL keeping to the 'rules of the game', according to which Cabinet decisions had to be unanimous, was an infringement of the independence of the party and contradicted its general line.[45]

Agreement could not be reached either on the anniversary history of sixty years of the Finnish Communist Party written by two members of the 'minority'. But in order to avoid an open vote at the congress, the matter was referred to the new Central Committee for revision. The main criticisms of it were that it failed to mention the impact of the 'cult of personality' on the party in exile in the Soviet Union in the 1930s; that it presented too negative a view of the party's experience in government since 1966 and failed to mention the changes in the party programme in 1969, including the emphasis on the peaceful means to socialism in Finnish conditions.[46]

The matter of the division within the party again occupied Saarinen and Sinisalo at the congress. Repeating much of what he had said at the Seventeenth Congress, Saarinen gave a frank appraisal of his view of the division:

> The kind of division into two based on a quota is probably quite a unique phenomenon in the Communist movement and in party life in general. It is a question of a co-operative organisation within which two fairly independent factions fight for support inside and outside the party.

This situation had been fully demonstrated only a few days before the congress by the abstention of the 13 'minority' members of Parliament in a vote of confidence on the government.[47] Nothing had happened to give him cause to rethink his view on the split, Saarinen reported. But he did extend his analysis of its causes:

> The question of the government is not the basic cause, the causes are much deeper, they are social, in the different social positions of Communists, in different personal experience, in differences of education and consciousness, in feelings, personal expectations and strivings and in the past of our party, in its eventful history. The brains of the past generations

are pressing on the brains of the living, as Marx said in his time.

The actions of the 'minority' aggravated the division and they often behaved 'to put it mildly, irresponsibly', threatening to split the party in order to have their way. The continued existence of *Tiedonantaja* was 'a very sore point' with Saarinen. Its publication was against all the party rules and his efforts to find a way out, such as to make it the paper of the united Central Committee, had been rejected by Sinisalo.

The atmosphere of the party had been severely soured by the dispute: 'quarrelling has taken up the energy of the party leadership so completely, that there has not been enough energy for conciliation.' The party must come together on the basis of the correct Marxist-Leninist views, but 'here is the core of the problem: which are the right Marxist-Leninist views and above all, what are the right adaptations in Finland of those views?' The problem could not be solved by repetition of revolutionary terminology but only by a serious analysis. Why was it that the two Finnish working-class parties' share of the national vote had not increased significantly for seventy years, even though the working class was the majority of the population?[48] There must be something wrong with the parties and in particular with their mutual relations. Rejecting the relevance of recent French experience, Saarinen called for bold and unprejudiced actions to bring the Communists together with the social democrats on the basis of a common programme of aims to be put before the electorate, and to which the trade union movement also could give its support.[49]

Saarinen, however, denied that this amounted to a new brand of Communism. It was natural, he thought, for there to be similarities in the roads to socialism of the West European powers, as they had much in common. But he no more than Sinisalo sympathised with the emergence of a separate 'Eurocommunism', denying the value of other countries' experiences. It should be possible for there to be a full and frank discussion between all Communist parties, which should not be reduced to an uncomradely polemic, and which should of course not be distinguished by hostility towards the Soviet Union.[50]

Since the 1978 congress Saarinen's hopes for the co-operation of the left have been dashed by the Social Democrats' rejection of a common programme of action. Sorsa feared the differences of ideology would bring conflicts on long-term aims, but he valued the experience of co-operation in the government with SKP: 'Let us continue therefore our co-operation along the road we have found best in practice – and is it not in this way, in the length of our practical experience and its success that we are unique in the world?'

There were, however, in August 1978 signs of a revival of discussions within the SKDL on 'models of socialism'. Ilkka-Christian Björklund, one of the SKDL socialist members of Parliament and a critic of Soviet-style socialism, called for an open discussion with the Communists. His views were published in *Kansan Uutiset*. Saarinen expressed readiness to enter the debate but has little prospect of taking his whole party with him. Björklund was heavily attacked in *Tiedonantaja* as an opponent of socialism as a result of his comments on the question of 'human rights' in the Soviet Union. At a meeting of the SKDL board, Alenius defended Björklund and tried to establish a sound basis for the discussion. He emphasised strongly that it should be understood from the start that if such a discussion involved critical evaluations of already established socialist societies, this should not be considered as being hostile to the very principles on which those societies sought to base themselves. Such criticism, Alenius claimed, had nothing to do with the campaign against the Soviet Union by the bourgeois press, which itself had no sympathy for any kind of socialism.[51] It is evident that there is a continuing lack of trust between the SKDL socialists and the SKP 'minority'.

The party approached the general election campaign of March 1979 as divided as in 1975 on the issue of the policy to be pursued if it participated in government and on the shape of its ultimate socialist aim. This probably in part accounts for the results of the election for the Communist Party. It was a general setback for the left and for the coalition of parties in the government. Ignoring warnings from the Soviet press about the impact on Soviet-Finnish relations, the electorate gave the conservative Kokoomus 12 new seats and a total of 47, leaving the non-socialists with a majority in Parliament of 113 to the socialists' 87. The representation of the SKDL was reduced by 5 seats to 35, their lowest since the Second World War. Their share of the vote fell from 18.9 per cent in 1975 to 17.9 per cent, and the votes cast for them from 519,483 to 517,308, although the total votes cast in the election altogether increased by 140,000 to 2.88 million. The balance of seats for the different elements comprising the SKDL as a result of the election stood at 18 'majority' Communists, 11 'minority' and 6 SKDL socialists. The latter increased their share of SKDL representation from 4 to 6 seats. The Communist Party 'minority', however, lost 1 seat and the 'majority' lost 4. But this was a result of the manner in which the electoral system works rather than of any swing of votes against the 'majority'. Actually, 'minority' candidates received only 143,000 votes, a drop of 11,000 compared with 1975, while the 'majority' and the SKDL socialists received 374,000 votes, 10,000 more than in 1975. The 'minority' candidates only secured a majority of the votes cast for SKDL in one electoral district (north Karelia), compared with 3 in 1975, and they suffered a setback as two of their leaders, Sinisalo and Kainulainen, lost their seats to 'majority' candidates. In fact the election seems to have intensified still further the division within the Communist Party, Saarinen himself attributing the loss of seats by the SKDL overall to the votes lost by the candidates of the 'minority' of the party.[52]

There is no doubt that the SKP/SKDL has become more integrated into the Finnish political system since 1966. Of the four major parties in the period 1966–79 it tended to be the conservatives (Kokoomus) who were left out of government. There may now be a trend to the right after the election of March 1979, but the SDP leadership regards its experience of co-operation with the SKP 'majority' since 1966 as valuable and worth continuing.

The SKP/SKDL achieved their aim of breaking the monopoly of the centre and right, which resulted from the division of the left. For the 'majority', willingness to participate in government continues to be necessary for this reason. But also, although the distinctively Communist achievements of their representatives in government have been limited, the SKP/SKDL have been able to use their participation to secure a larger share of political appointments. This reflects also the changes in the composition of the party and the influx of more members of the intelligentsia.

The internal life of the party has clearly become more open. Readiness to discuss, to co-operate, to ask embarrassing questions of the party and to accept inconvenient facts have been keynotes of Saarinen's period of leadership. This has been part of his strategy to make the party more acceptable, and so to acquire influence and support to bring about more radical changes. The completion of this transformation of the party is considerably inhibited by the existence of the 'minority'. But the organisational principle of democratic centralism has not been rejected by the 'majority'. It is merely inconvenient to operate it at the present time. The 'minority' retains the hope that traditional tactics and views may come to dominate and be the basis for restored unity. The 'majority' cannot dispense with the 'minority' because this will deprive it of a substantial group of party activists and divide their electoral support. This in turn would give the party even less weight in a government coalition.

A break between 'majority' and 'minority' would also have implications for the party's relationship with the Soviet Union. Saarinen feels that it is important for the party to maintain fraternal relations with the Soviet Communist Party, while still emphasising the independence of his party. The maintenance of this link helps to moderate the attacks of the 'minority' on the leadership and therefore to hold the party together. But it raises queries amongst the party's allies and coalition partners over the nature of their eventual aims. As Saarinen commented at the Eighteenth Congress, looking back to the programme of 1969:

> Our party has always fought for freedoms of speech, press and meeting, for the right to strike and in general for the extension of democracy. This is certainly known but it is not believed that we would respect these freedoms and rights if we had a decisive position in the exercise of power. The problem is that we have not yet had an opportunity in practice to show that these kinds of suspicion are wrong. Mere declarations and assurances are not enough.[53]

Therefore in order to give more conviction to their own programme the party was vitally interested in the extension of democracy in the socialist countries, where Communist parties did have the opportunity to put their ideas into practice.

The old image of the SKP as unpatriotic is still retained by the Sinisalo 'minority' of the party. The road which the party is to take is by no means decisively chosen, but although the 'minority' is still a substantial factor, the election results of March 1979 suggest that its appeal is declining amongst Communist supporters. Nevertheless, when Saarinen retires in 1981, a leader will still be required with his gifts for holding together the irreconcilables.

Notes

1. *Suomen kommunistisen puolueen toiminnasta 17 ja 18 edustajakokouksen väliseldä* (Pori, 1978), pp. 32–3; *Helsingin Sanomat*, 28 May 1978.
2. For the history of the Communist Party of Finland to the mid-1960s see A.F. Upton in *The Communist Parties of Scandinavia and Finland* (London, 1973), pp. 205–352, Also J.H. Hodgson, *Communism in Finland: a History and an Interpretation* (Princeton, 1967); Ilkka Hakalehto, *Suomen kommunistinen puolue ja sen vaikutus poliittiseen ja ammatilliseen työväenliikkeeseen, 1918–28* (Helsinki, 1966).
3. Upton, *Communist Parties*, pp. 125–42.
4. Ibid., pp. 223–31.
5. Hertta Kuusinen, quoted in Upton, *Communist Parties*, p. 249.
6. On this episode see ibid., pp. 237–44.
7. On the impact of the Twentieth Congress on the Finnish party from the inside see A. Kovanen, *Kommunismin kriisi* (Helsinki, 1970), pp. 70–8. Also Upton, *Communist Parties*, pp. 331–6.
8. See *SKP: n asiakirjoja vuosilta 1944–8* (Helsinki, 1974), pp. 183–4.
9. R. Setälä, *Uusstalinistin uskontunnustus* (Helsinki, 1970), pp. 36–7; Bengt Matti, 'Finland' in W.E. Griffith (ed.), *Communism in Europe* (London, 1967), vol. 2, pp. 390–2; K. Haikara, *Isänmaan vasenlaita* (Helsinki, 1975), p. 167.
10. Kovanen, *Kommunismin kriisi*, pp. 75–6.
11. Upton, *Communist Parties*, pp. 349–50.
12. *SKP 13. Edustajakokous* (Helsinki, 1963), pp. 71–2, 86–9.
13. Ibid., pp. 57–8, 66, 107–8.
14. Kovanen, *Kommunismin kriisi*, pp. 80–9; Matti, 'Finland', p. 394.
15. K. Immonen (ed.), *Puolueiden puheenvuoro* (Helsinki, 1965), pp. 11–16.
16. Matti, 'Finland', p. 399; Kovanen, *Kommunismin kriisi*, pp. 80–9.
17. E. Rautee, *Puheenvuoroja marxilaisuudesta* (Helsinki, 1966), p. 141. Rautee is chief theoretician of the party.
18. SKP, keskuskomitea, *Marxilaisesta valtioteoriasta ja Suomen tiestä sosialismin* (Kuopio, 1965), particularly pp. 15–16; Kovanen, *Kommunismin kriisi*, pp. 89–90.
19. Ibid., pp. 90–1.
20. P. Pesonen (ed.), *Protestivaalit nuorisovaalit* (Helsinki, 1972), p. 250.
21. Setälä, *Uusstalinistin uskontunnustus*, p. 65.
22. On the motivations for the Communist vote in Finland see J. Nousiainen, *Kommunismi Kuopion läänissä* (Joensuu, 1956); E. Allardt, 'Social Sources of Finnish Communism', *International Journal of Comparative Sociology*, vol. 5, no. 1 (1964); P. Pesonen, *An Election in Finland* (Yale University Press, 1968).
23. Pesonen, *Election in Finland*, pp. 396–405; E. Alenius, *Suomalainen ratkaisu* (Helsinki, 1974), pp. 41–5. See also *Helsingin Sanomat*, 19 May 1978 for a report on the views of Finnish sociologists and political scientists on the origins of Communist participation in government.

24. Kovanen, *Kommunismin kriisi*, pp. 94–8; *SKP 16. Edustajakokous* (Kuopio, 1972), pp. 52–3 for Saarinen's account of the origins and development of the conflict in the party.

25. Kovanen, *Kommunismin kriisi*, pp. 100–1; *Kansan Uutiset*, 22 August 1968.

26. A. Saarinen, *Puolue-yhtenäisyyttä rakentamaan* (SKP Helsinki branch) (Pori, 1975), p. 10; Kovanen, *Kommunismin kriisi*, p. 102.

27. *SKP 15. Edustajakokous* (Kuopio, 1969), p. 75.

28. Ibid., pp. 77–8, 80.

29. Ibid., pp. 22, 55, 64.

30. Ibid., pp. 52–66; *SKP 15. Edustajakokous Päätös ja julkilausumat* (Helsinki, 1969), p. 2.

31. Ibid., p. 3.

32. Kovanen, *Kommunismin kriisi*, pp. 102–3. Also for Saarinen and Sinisalo's views in 1970 see their contributions to K. Savolainen (ed.), *Vasemmiston tunnonvaivat* (Tampere, 1970), pp. 45–75.

33. On this point see Saarinen's statement in *Helsingin Sanomat*, 28 May 1978.

34. *SKP 16. Edustajakokous* (Kuopio, 1972), pp. 137–58 for the decisions of the Extraordinary Congress. Also Kovanen, *Kommunismin kriisi*, pp. 103–8.

35. Ibid., p. 111; Pesonen, *Election in Finland*, pp. 16, 412–15.

36. *SKP 16. Edustajakokous*, pp. 52–72.

37. Alenius, *Suomalainen ratkaisu*, pp. 80–90, 99–108, 120–3, 192.

38. *SKP 16. Edustajakokous*, Appendix II, pp. 155–8.

39. Haikara, *Isänmaan vasenlaita*, p. 448.

40. Ibid., pp. 445–62.

41. Saarinen, *Puolue-yhtenäsyyttä rakentamaan, passim*; *SKP: n puolueen toiminnasta 17 ja 18 edustajakokoukseen väliseltä* (Pori, 1978), pp. 32–3.

42. *Kommunisti*, no. 6 (1978), pp. 456–8. These same Ministers continued in the reorganised Cabinet of Sorsa in March 1978.

43. *Scandinavian Political Studies*, no. 11 (1976), p. 186. The branches in minority control are Tampere, Lahti, Turku, Uusimaa, Kuopio, Joensuu, S. Karelia and Kymenlaakso (*Demari. Suomen Sosialidemokraatti*, 3 June 1978, p. 6).

44. *Kommunisti*, no. 6 (1978), pp. 472–3; *Kansan Uutiset*, 2 June 1978; *Tiedonantaja*, 2 June 1978.

45. For various sections of Sinisalo's speech see *Kansan Uutiset*, 2 June 1978 and *Tiedonantaja*, 2 June 1978 and for a shortened version, *Kommunisti*, no. 6 (1978), pp. 469–77.

46. *Helsingin Sanomat*, 4 June 1978, p. 7.

47. *Kommunisti*, no. 6 (1978), p. 461; *Helsingin Sanomat*, 27 May 1978.

48. The united Social Democratic Party received 37 per cent of the vote in 1906; in 1975 the two working-class parties took 43.8 per cent of the vote. The maximum of 103 members of Parliament from these parties achieved in 1966 had also been held by the undivided social democrats in 1916.

49. *Kansan Uutiset*, 2 June 1978, p. 14; 4 August 1978, p. 8.

50. Ibid. For the more fearful expressions of the 'minority' on Eurocommunism, see *Tiedonantaja*, 9 May 1978, p. 10 and 16 May 1978, p. 10.

51. Ibid., 22 August 1978; *Kansan Uutiset*, 20 August 1978; *Demari*, 9 June 1978, p. 13; 13 June 1978, p. 19.

52. Saarinen and Alenius in *Kansan Uutiset*, 21 March 1979, pp. 1–2. The figures for 'minority' and 'majority' support in each electoral district were fully reported in *Kansan Uutiset*, 22 March 1979, p. 6.

53. *Kansan Uutiset*, 2 June 1978, p. 13.

7

COMMUNISM IN THE NORDIC COUNTRIES:
DENMARK, NORWAY, SWEDEN AND ICELAND

Trond Gilberg

1 Russian Bolshevism and Scandinavian Individualism: the Cultural Context of the Nordic Countries on the Eve of the Russian Revolution.

When the Russian Revolution took place in the autumn of 1917, it produced great enthusiasm in the political left of Scandinavia. Even the classical social democrats of the Danish, Norwegian and Swedish labour movements hailed November as a momentous political event which would set history in motion towards universal peace, greater social justice and a better society for all in the years to come. In many of the youth organisations, as well as in some trade unions, and, above all, in the left wing of the three social democratic parties, there was outright jubilation. The revolt in Petrograd had finally ushered in an era in which the programme of Karl Marx would be realised in the political, socio-economic and cultural spheres. Finally, social justice would be done. Finally, the 'nouveaux riches' of shipowners and speculators who had profited enormously from Scandinavian neutrality during the war would be expropriated. But above all, the Russian Revolution was seen as the dawning of a new era in which the individual would be free – free of the social bondage of old and outmoded class systems; free of economic dependence and poverty; and, finally, free to relate to authority and power in terms of co-operation rather than subjugation.[1]

The emphasis on Marxist humanism was an important element in the Scandinavian endorsement of the Russian Revolution, and it exhibited a fundamental misunderstanding (or disregard) of the nature of Bolshevism and the main elements of the 'later', as opposed to the 'earlier', Marx. In a nutshell, the Scandinavian labour movement envisioned the practice of Marxism as a policy of Western humanism, where the emphasis would be on the individual, whereas the Bolsheviks, led by Lenin, emphasised the collectivism of the Eastern tradition. Furthermore, Lenin's authoritarian attitudes on matters such as party organisation, bureaucracy and coercion harked back to the experience of the Russian underground in its struggle with Tsarist autocracy. Thus the Bolsheviks represented basic traditions of the Eastern, orthodox, and partly Byzantine heritage, while the Scandinavian political cultures were formed by the experiences and influences of the Western, Judeo-Christian tradition and the momentous events of the Reformation and the Enlightenment. It may be argued that the entire history of Scandinavian Communism revolves around this dichotomy of attempted 'cultural transfer' from the Bolshevik, Eastern tradition to the Western, social democratic traditions of Scandinavia.[2]

Other, more specific, discrepancies existed between the Soviet system as it evolved, and Scandinavian political reality in the post-revolutionary era. Russian history is essentially a history of despotism, where political leaders tended to rule in supreme disregard of the individual, or even of the collectivity of the people, the *narod*, the masses. Despite occasional experiments with local government and limited participation therein (the *zemstvo* system), and then, at the central level, the ill-fated attempts to establish a Duma as the Russian version of Parliament, there essentially was no tradition in the Russian lands of political participation by the masses. And through the system of the peasant commune, the *mir*, the individual was raised and steeped in the spirit of collectivism. A highly centralised and rigid bureaucracy arrogated for itself the lion's share of decision-making and policy implementation. Local autonomy was more a result of lacking ability to enforce centralised rule than a conscious government policy.[3]

The Scandinavian political tradition was vastly different. The kingdoms of Denmark, Norway and Sweden had been grudgingly united around the year 1000, but local autonomy had been maintained, for many as a necessary guarantee against despotism. Geographical conditions, especially in Norway, helped maintain regional differences and the tradition of local autonomy. At the same time, the Scandinavian countries were among the very first in medieval Europe to establish unified systems of law, in which the rights of the individual and of specified economic strata were carefully laid down. The Scandinavians also resurrected the principles of representative assemblies of freeholders at a very early stage, and the principles of executive responsibility and representative supervision were established early and assiduously honoured throughout generations, until autocracy temporarily (but only temporarily and in limited degree) superseded this practice. The Scandinavians were free farmers and thought of themselves as such, whereas the Russians were peasants in the Eastern tradition and, for long centuries, actually serfs. From such fundamental differences arose quite different outlooks towards authority and political power.[4]

The introduction of Christianity to the pagan populations of Russia and Scandinavia also had quite different results. In the Russian lands, the Orthodox Church became an instrument of *secular* authority as well, and the very heart of Orthodoxy is collectivism, not individualism. In Scandinavia, the introduction of Catholicism in the eleventh century first established the principle of spiritual power as separate from the secular realm (although Christianity in Scandinavia was introduced by means of the sword of converted kings); after the introduction of Protestantism, the unification of Church and state in the form of Lutheran state churches did not fundamentally alter the fact that Martin Luther had also emphasised the right of individuals to converse *directly* with the highest authority, God, without the need for human intermediaries. This emphasis on individual worship helped maintain the spirit of individualism even during the centuries of Nordic Lutheranism.[5]

Several other factors also helped differentiate the Scandinavian political cultures from the traditions of Russian Bolshevism. The idea of representative oversight over executive authority was embodied in the principle of the Ombudsman – an office specifically designed to help the individual and protect him from excesses of the bureaucratic and executive powers. Sweden instituted such an office as early as 1809; in the other Scandinavian countries, the principle was upheld primarily through the court system and the tradition of executive restraint. Furthermore, the Swedish nobles repeatedly toppled kings and rearranged their authority systems, and even the Danes (and the Norwegians, for four hundred years under Danish rule) modified the principle of absolutism in such a way that the Nordic variant thereof differed drastically from the Eastern interpretation and Eastern practice. The Russian tradition in this area is certainly well known, and in most respects, differs fundamentally from the Nordic experience.[6]

One final difference should be noted. The Scandinavian countries were among the first in Europe to establish a national school system, thus providing universal elementary education for their populations. This goal was achieved during the nineteenth century, to a considerable extent even before 1850. Such an impressive achievement acted as a major catalyst for organisational activity in Denmark, Norway and Sweden. Even long before the introduction of universal suffrage, therefore, the Scandinavians had generations-long experiences with political participation and political competition. Against this background, the Russia of 1917, with its illiterate peasantry and virtually non-existent political participation, looms as a system fundamentally different in its major manifestations.[7]

The main political and social traditions which characterised the three Scandinavian countries basically held for Iceland as well. Iceland was settled by rebellious Norwegians who refused to pay taxes to the chieftains whose goal it was to unify the many local authorities of the country. Small wonder, then, that the Icelanders jealously guarded against despotism and held high the banner of representation and legislative oversight as well as the principle that the law stood above *any* authority, including that of the King. At the same time, the occupational structure of Iceland, emphasising fishing as the primary means of living, helped foster a tradition of individualism and a sense of 'man against nature' – an outlook which ensures collectivism in the form of co-operation *among* individuals rather than collectivism perpetrated *upon* individuals. Even Danish attempts to enforce the principles of absolutism on the Icelanders foundered on the fact that the island possession was far away, and the means of Copenhagen were severely restricted and constrained, since the Danes also had to rule Norway and periodically engage in war against the Swedes. Thus, foreign nominal rule did not succeed in stamping out the specific elements of the *Icelandic* tradition. The Icelanders and the Norwegians, both victims of foreign rule, became intensely nationalistic and thus resistant to change imposed from the outside. This was to have important repercussions for the implementation of *universalist* revolutionary principles in the Comintern and subsequently.[8]

2 **The Bolshevisation of International Communism and Nordic Developments**

The cultural and historical differences between the Nordic countries on the one hand, and Russia on the other, had profound implications for the development of Communism in Denmark, Norway, Sweden and Iceland. These differences, which were certainly perceived by left-wing leaders and intellectuals in the Nordic countries prior to 1917, were nevertheless minimised in their minds, and the internationalist ethos of Marxism helped foster the belief that national and cultural differences would be swept aside in the great rush towards the fulfilment of historical necessity under the auspices of proletarian solidarity. This vision was further enhanced by the unmistakable fact that Lenin, Trotsky, Bukharin, Zinoviev, Kamenev, Radek and many others among the Bolsheviks were emphatic 'Westernisers' who vehemently opposed the Slavophiles' and Pan-Slavs' emphasis on a specific *Russian* and agrarian road to the hallowed epoch of human fulfilment. Thus, internationalist optimism and a false emphasis on the 'Western' aspects of Bolshevism, Lenin-style, helped pave the way for the Nordic endorsement of the 'Great November'. The problems of actually relating *policies* to this confident image of Eastern and Western convergence under the banner of Karl Marx developed only after the successful seizure of power in November 1917. Now, the question before the European left was not revolutionary rhetoric, but rather practical policies of fundamental impact for all leftist movements and parties. Lenin's famous statement, 'We shall now proceed to construct the socialist order' in Russia was matched by the intentions of the rulers in Petrograd and Moscow to further revolution abroad – it was *world revolution* that now was on the agenda, in the Nordic countries as well as elsewhere.

Within a year of the Revolution, Nordic leftists were introduced to the fundamental problems of relating to the new rulers in the Kremlin. The centralist and collectivist elements of Russian Marxism had been visible during the early stages of internal development in the post-revolutionary period, and during 1919 and 1920 they became the main elements in the drive to establish the Communist International and furnish the new international organisation with its basic operating principles. The celebrated 'twenty-one points' concerning the rules of membership and the fundamental duties of the revolutionary vanguard clashed with tradition and practice in the Nordic countries on many points, chief of which were the following.

(1) Organisationally, the 'twenty-one points' posited a strictly centralised structure, in which the principles of 'democratic centralism' ruled supreme. Furthermore, membership affiliation was to be exclusively individual, and members must agree to subordinate themselves to strict party discipline *à la* the principles which had been laid down for the Russian social democrats in 1903. International Communism was to be subjected to similar centralising principles, whereby the word of the 'general staff of the revolution', the Executive Committee of the Comintern, was to determine the behaviour of *all* Communist parties, both in terms of domestic policies and in relations with other fraternal organisations.[9]

The Scandinavian parties found these organisational principles exceedingly hard to accept. In all three countries, the existing social democratic parties functioned by means of a mixture of collective affiliation through trade unions and individual membership. There was a great deal of autonomy for local organisations within each party, and 'centralism' had long been abhorred by many regional and local leaders as well as the rank and file. Internationally, the Scandinavians had been used to the relatively free exchange of ideas in the Second International and other forums of the pre-war era, and the concept of a revolutionary centre which could in fact dictate behaviour to the local affiliates was rejected (or at least mistrusted) by many.[10]

In Iceland, there was no real left-wing party at this early stage. Left-wing elements existed in several organisations, but their ties were rather loose, and the principles of tactical and strategic manoeuvrability and flexible organisational forms were even more important on the island. For the Icelandic left, therefore, the 'twenty-one points' represented a fundamental break with existing practice.[11]

(2) The 'twenty-one points' also posited the principle of clandestine organisations, which could at any time move between legality and illegality. Such organisations must of necessity operate on the basis of strict discipline and organisational hierarchy.[12]

Once again, this major principle of the Comintern clashed fundamentally with existing practices in the Nordic countries. In all of these states, the principles of political pluralism had been established early, and had become major operational principles by the First World War. To demand underground organisations in such a political setting seemed completely alien, and the idea of 'iron' discipline akin to military organisations also had a strange ring in societies in which individualism and anti-militarism were potent political facts. Many of the leaders of the Scandinavian left rejected the idea of clandestine political organisations both for ideological reasons and also as politically dangerous; it was felt that public opinion, attuned to genuine political competition, would look askance at such behaviour, and would turn against the labour movement in a decisive manner.[13]

(3) The operational principles of the Comintern demanded a resolute struggle against religion, in line with the Marxist view that 'religion is the opium of the masses,' and consequently a major weapon in the class domination of the bourgeoisie. Atheism was forcefully supported by Lenin and the Bolsheviks as a necessary vehicle for capturing power in a society where the very leadership of the *secular* realm in fact claimed *divine* guidance and protection.[14]

For the Nordic peoples, anti-religious propaganda seemed yet another alien manifestation, which could only have negative consequences in the competition for power. Furthermore, Lutheranism as a cultural phenomenon had permeated large strata of the industrial working class, and religious feelings were important among the freeholders, smallholders and fishermen, from whom the new urban proletariat was recruited. To endorse and implement atheism and anti-religious campaigns therefore became both politically inexpedient and morally wrong, and the Nordic left once again found itself in opposition to the Comintern leadership in the Executive Committee (ECCI).

(4) Finally, the Bolsheviks in the ECCI, supported by important elements in other parties (notably the German Communists) insisted on a revolutionary path to power that would be feasible only through violence. This attitude once again clashed with existing outlooks among the Nordic left; for many, revolutionary armed struggle, perhaps even civil war, seemed to be very painful alternatives which might be appropriate in less 'civilised' systems, but certainly inappropriate in cultures where the basic decency of many in the ruling classes had to be acknowledged. Even the most activist of the Nordic

left tended to deal with this problem by insisting that violence in the transition to socialism would be perpetrated by the *bourgeoisie*, and that the proletariat therefore would be forced to *defend* itself. This notion was of course quite different from Lenin's insistence on *offensive* violence.[15]

The doctrinal differences between the Russian-dominated leadership of the Comintern on the one hand, and many within the Nordic left on the other, were fundamental. They represented, in fact, a basic dichotomy between Eastern, or Russian, Communism, and the Western, European variant. As such, this set of differences produced the first clash between 'Eurocommunism' and ruling Communism, and the ideological struggles of the early 1920s strongly resemble the current debate between the French, Italian and Spanish parties (together with assorted allies throughout Western and Northern Europe) on the one hand and Soviet leaders, together with their trusted allies in the Communist-ruled states of Eastern Europe, on the other hand. Then, as now, the issues are, essentially, the question of whose 'model' is to be followed, and whether or not there is an international centre of Communism. Then, as now, the debate flares up over the question of relations between Communists and the rest of society in each country. Then, as now, the path to socialism and Communism is debated: is it to be peaceful and evolutionary, or violent and revolutionary? How, in essence does a party ideologically dedicated to the establishment of a *new* political order act in the *existing* system, which in Western Europe is genuine political pluralism? Then, as now, Communists debate the relationship between the secular and spiritual realm, at a time of grave moral and religious crisis. The student of European Communism in the 1970s gets a distinctive feeling of *déjà vu* when comparing the present epoch and the current debate with the great clashes in the Comintern prior to the successful 'Bolshevisation' of that organization in 1923/4. The Nordic countries fit this pattern as well as any in non-Communist Europe.

3 Sectarian Communism, Nordic Style: a Chronology

Given the fundamental differences between basic attitudes and behaviour patterns in the Nordic left and the operational practices of the Russian-led Comintern, developments in left-wing politics in Denmark, Norway and Sweden took predictable turns during the decades after the establishment of the Third International. In Denmark and Sweden, a small group on the left of the Social Democratic Party split off and became the local Communist party, which in turn became a pliant tool for the ECCI, both in terms of policy and doctrine.[16] In Norway, on the other hand, the left captured the machinery of the mother party and enrolled the Norwegian Labour Party (DNA) in the Comintern.[17] This apparent deviation from the general Scandinavian (indeed Western European) pattern was based upon a misunderstanding of the true nature of the Comintern and the extent to which Lenin and his close associates would sacrifice political opportunities in the West for the sake of maintaining internal control over the Comintern. In the end, the Norwegian 'deviation' proved to be very temporary; in November 1923 the DNA was excluded from the international organisations for having violated a number of the 'twenty-one conditions' and also for recalcitrance (the ideological leader of the DNA, Martin Tranmael, and his associates had accused the Russians of right-wing deviationism when the Comintern switched to a policy of 'united fronts' and limited co-operation with 'bourgeois' parties in 1921).[18]

In Iceland, no Communist party as such existed until 1930, and the factional struggles, tactical policy changes and sterile ideological debates so familiar in Copenhagen, Oslo and Stockholm seldom disturbed the flexibility and manoeuvrability of the Icelandic left. In an international movement which was increasingly beset by ideological rigidity, this position of the Icelanders represented a major deviation, but the island was isolated, and little was known about it among the leaders of the 'general staff of world revolution in Hotel Lux and in the Kremlin. Thus the Icelandic deviation passed almost unnoticed.[19]

During the period 1923/4 to the Second World War, the policies of the Comintern underwent a series of drastic changes, all of which reflected both the changing political situation in the world (especially in Europe) and the fact that the international Communist movement increasingly became a mere instrument of Soviet foreign policy. Thus, in 1921, the ECCI decreed a switch from an offensive to a defensive revolutionary line, and this necessitated a major policy change of political relations with non-Communist parties and a temporary shelving of the visions of world revolution.[20] In 1927/8, on the other hand, the ECCI demanded a new offensive surge within the international movement; this policy was instituted to forestall a capitalist attack on the Soviet Union, now in the beginning throes of rapid and forced industrialisation and collectivisation of agriculture. Overnight, Western European Communist parties were asked to terminate their united fronts with non-Communists, and instead wage ruthless political war upon them.[21] A few years later, Stalin's fear of resurgent Germany and the general rise of Fascism in Europe forced yet another policy change in the international movement. At the seventh congress of the Comintern in 1935, the policy of 'popular fronts' of all anti-Fascist forces, regardless of policy programmes, demanded yet another *volte-face* of Western European Communists.[22] By the same token, the Hitler-Stalin pact of August 1939 forced abandonment of the anti-Fascist 'popular front' policy and put the Western European Communist parties in the untenable position of defending a political agreement which had caused consternation throughout the world. Indeed, the local Communists were forced to defend, or at least to redefine, Nazi aggression in Europe, thereby putting the blame for the outbreak of the war on France and Britain.[23] This policy change was of particular local importance in the Scandinavian countries, in so far as it forced the Danish, Norwegian and Swedish Communists to support the Soviet Union in its war with Finland, while the rest of public opinion and organised political life in the three countries strongly endorsed the Finnish struggle for survival.[24]

During these many abrupt changes of policy the Danish Communist Party (DKP), the Norwegian Communist Party (NKP) after November 1923, and the Swedish Communist Party (SKP) faithfully followed the lead from Moscow. To be sure, such extreme tactical flexibility could not be implemented without internal strife, and the history of Scandinavian Communism in the inter-war period is also a history of factional in-fighting and numerous purges of 'unreliable elements'. In some of these purges there is evidence of direct Comintern involvement.[25] But despite such problems, the three parties always followed the approved Comintern line after the internal dislocations had been overcome. Thus, the change to a more

offensive policy *vis-à-vis* 'bourgeois' society in 1927/8 saw the
DKP, NKP and SKP pull out of any joint ventures with the
local social democrats, and in the trade unions the Communist
attitude changed from co-operation of leftist forces against the
capitalist class enemy to civil war of the left in an attempt to
'unmask' the 'renegades' and 'social fascists'.[26] Those same
'social fascists', as well as the 'merciless exploiters of working
people', in 1928 became 'progressive forces in the struggle
against Fascism' in 1935.[27] And the following two quotes from
the NKP Central Committee's official commentary can well
illustrate the facility of accepting Moscow's line at the time of
the outbreak of the Second World War and the inception of the
Russo-Finnish Winter War, respectively:

> Finally the following facts shall be emphatically established:
> the war between England, France, Poland and Germany is an
> imperialistic war. In the reckoning between four capitalist
> powers the Soviet Union, like Norway, remains outside, and
> will remain there as long as it is not attacked. If it is attacked,
> it will answer each blow with two blows.[28]

> While Mannerheim Finland collapses the Norwegian people
> want to live in peace. Therefore they wish the government to
> maintain their neutrality in the war which English imperialism
> attempts, by all means, to expand. That means that the war
> activists [must] be stopped in their trafficking, which is
> treason to the people. It furthermore means that the foreign
> policy of our country must be made independent of Sweden.[29]

The policies of the Scandinavian Communists in the inter-war
period had entirely predictable results. Public support for *some
form* of left-wing policy, which had been considerable in Norway
and had had some impact in Denmark and Sweden towards the
end of the First World War, dwindled with each new tactical
move dictated in the Kremlin. By the late 1930s, the DKP,
NKP and SKP had become mere sects on the fringes of the
political scene in Scandinavia. Not even the Depression, which
caused great political and social dislocations in the three
countries, could revive the fortunes of the extreme left; instead,
it was the social democrats who capitalised on the need for
governmental intervention in the economy, so that in all three

countries these moderate leftists became the dominant political forces by the Second World War.[30]

While the domestic fortunes of Scandinavian Communism suffered repeated blows throughout the inter-war period, the international relations of the three parties remained firmly locked in total dependence on Moscow, and the three parties became typical *apparatchik* organisations whose leaders by and large adopted any directive from the East in an automatic manner. Those who had questions could always be purged for 'deviationism'. It seems clear that the Scandinavian Communists in fact redefined their *function* in a most fundamental way, so that the relevant constituency of the DKP, NKP and the SKP became the Kremlin and the ECCI, not the Danish, Norwegian or Swedish political systems. With such a redefinition of function came a re-evaluation of *achievements*: success was measured in terms of adherence to the policy line in Moscow, while electoral failures were downplayed. Thus the almost total lack of relevance for the three parties in their domestic environments could be tolerated.[31]

4 Reassessment of Policy: the War Years in Scandinavia

The Nazi invasion of the Soviet Union on 22 June 1941 became a major turning-point for the Scandinavian Communists (as well as for all Communists in Europe). The German attack on the socialist fatherland clearly established the need for local Communists parties to abandon their collaborationist stance *vis-à-vis* Germany and thus enter the broad anti-Nazi coalition of political forces which had sprung up with the occupation of Denmark and Norway. In neutral Sweden, a more cautious policy towards Berlin was easily understandable, but even here there was little doubt as to where public – and organized – opinion could be found.[32]

Into this broad national coalition, then, came the three Scandinavian Communist parties. Due to their experience in organisational rigidity and internal discipline the DKP and the NKP soon became major elements in the resistance; in fact, these two groups were among the foremost advocates of 'active' underground activities such as sabotage and liquidation of pro-Nazi elements in the local population. As a result of this kind of activity, the Danish and Norwegian parties gained considerably in public esteem, and the willingness of their cadres to work alongside other, national-minded individuals and groups created the impression that Communists were patriots and political activists with goals and dreams similar to those of the rest of the population. The war, therefore, became a great vehicle for *political legitimisation* of Danish and Norwegian Communism. And in Sweden, the strong support of the SKP for the maintenance of national defence and foreign policy neutrality coincided with the views of the popular majority, thus creating the image of a Communist party squarely in the mainstream of the 'national interest'.[33]

The startling reversal of political fortunes for the three Scandinavian Communist parties stood in direct relationship to the latters' position on internationalism and national needs. Since the DKP, NKP and SKP now took positions very similar to the rest of the political forces in their respective countries, their public image of 'foreign-ness' began to dissipate. At the same time, the heroic struggle of the Soviet Union against the Nazi juggernaut created a very favourable image for the Kremlin throughout the entire world. Even staunch conservatives realised that the survival of *their* civilisation was dependent upon the success of the Red Army in its life and death struggle against Nazism. Consequently, history had turned the Soviet Union into one of the chief protectors of Western civilisation rather than a mortal threat to it. This amazing *volte-face* of history also helped legitimise the followers of the Kremlin, the local Communists.[34]

Stalin, fully aware of these developments, and certainly worried about the consequences of 'national Communism' in Western Europe, nevertheless made the decision (probably inevitable under the circumstances) that the very survival of the Soviet Union hinged upon maximum support for his desperate war effort from *all* quarters, and he therefore accepted the national stance of Western European Communists and indeed made certain moves to encourage such developments, as exemplified by his dissolution of the Comintern in 1943.[35] This decision, which had little practical significance at the time, nevertheless helped to further alleviate the images of world revolution and centralised control over the international Communist movement.

The experience of Scandinavian Communists during the Second World War foreshadowed all of the major debates currently rocking international Communism. During the war, local Communist parties operated outside any real influence from Moscow, since the Kremlin was cut off from its usual channels of communication and engaged in a struggle for the very survival of the Soviet *state*. Furthermore, the DKP, NKP and SKP produced policies which in fact identified them as legitimate members of the *national* polity: they emphasised nationalism, sovereignty and independence, the need for co-operation of all anti-Nazi forces and the identification of a common enemy, which must be defeated at all cost. In this process, the old dividing lines based on socio-economic class and function were reduced to relative insignificance, and national political integration became the primary political manifestation. In fact, the three Communist parties became more nationalistic than most other political groups. In their defence of political pluralism and the institutions of democracy they harked back to Nordic history and the political traditions of the Viking era. This enormous change in the political platform, coupled with a demand for increased social justice after the war which was also a major focal point for the social democrats and others, helped establish the three parties as full-fledged participants on the *national* scene, as the first national Communists in the Scandinavian countries.[36]

5 The Early Confluence of Nationalism and Radicalism: the Case of Iceland

While the three Scandinavian Communist parties underwent rather similar experiences during the inter-war period and the years of the Second World War, the history of Icelandic leftism differed considerably from the Scandinavian developments. The primary political goal of the Icelanders was national independence, and this status was not obtained until 1944. Thus, Icelandic political groups (as well as general public opinion) grappled with questions which had been settled much earlier in Denmark and Sweden, and whose solutions had been found in Norway in 1905. The quest for independence superseded all other political controversies in Iceland during the 1920s and 1930s. Consequently, policies based on class antagonisms and Communist internationalism simply fell by the wayside as major issues. Icelandic leftism, therefore, was faced with the choice of either addressing issues which were relevant to the electorate, or conversely, to accept the Comintern's definition of what was relevant and important, risking political obliteration.

Most Icelandic leftists had little trouble in identifying their own interests with that of domestic nationalism.[27]

This policy choice was facilitated by the fact that much of the local wealth of Iceland was in fact controlled by foreign individuals and co-operatives, primarily Danish. Thus the class struggle could be subsumed under the quest for national independence; the exploiters of the workers, farmers and fishermen were also foreigners, and this fact helped integrate the Communist elements of the Icelandic left into the mainstream of political life on the island. The stage was thereby set for a close correlation between nationalism and leftism – a correlation which continues to represent one of the main tendencies in Icelandic policies to this day.[38]

The combination of nationalism and radicalism, which had strong support among the farmers and fishermen of the island, was further enhanced by the centuries-old tradition of 'individualism in a collective society', which characterised the social organisation of the Viking era and appears to have been maintained in Iceland to the present day. Briefly put, social relationships in Viking society were characterised by a strong emphasis on individualism, but at the same time the social cohesion of people facing a hostile environment was remarkable, ensuring a great many support mechanisms for those who were inside the collectivity while erecting strong barriers against outsiders. Icelandic society therefore tends to exhibit clannishness and internal collectivism while at the same time endorsing considerable individualism in the form of privacy and hard work for personal advancement. Under these circumstances, rebellion against authority which was perceived as unfair could coexist with a rejection of the collectivism of the Russian peasantry, which had a considerable impact on Leninist notions of class cohesions and solidarity. Thus, Icelandic radicalism was fundamentally different from the variety considered the norm in the Comintern, and it was therefore predictable that the policies of Icelandic Communism would deviate considerably from the model of 'Bolshevised' parties.

The formation of the Icelandic party in 1930 provided a

vehicle for the realisation of left-wing policies which experienced considerable successes. The Icelandic Communists early on opted for organisational forms which would allow for broad coalitions left of centre rather than ideological exclusivism. Thus in 1938 the party arranged for the inclusion in its ranks of the left wing of the social democrats. On this occasion, the party took the name United People's Party-Socialist Party (SA-SF) in Icelandic). This coalition of left-wing forces existed until 1956, when another, broadly based party of the left was formed, this time with the name People's Alliance (AB in Icelandic).[39]

Organisational flexibility and a willingness to accept a variety of groups into a broadly based party necessitated flexibility in policies as well. The SA-SF emphasised nationalism, social welfare, economic justice and a certain redistribution of wealth – all platforms which could find considerable support in the general population, even among individuals who could not be classified as left of centre ideologically. At the same time, the SA-SF downplayed ideological rigour and appealed instead to the considerable populism and egalitarianism present in Icelandic society.[40]

The result of such policies was a popular support unknown in the three Scandinavian parties. In fact, the SA-SF participated in coalition governments during the periods 1944–7 (and again in the 1950s, 1960s and 1970s, as will be discussed below). Support for the SA-SF was considerable in the trade unions, and the Communists have a long tradition of political control over many important locals, such as the union of general workers in the capital of Reykjavik.[41]

The Icelandic case, then, deviates sharply from the Danish, Norwegian and Swedish 'models' during the period 1918–45. Only during the war years (and in the immediate post-war period) did the DKP, NKP and SKP match the SA-SF in popularity or policy. The Icelandic experience was an early lesson which now appears to have been internalised well by the 'Eurocommunists': a party of the left which pays due attention to the political conditions in its local environment and conducts a flexible policy oriented towards national and pragmatic economic issues may do well in the Nordic countries. Conversely, parties concerned primarily with ideological rigidity and adherence to a foreign centre and its imposed model are likely to end up as frustrated and isolated political sects. The

Icelanders, being the first 'Eurocommunists', never suffered this ignominious fate.

6 People's Democracy and Stalinism: from Relevance to Sectarianism

For the first time since the early 1920s the political scene appeared uniquely favourable for the Scandinavian Communists in the spring of 1945. Nazi Germany had been defeated, and the Danish and Norwegian Communists had amassed considerable support as important forces in the resistance. Better still, wartime co-operation between the political elites in the two countries, united in the struggle against the Nazi occupation and local Quislings, had brought about the admission of Communists to important committees and a general acceptance of the DKP and the NKP as legitimate political participants. Best of all, the largest political parties in Denmark and Norway, the social democrats, had accepted the principle of unity of the working class – a prospect which ensured that the Communists would be able to 'come in from the cold' of political isolation, both in party politics and in the trade unions. In Sweden, the nationalistic stance of the SKP had also secured legitimacy for the party and added influence in many mass organisations.[42]

During the years 1945 and 1946, Scandinavian Communists experienced the luxury of considerable political success, based upon flexible policies and party platforms geared to the needs of their local populations. This luxury was possible because the Soviet Union and the CPSU, reeling from the almost Pyrrhic victory in the Second World War, chose to emphasise domestic consolidation, while the foreign policies of party and state concentrated on providing maximum leeway for local Communists whose prospects for power seemed good in devastated Western Europe. Thus, all three Scandinavian Communist parties experienced unprecedented successes in the first post-war elections, both at the national and local levels, in all three countries. In Denmark and Norway, the two Communist parties received over 11 per cent of the vote in the parliamentary elections of 1945, and the SKP was not far behind. Communists participated in the first coalition governments of 'national unity' in both Denmark and Norway. Subsequent local elections in the three countries confirmed considerable public support for these erstwhile pariahs of the Scandinavian political scene.[43]

This favourable situation did not last past 1946. In the international Communist movement the CPSU was re-establishing its position, and in Soviet foreign policy generally, state interests, as perceived by Stalin, dictated the need for an 'Iron Curtain', while the consolidation of Soviet hegemony in Eastern Europe proceeded apace. With the formation of the Cominform and the formulation of the 'two camp theory' in mid-1947, Nordic Communists, as well as their colleagues throughout Western Europe, were once again confronted by the agonising choice between 'international solidarity', as defined and executed by Moscow, and meaningful policies in their domestic environments. As was the case in the inter-war period, CPSU domination and international solidarity won out. But the very success of the Soviet attempt to re-establish unquestioned control on the movement represented the last substantial success in this arena; after Stalin's death, 'localism' and 'national Communism' became the order of the day.

The re-imposition of Moscow's control over Western European Communist parties was manifest in a whole range of fields and policy topics. In terms of international organisation, solidarity and ideological orthodoxy, Western European Communists were required to profess their allegiance to the universality of the Soviet model, and to the need for applying this model to their own political programmes. Embedded in this wholesale acceptance of Moscow's road was the need for purges of 'elements hostile to the socialist order' who had 'wormed their way into the socialist edifice'. Such purges were to be conducted against 'Zionists', 'cosmopolitanists' and, as the rift with Yugoslavia widened, against 'Titoists' and other renegades. Relations with the social democrats were once again to be carried out under the auspices of 'united fronts from below', in which leftist organisations would co-operate for specific reasons, but would abstain from organisational unification (the latter process was called 'united fronts from above'). 'United fronts from below' allowed for constant Communist efforts to gain inroads into the mass membership base of other leftist organisations, notably the rank and file of the social democratic parties and the trade unions dominated by the latter groups.

Under these policy guidelines, local Communist parties were

also required to relate to 'bourgeois' parties and organisations in a more hostile, 'class-oriented' manner. This signalled the end of the era of the 'progressive coalition', which had included all anti-Nazi forces during the immediate post-war period, and set the stage for a much more clear-cut delineation between Communists and other political organisations. After mid-1947, Communists were also required to take sharp issue with any political organisation considered to be pro-Western rather than oriented towards Moscow.[45] Foreign policy pronouncements by local Communists, which had emphasised many of the aspects of the war alliance between the Soviet Union and the Western powers, were now required to attack the 'imperialist camp under the leadership of the United States'.[46]

The Communist parties of Scandinavia did not hesitate to follow the lead of Moscow in this massive policy reorientation. Beginning even in 1946, the DKP, NKP and SKP escalated their demands for concessions from the social democrats in any future unification of left-wing forces. This gradual change in policy, which appeared to coincide well with the cooling of relations between the Soviet Union and its Western allies, became very definite and drastic after the formation of the Cominform and the enunciation of the two-camp theory. The three Scandinavian parties ran their campaigns for local elections in 1946 and 1947 on a platform which sharply distinguished itself from the programme of reconstruction offered by the Danish, Norwegian and Swedish social democrats. In the trade unions, Communists started another organisational drive to capture locals and thereby expand their representation on the trade union national councils, only to be met by determined counter-moves by the social democrats, who pointed out the extent of collaboration which the DKP and NKP had proffered the Nazi occupying forces in 1940 – June 1941; in Sweden, the Communists were reminded of their splitting efforts during the period of the struggle against 'social Fascism' during 1928–34.[47]

The three parties also rose to the demand of class struggle with the local 'bourgeoisie' and internal purges. By the end of 1947, the three parties had forcefully denounced their erstwhile allies in the 'progressive coalitions' of 1945; the Danish, Norwegian and Swedish publics were now frequently reminded of the profit-mongering of the factory-owners during the war,

and the farmers of all three countries were likewise charged
with undue advantages during this period. These charges were in
fact extended to the social democrats as well, especially in
Denmark and Norway; here, the accusations mostly revolved
around the presumed unwillingness of the ruling social
democrats in exile to engage in 'active' warfare such as sabotage
and guerrilla attacks.[48]

Perhaps the most dramatic demonstration of the *volte-face*
which the Scandinavian parties had undertaken towards
subservience to Moscow came in the form of internal party purges,
carried out under the auspices of a struggle against Titoism. The
models for these undertakings were the drastic purges which
decimated the Eastern European parties during this period as an
integral part of the massive restructuring of the social and
political systems of the area now under way. The presence of
the Red Army in the Eastern European states during much of
this period set the stage for the successful completion of such a
programme (successful, that is, from the point of view of
Moscow), and the total dependence of the local Communist
leaders on the Kremlin and Stalin personally made subservience
a necessity for political survival.[49] By the end of the Stalinist
era, the massive purges had destroyed much of the pre-1945
leadership of the Eastern European parties, thus setting the
stage for the recruitment of Stalin-type *apparatchiki* to the
leadership positions there.

In the Scandinavian countries, the pre-conditions for such
purges did not exist. Executive power was firmly in the hands of
non-Communists, and they were not about to underwrite any
internal reckonings in the local Communist parties. There was
no Red Army to help with the execution of policies, and
Moscow's political influence, which had been considerable
during the first few years after the war, was clearly on the wane.
Instead, the Scandinavian political systems (especially in
Denmark and Norway) were in the process of foreign policy
reorientation towards a much closer relationship with the West
than traditional neutrality had warranted earlier. Under such
circumstances, Eastern European-style purges could only raise
once again the spectacle of political parties acting in a very
strange way, following a foreign and alien model in political
systems which were in full democratic and pluralistic
reconstruction.

Despite these warning signs, the purges of 'Titoists', 'nationalists' and 'cosmopolitanists' proceeded apace in the DKP, NKP and SKP. Dozens of political scores were settled, but, due to the omnipresence of 'bourgeois' justice, the ramifications were minor; there were no liquidations, only wrecked careers. The purges nevertheless altered the make-up of the leadership cadres in the three parties significantly and ushered in a period in which the nationally oriented heroes of the anti-Nazi underground were reduced to political insignificance, while the trusted *apparatchiki* with an impeccable record of Stalinist loyalty and trustworthiness came to the fore.[50]

This major change was exemplified by the purges in Norway, which were the most spectacular in the Scandinavian countries. There, the successful leader of the Communist underground, Peder Furnbotn, was forced out of the party in 1949 after a bitter struggle in which the resistance leader was accused of Titoism, undue willingness to co-operate with the social democrats and the 'bourgeois' leaders, and of collaborationism with the German occupying forces; Furnbotn was even charged with being a Gestapo agent.[51] The charges against this one-time leader in fact ran the gamut of every successful policy which the latter had instituted during the war – policies which had resulted in a significant increase in the position of Norwegian Communism, both in the general population and in relation to other political groups and elites. Such successes, of course, were turned to serious liabilities at a time when the main criterion of political performance was not influence in the domestic political system, but rather blind obedience to Moscow and the CPSU. It therefore stood to reason that Furnbotn's successor as the unquestioned leader of the NKP was Emil Lövlien, a more colourless party *apparatchik* who had led the party during the disastrous thirties, when the fortunes of the NKP sank so low that the party even refrained from establishing a full national ticket in the elections of 1936.[52]

The policies of internal purging, ideological rigidity and hostility to all other political manifestations in Scandinavian society continued throughout the rest of the Stalinist era, with predictable results. In 1950, all three Scandinavian Communist parties had been reduced to insignificance, exemplified by the fact that the DKP obtained 4.6 per cent of the total vote in the parliamentary elections of 1950, while the NKP and SKP received 5.8 and 6.3 per cent respectively, in the Norwegian national elections of 1949 and the Swedish elections of 1948.[53]

7 Iceland: the Policy of Influence Continues

The policies emanating from the Communist Party headquarters of Copenhagen, Oslo and Stockholm stood in sharp contrast to the programmes and platforms of the SA-SF in Reykjavik. Having succeeded in producing policies which were acceptable to relatively large numbers of their fellow countrymen during the inter-war period and indeed up to the establishment of national independence in 1944, the Icelandic Communists chose to continue their flexible policies during the second half of the 1940s and indeed well into the 1950s. This policy continuation emphasised the need to safeguard national sovereignty, so recently acquired, and to produce programmes which emphasised economic issues with a wide appeal. Furthermore, the formula of pragmatism precluded ideological rigidity; the party leaders, having made their decision to maximise *domestic* influence had also, *ipso facto*, relegated ideological orthodoxy to a back seat. The programmes and statements of the Icelandic Communists in this period naturally refer to Marxism as the main guideline for their policies, but the *specific* platforms promoted often belie such a tie with formal ideology, and the policies actually carried out clearly show that the SA-SF leadership was not about to let 'the scriptures' detract from policy programmes.[54]

The pragmatism of the SA-SF also had far-reaching consequences in the relationship between the Communists and the so-called 'bourgeois' parties in Iceland. As noted above, there was a good deal of native radicalism and populism in large segments of the population, and this meant that the specific platforms of several parties had considerably more in common than separated them. In addition to this, *all* political parties had been partners in the struggle for national independence, and this experience was only a few years in the past, with considerable camaraderie still left in personal relationships. All of these factors helped produce Communist policies in Iceland which deviated sharply from the experiences of other Communists in the Nordic countries. The most startling of these 'deviations' was SA-SF participation in a coalition government during the period 1944 to 1947, the latter part of which period coincided with the sharpest attacks on 'bourgeois democracy' elsewhere among Communists, even in Scandinavia.[55]

The Icelandic success story in the midst of dismal failure on the part of almost all other Western European Communist parties raises several interesting questions. Why did the SA-SF leadership refuse to accommodate themselves to the policies decreed by the CPSU in the international movement? How was it that the Kremlin was unable (unwilling) to seriously enforce its policies in Iceland? Any answer to these questions must of necessity remain very tentative, since the query turns on motivations – a very difficult case for establishing causality. But given these analytical difficulties, it seems clear that *some* indications nevertheless can be found, chief of which are the following. The SA-SF leadership, confined to a relatively isolated island, far away from the main political turmoil of the continent, and required by the very success of their policies during the struggle for liberation to spend their productive time at home rather than in political seminars in Moscow, had an inadequate understanding of the true nature of Stalinism, just as Martin Tranmael and his followers in the Norwegian DNA misunderstood Leninism during the early 1920s. Such a misunderstanding may have induced the Icelandic Communist leaders to take Stalin seriously when the latter spoke of national sovereignty and the Soviet Union's acceptance of different roads of development, which had been a major part of the CPSU's international programme up until mid-1947. When the line changed, it was not clear to the SA-SF that an immediate *local* change had to be effected.

By the same token, the Icelandic deviation escaped the wrath of Moscow because of the remoteness of the island and the determination of the SA-SF not to become involved in the factional struggles over the proper roads to socialism and Communism which produced the purges in the other Western European parties. There were other deviations of a much more serious nature, and these occupied most of the Kremlin's time and energy during this period; of particular importance was Titoism, which not only claimed the right to establish a 'national road', but in fact postulated the Yugoslav road as a possible alternative to the path demanded by Moscow. The isolationist stance of the SA-SF seemed much less dangerous by comparison, and the CPSU therefore chose to ignore this challenge. For the time being, this may have been a rational choice. But by the mid-1970s, many of the challenges to the Soviet model which the Icelanders had posited by means of their practical policies in the era of Stalinism were to re-emerge as major points in the current struggle between 'Eurocommunists' and 'ruling Communists'.

8 The Decline of Soviet Hegemony, Stage One: Questioning the Idol

The death of Stalin in March 1953 sent shock waves throughout the international Communist movement. The tight, hegemonistic control established by the CPSU in the movement hinged upon the unquestioned rule of the dictator internally, coupled with his ability to cement relationships with the puppet leaders of the satellite states in Eastern Europe. Many of the control mechanisms cementing the Soviet bloc were therefore informal in nature, and under such circumstances, the death of the linchpin had serious consequences indeed. In addition to these repercussions, there was always the danger of a protracted power struggle in the Kremlin, which would further jeopardise the hegemonic position of the CPSU in international Communism.

All of the fears felt in the Kremlin after Stalin's death materialised, at least to some extent. There *was* a protracted power struggle in the CPSU, and this contest was not settled until 1955. Krushchev's position was only partly consolidated even at that time, and he needed further ammunition for his attack on major rivals who had remained powerful figures in the party. This ammunition came in the form of the secret speech at the Twentieth CPSU Congress in early 1956. It is safe to say that international Communism has not been the same since.

The Scandinavian Communist parties found themselves in much the same quandary as did the other 'fraternal' parties in Western Europe. Having undergone the rather traumatic experience of the internal purges in the late 1940s, the DKP, NKP and SKP had been thoroughly 'Stalinised' (with the exception of the very top of the DKP, where Aksel Larsen still maintained his position despite criticism of his 'unprincipled' position on many issues; Larsen's colleagues at the top were predominantly Stalinists, however, and it seemed clear that another purge would soon ensue).

Now, the 'model' was indeed gone, and the insecurity of succession in the Soviet Union made it difficult to predict future policy lines. The Scandinavian Communists therefore assumed a wait-and-see attitude, during which period they continued to adhere to the general policy line as it had existed during Stalin's lifetime. At the same time, however, there were cautious attempts to re-assess the situation and perhaps consider possible alternatives to the close adherence to the CPSU line in all aspects. One example of such trial balloons can be found in the revised NKP programme of 1953, which held out vague hints about the need for unity of the left and a Norwegian road to Socialism and Communism while maintaining its essential Stalinist features.[56] In Sweden, the first split of the Scandinavian Communist parties since the 1920s came in the form of the SKA (Swedish Workers' Party) which considered itself a Marxist party but espoused a programme of modified Maoist overtones, thus being a forerunner of the many Maoist groups to develop in Scandinavia during the 1960s.[57] In Denmark, Aksel Larsen, who had never been comfortable with the Stalinist strait-jacket, began to express his misgivings with more zeal than usual.[58] This, then, was a time of ferment in the three Scandinavian Communist parties.

The uneasiness which spread throughout the Communist parties of Western Europe in the aftermath of Stalin's death and the ensuing power struggle rose to a crescendo after the secret speech, and international Communism now proceeded from crisis to crisis. The secret speech marked the end of the Stalinist era and cast doubts upon the legitimacy of certain aspects of the Soviet political and socio-economic model which had hitherto been sacrosanct. The reverberations of this speech throughout the Communist movements of Europe resulted in internal recriminations, bickering and, ultimately, a process of de-Stalinisation which gradually forced substantial changes in both personnel and policy. This, then, was the beginning of a process which ultimately gave rise to the autonomist stance of many Western European parties in the 1970s, among them the Swedish and Norwegian parties (not to mention the Icelandic party, whose 'deviations' continued as before).[59]

In Denmark, Norway and Sweden, the revelations of the secret speech gave rise to considerable soul-searching. Why

were we not told? How could such unspeakable crimes be
perpetrated in the name of socialism and Communism? – these
were the main questions asked. These questions, asked in
bewilderment during the spring and summer of 1956, rose to
insistent demands for full explanations after the 'Polish October'
and the Hungarian Revolution in November. Some parties,
notably the NKP and the Swedish comrades, openly criticised
the Soviet invasion of Hungary and began to quote approvingly
from the writings of Palmiro Togliatti on the subject of
'polycentrism'. Others, such as the leadership of the DKP, took
a more cautious attitude, reflecting the tendency towards
'solidarity' so often found in the past. The exception to this
tendency was Aksel Larsen, who rejected Soviet policy in this
instance in no uncertain terms. This open stance of defiance
resulted in a full-scale crisis in the DKP. Larsen was ultimately
forced to resign, and promptly set about organising his own party,
the Socialist People's Party (SF). In Norway, too, elements of
the left wing of the DNA (Social Democrats) and disaffected
Communists established a Socialist People's Party (SF) which
drew significant support from those elements of the population
who advocated radical socio-economic policies, but were unable
to accept Soviet foreign policy and the attempts by the CPSU to
re-establish unquestioned hegemony in the movement in the
aftermath of the 1956 crisis.[60] In Sweden, no formal party split
took place, but there was a gradual shift in policy and personnel
towards the 'autonomists' around C. J. Hermansson, whose
outspoken criticism of the Soviet Union and the CPSU became
legendary.[61]

The problems created by the events of 1956 indeed revealed
the major weakness associated with the Soviet claim to
pre-eminence in the world Communist movement. Close
reliance on such a centre can only be maintained as long as that
centre is internally strong and capable of sending consistent
signals to the flock. Once that ability is damaged, few policies
can re-establish it. This fact became painfully evident
throughout the year 1957, when the Kremlin scrambled to
compensate for its unquestioned losses of prestige and influence
during that catastrophic year. And for the first time, the Chinese
appeared as factors of importance in the European sector of the
international movement; so far, it was true, Chou En-lai acted
predominantly as a spokesman for those who maintained that

the unity of the movement must be preserved at all cost, including that of strengthening the position of the CPSU once again, but the very fact that a 'junior partner' such as the Chinese Communist Party (CCP) now had to throw its weight behind the Kremlin attested to the sorry decline of the latter in power terms. Thus the assistance from Peking became something of a liability during the immediate period after Hungary.

There was also the problem of Titoism. Khrushchev's overtures to the Yugoslav leader in 1955 had failed to reconcile the differences between the two parties, and sharp controversies continued to flare up after the autumn of 1956, despite Tito's half-hearted support for the second invasion of Hungary. The conflict between Moscow and Belgrade, always simmering, broke out repeatedly during the first years after the 'Hungarian events' and provided a clear example of the decline in Moscow's ability to control the movement.[62]

While the problems associated with the Soviet attempt to re-establish the ideological centre and the Titoist challenge to it were formidable, the very successes of the Soviet *state* in other fields of activity further complicated matters on the *party* level. When the Kremlin launched the first satellite in 1958, the CCP immediately seized upon this memorable occasion to postulate the idea that 'the east wind prevails over the west wind,' and that the military and strategic advantages of the Communist-dominated world now must be utilised forcefully in the political realm as well, for maximum leverage against the Western 'paper tigers'. Peking, in short, argued that the time had come for a new revolutionary wave in international affairs, and the CCP called upon the Soviet Politburo to assume an activist position, if the latter were to claim the mantle of leadership in the Communist movement. The rest is history; after 1960, the Sino-Soviet rift became common knowledge, and today it represents one of the foremost facts of international life, both in relations among states and also in the international Communist movement.

With such momentous events crowding the international calendar during the period 1957–60, it was clear that the Scandinavian Communist parties could not remain untouched. In fact, several processes of internal development had been under way since the death of Stalin, and these tendencies were now strengthened by the new elements of the Sino-Soviet dispute. The most important of these developments were the following.

8.1 The Problem of De-Stalinisation and the Recycling of Party Elites

The first serious fragmentation in the DKP, NKP and SKP since the purges of the late forties arose in the aftermath of Stalin's death and especially after the Twentieth CPSU congress. On the one hand, there were those who argued that the revelations of Khrushchev during the secret speech should have no direct impact on the party, its organisation and its policies; in fact, it was imperative that the 'correct line' be maintained in the face of the prevailing chaos in the international movement. This group also emphasised the need to maintain the principles of international solidarity and the supremacy of the Soviet Union and the CPSU. This view was represented in the NKP by Jörgen Vogt, who had been editor of the party organ *Friheten*. In Sweden, the group around Hilding Hagberg and the strong party group in Norrbotten (northern Sweden) occupied a similar position. In Denmark, Knud Jespersen became the foremost spokesman for some of the same ideas, and he was supported in this by Ib Nörlund and others. Jespersen was nevertheless considerably less dogmatic in domestic affairs than Hagberg in Sweden or Vogt in Norway.[63]

Against these local 'Stalinists' were pitted a considerable number of individuals who claimed significant organisational backing as well as support from many elements in the rank and file. The main attitudes of this group reflected concerns which have recently gained a great deal of publicity as mainstays of 'Eurocommunism'. Basically, the main focus here was on policies geared to national conditions, and international solidarity, but only under the auspices of the principle 'mutual benefit and non-interference in internal affairs'; furthermore, this group demanded a reckoning with Stalinism and its representatives, both domestically and internationally.

In the category of emerging 'national Communists' and 'anti-Stalinists' could be found Reidar Larson in the NKP, C. J. Hermansson in the SKP, and, up to 1958, Aksel Larsen in the DKP.[64]

8.2 The Organisational Fragmentation of Scandinavian Communism

Would-be monolithic parties tend to be prone to factionalism, and the three Scandinavian Communist parties have traditionally fitted well into this pattern, as discussed above. The factionalism which emerged in the three parties after the secret speech and the Sino-Soviet rift was nevertheless quite unprecedented. During the 1960s, the DKP, NKP and SKP experienced a series of splits and endured the development of splinter movements in considerable numbers. This tendency has continued up to the present time, creating in the Scandinavian countries an extremely confusing and fast-changing situation on the political left. During the 1960s and 1970s the Danish left sustained the emergence of a plethora of groups and parties, chief of which are the following:

(a) Communist Labour Circle (KAK), founded in 1964 (pro-Chinese);

(b) Left Socialists (VS), which was established in 1967 as a result of a split in the KAK;

(c) Communist League (Marxist-Leninist) – or KFML, another splinter group, this time emanating from the VS;

(d) Communist Youth League (KUF), founded in 1968;

(e) Communist Youth (Marxist-Leninist), or KUML, founded in 1969;

(f) Socialist Youth League (SUF), founded in 1969 by a group of dissident VS members who had been excluded from the parent organisation;

(g) Revolutionary Socialists, a Trotskyite group, founded in 1969.[65]

The many Danish groups and splinter movements which emerged during the 1960s had their counterparts in Norway and Sweden. In Norway, several splits and mergers have created a bewildering scene on the political left, to wit:

(a) in 1967, the Norwegian Communist Youth League (NKU) split; the dissenters established themselves as Communist Youth (KU); the latter group was pro-Soviet, and objected to the NKU's frequent criticism of the CPSU and the Soviet Union;

(b) in 1968, the SF's youth group broke away from the parent party and adopted a Maoist policy. The new group took the name Socialist Youth League (SUF); in 1969, the SUF became a political party in its own right, named Socialist Youth League (Marxist-Leninist) or SUF (ML);

(c) the establishment of the Marxist-Leninist Groups (ML-gruppene), which became a formal political party (MLG);

(d) in 1970, dissidents in the NKP established the Marxist-Leninist Front (MLF);

(e) in 1973, several of the splinter groups reformed under the name Workers' Communist Party Marxist-Leninist or AKP(ML). This party is still in existence and has adopted a Maoist policy. The AKP(ML) maintains close relations with the Chinese Communist Party;[66]

(f) in 1975, the NKP split, and parts of the rank and file as well as the leadership went over to the Socialist Left Party (SV) which had originated as an electoral alliance before the parliamentary elections of 1973;

(g) the AKP(ML) has run in recent parliamentary elections as the Red Electoral Alliance (RV).[67]

In Sweden, the schisms of the left have resulted in the formation of a new party, the pro-Soviet APK (Workers' Party of Communists) in 1977. In addition, the following organisational developments took place during the post-Stalin era:

(a) in 1967, the SKP dropped its name and adopted another, the Left Party of Communists (VPK);

(b) in 1953, pro-Chinese dissidents in the SKP established themselves as the Communist Workers' League of Sweden (SKA);

(c) in the 1960s, there was established a Communist League (Marxist-Leninist), or KFML, with a Maoist bent;

(d) the KFML split in 1970; the new body of dissenters established itself as KFML (R) – the 'R' denoting the group's dedication to revolution;

(e) in 1973, the KFML took the name SKP, which had been abandoned by the Communist Party in 1967;

(f) in the early 1970s, the VPK youth organisation split from the parent body and became the Marxist-Leninist League of Struggle (MLK), with a pro-Maoist programme;

(g) in 1973 the pro-VPK elements in the youth organisation MLK, resenting the Maoist programme of the group, split out and formed the Communist Youth (KU);

(h) during the 1970s, two Trotskyist groups, the

Revolutionary Marxists and the Bolshevik Group, were formed.[68]

8.3 The Realignment of Relationships

The development of large numbers of left-wing organisations, all of them challenging the position of the Scandinavian Communist parties, has resulted in a considerable change in the 'alliance system' of the DKP, NKP and VPK. This realignment has come about partly as a result of the programme and platform changes which have been undertaken during the 1960s and 1970s (see below); in part, the rearranging of such relations has come about because of the emergence of new ideological 'centres' during the last fifteen years. Extremely complex events and developments have helped foster such diversity during this period, and the Scandinavian Communist parties have partaken fully in these developments, to the delight of political 'autonomists' and to the despair of analysts.

The process of proliferation was under way already by 1960, when the Sino-Soviet conflict became the primary catalyst for further developments in the movement, but the latter event accelerated the developments towards the present state of international autonomism. The notions of polycentrism and Titoism had certainly raised the question of national roads to socialism and Communism, but these two phenomena, important as they were, did not represent anything basically new; 'national roads' had been quite the fashion already in the period 1944–7. With the advent of the Chinese challenge, however, there *was* a distinctly new element in the game. For the first time there appeared now a Communist party, backed by considerable actual and enormous potential *state* power, which openly rejected both the notion of CPSU international leadership and the veracity of Soviet policy and ideology; indeed, the CCP charged the Kremlin with major deviationism and outright betrayal of the cause. Here was a real opportunity for choice in the movement for those who had been looking for it.

Several Communist parties utilised the new opportunities for choice. In Eastern Europe, Albania chose to accept the Chinese view of international Communism and Soviet policy. Rumania began to consider itself a mediator in the struggle between Moscow and Peking, thereby considerably enhancing its autonomy within Comecon, the Warsaw Pact, and in the international movement. Yugoslavia was able to exert increased influence, since its views on the need for autonomy and national sovereignty were now accepted by increasing numbers of parties.

In Western Europe, the emergence of new 'centres' in Eastern Europe and the continued escalation of animosity between the CCP and the CPSU provided unheard-of opportunities for expanding individual autonomy and influence. The Italian Communist Party (PCI), the seat of original polycentrism, became an early convert to the idea of expanded relations with the Rumanian Communist Party (PCR) and the League of Communists of Yugoslavia (LCY). The Spanish Communist Party (PCE), still in exile, lined up with the PCI on the international question. Similar positions emerged among the British and Dutch parties. Throughout the 1960s and 1970s, increasingly frequent consultations took place between the Rumanian, Yugoslav, Italian, Spanish and British parties (as well as other mavericks).

Among the Scandinavians, the reactions to these new opportunities varied considerably. In the VPK and the NKP, the post-Stalin leadership became increasingly enamoured with the new opportunities, and there was a major expansion in their relations with other parties in Western Europe, expecially the PCI. At the same time, the Swedish and Norwegian comrades became quite vocal in their denunciations of Soviet policies, especially the treatment of dissenters in the Soviet Union, as well as the constant efforts by the CPSU to re-establish the principle that the Soviet model must be considered the primary development model, and the CPSU the continued leader of the international movement. The criticisms emanating from party headquarters in Oslo and Stockholm rose to a crescendo at the time of the invasion of Czechoslovakia; both the NKP and VPK denounced the invasion as unforgivable imperialism by a big power, and the two parties became active members in an increasing circle of European Communists dedicated to the maintenance and expansion of 'national sovereignty, non-interference in domestic affairs and mutual advantage' as the principles underpinning relations among Communist parties.[69]

During the years of VPK and NKP disenchantment with the CPSU and aspects of policy in the Soviet Union there was a considerable expansion of relations between the two

Scandinavian parties on the one hand, and the PCR on the other. Thus, during the 1960s and 1970s, the following meetings between the Rumanian Communists and their Swedish and Norwegian counterparts took place:

(a) PCR delegation in Norway and Sweden, August and October 1967, respectively;

(b) NKP delegation in Bucharest in January 1968; PCR delegation in Sweden in February of the same year. In September 1968 the NKP sent another delegation to the Rumanian capital;

(c) PCR talks with the NKP in June 1969. Both the NKP and VPK were represented at the PCR Tenth Congress in August of that year;

(d) both the NKP and VPK participated in the meetings of Communist parties on the Rumanian Black Sea coast in the summer of 1970 and 1971 (this was a 'counter-summit' called at a time when the more pro-Soviet parties were meeting in the Crimea);

(e) in April 1974, Reidar Larsen of the NKP visited Bucharest;

(f) there were informal talks between the PCR representatives and Norwegian and Swedish delegates to the Conference of Communist and Workers' Parties in East Berlin, June 1976;

(g) in April 1977, Bo Hammar of the VPK visited Bucharest.

By comparison, the DKP took a much more cautious attitude in most policy questions (see below), and the Danes were also less prone to attack the CPSU in the international movement. Thus, after much lamenting and soul-searching, the DKP endorsed the invasion of Czechoslovakia, and the party also supported the CPSU's efforts to call another world conference of Communist parties to deal with the 'Chinese question'.[70] These attempts were rejected by the NKP and VPK, and the two latter parties tended to take a neutral stance in the polemics between Moscow and Peking; at times, the Swedes and Norwegians in fact went out of their way to demonstrate their support of the CCP's right to determine its own policies and positions in the international movement, even though the two Scandinavian parties found little in the Chinese party's domestic policies that had direct relevance for themselves.[71]

Despite the more orthodox policy of the DKP, the Danes did

maintain close contact with the 'other' centres of Communism, as witnessed by frequent contacts with the PCR and other mavericks during the late 1960s and 1970s (PCR delegation in Denmark in September 1967; DKP delegation in Bucharest, February and June 1968; DKP delegates at the Tenth PCR Congress in August 1969; DKP participation in the 1970 and 1971 Black Sea coast meetings; August 1972, Knud Jespersen, head of the DKP, in Bucharest; Jespersen came back in August 1974).[72]

By the mid-1970s, then, the NKP and the VPK had engaged in policies which represented a major challenge to the traditional hegemony of the CPSU in the international movement. Both parties had rearranged their political alliances and could be found in a large group of European Communist parties emphasising 'national roads' to socialism and Communism, thereby rejecting the CPSU's claims to a position of 'first among equals'. This 'Eurocommunist' position had been matched by internal developments, which had propelled a new set of leaders to the fore, thus reducing (but not eliminating) the influence of the 'Stalinists', the traditionalists, in the two parties. But these policies and developments, which certainly seemed sensible in terms of relations with the other political actors and competitors in the national political systems of Norway and Sweden, had not resulted in appreciable gains in the local electorates; in fact, the erosion of ideology and the proliferation of leftist groups had made it even more difficult to maintain a Communist presence in these two countries.

The Danish position was different. In the DKP, the chief proponent of 'national roads' had been purged and Aksel Larsen became the main organiser of the SF, which in turn proceeded to reduce the influence of Danish Communism considerably. The DKP leadership under 'Red Knud' Jespersen was much more positive in its views of the CPSU, as could be expected from a leadership which had emerged not as a result of de-Stalinisation but, on the contrary, in response to a 'rightist' deviation by Aksel Larsen, the former head of the party. In one area, however, the DKP shared the fate of its Scandinavian colleagues; it was beset by organisational difficulties and factionalism, which resulted in innumerable splits and the formation of groups constantly challenging the position of the Communist Party on the Danish left.

9 The Hegemony Challenged: Scandinavian 'Eurocommunist' Policies

For the CPSU and the Soviet Union, the period since 1960 has been a trying one, in so far as the fragmentation of the international movement and the Chinese challenge resulted in considerable erosion of the power which had traditionally belonged to Moscow. During the latter part of the 1960s and throughout the 1970s, however, another challenge emerged which was even more demanding and in many ways even more demeaning for the erstwhile masters of international Communism. This challenge was one of policy; several parties in Western Europe openly questioned the main tenets of Soviet-style Communism, and instead posited a set of policies which they deemed more suitable for modern, 'mature' systems. By the same token, these parties, headed by Santiago Carrillo of the PCE and Enrico Berlinguer of the PCI, and strongly supported by French Communist theoreticians such as Jean Kanapa and Jean Elleinstein, classified Soviet-style Communism as 'primitive', or at least only suitable for less developed countries and economic systems. Thus the question was no longer merely of national roads to socialism and Communism, but, more generally, of the paths to this goal most profitably undertaken by modern societies, with the clear indication that 'state Communism', as it existed in the Soviet Union and Eastern Europe, had little to offer such societies.[73]

The Scandinavian parties, especially the NKP and the VPK, followed the lead of the Spaniards and the Italians with a great deal of enthusiasm and fanfare during the late 1960s and up to the mid-1970s. Policies which had been developed during the era of 'Bolshevisation of Communist parties' in 1923–4 were now subjected to considerable scrutiny, and in many cases redefined. Now policies were developed to deal with local opportunities, and for the first time since the immediate post-war era the Swedish and Norwegian Communists (and to some extent also the Danish comrades) developed policies which were designed to respond to the changing opportunities in their local environments. Such policy flexibility was matched by significant revisions in ideology. In the latter field, the following changes were the most important.

First of all, the Scandinavian parties began to reassess the *path to power*. During the decades since 'Bolshevisation' the three parties had steadfastly maintained adherence to the revolutionary path, at least in theory. It is true that this approach had been downplayed at times for tactical reasons, but it had never been removed as part of the ideological baggage of the DKP, NKP, SKP and VPK. During the era of 'Eurocommunism', however, there were many references to the dictatorship of the proletariat as an 'outmoded' concept, and, conversely, the notion of peaceful transfer of power to the Communists by means of the ballot box became more and more important. The Scandinavian Communists now appeared as staunch democrats, and they renewed their interest in a whole host of participatory mechanisms, such as worker participation in joint labour-management boards in industry. There were also many references to the need for 'advanced' Communist parties to devise ways of capturing power which would be more appropriate for the society in which they functioned.[74]

Second, there was an important reassessment of the nature of 'bourgeois democracy'. Just as the paths to political power now advocated appeared to be similar to the 'weapons' used by other political parties in a pluralist democracy, so the very nature of the latter political form began to endear itself to the erstwhile revolutionary groups on the left. On virtually all important occasions, and in their newspapers and policy statements, the Scandinavian parties emphasised their commitment to human rights, genuine party competition and the possible survival of pluralistic democracy, even after the assumption of executive power by the Communists. Such discussions, coming from parties with only a minuscule fraction of the electorate behind them, nevertheless suggested important, perhaps fundamental, revisions in policy and ideology.[75]

Third, and in line with the positions on democracy and individual human rights listed above, the Scandinavian Communists reassessed their relations with other elements of the political left in their respective countries. The vituperative attacks on ideological renegades, which had so often been levelled against the social democrats, were now predominantly directed against the many groups and movements to the left of the DKP, NKP and VPK, especially the Trotskyists and, to some extent, the Maoists. The social democrats, on the other hand, were often approached for common policies and actions, and the need for 'action unity' of the 'progressive forces' was often emphasised. While this policy line was consistent also with current Soviet and CPSU policies, it was clear that the primary reason for the interest in united fronts with the social democrats reflected the assessment of Communist leaders of the local political situation, rather than any deeply felt wish to please the leaders in the Kremlin.[76]

Fourth, the Scandinavian Communists, albeit critical of certain aspects of domestic policies in the Soviet Union and the attempts by the CPSU to re-establish its hegemony, continued to emphasise their support for 'progressive' forces everywhere, and this position also required anti-Americanism abroad and political struggle against pro-American opinion at home. In this policy area, the three Communist parties simply continued their traditional policies, albeit in a somewhat more muted form.[77]

These revised policies of the 1960s and early 1970s were undertaken in an atmosphere outwardly more favourable to Communist endeavour than had been the case since the Second World War. The Vietnam War produced considerable anti-Americanism in Scandinavia, and many parties, including the social democrats and liberal elements and groups in the non-socialist parties, roundly denounced the United States for its 'immoral' war. The Communist position on this issue was a given, but the considerable agreement which existed on the question in broad circles of Scandinavian public opinion served to legitimise the stand of the DKP, NKP and VPK to an extent rarely found in the three countries. Communists could be found in the many 'action committees' which sprang up in order to demand US withdrawal; Communists were also very active in the peace movements and the groups pledging solidarity with the Vietcong.[78]

The malaise which beset Western Europe during the American involvement in South-East Asia also served to jeopardise long-standing Scandinavian commitments to organisations such as NATO, and this development provided a welcome setting for the DKP and NKP programme of getting Denmark and Norway out of the Atlantic organisation. One alternative to this defence arrangement was a Nordic defence union, which would also involve Sweden and possibly Finland, and this alternative became a major focal point for the three Scandinavian Communist parties and their campaigns. Such a

242   *Communism in the Nordic Countries*

pact would remain outside the major power blocs, and this was seen as a considerable advantage by all three parties.[79]

The emphasis on neutrality in defence matters was but an element in the increased Communist awareness of the political advantages to be reaped from a nationalist policy stance in other fields. During the 1960s and 1970s, the Scandinavian Communists became ardent nationalists and regionalists. The arguments utilised to defend such a position were frequently rather chauvinistic in nature, emphasising the need to maintain the purity of national culture and the Scandinavian heritage in the face of 'cultural imperialism' from other powers, especially the United States. This policy could meaningfully count on some support in broad sectors of public opinion, whose uneasiness over the 'Americanisation' of Scandinavia in terms of life-style and even language had reached crisis proportions.[80]

The nationalistic stance of the Communists provided the Norwegian Communists with an unusual opportunity during the late 1960s and early 1970s. For several years, one of the most hotly debated topics in Norwegian politics had been the question of possible Norwegian membership in the Common Market (EEC). This issue split public opinion in unusual ways, and pitted erstwhile allies against each other, while former political foes found themselves forming alliances. The leadership of the Labour Party (DNA-Social Democrats) and the Conservatives, representing the banking, shipping and industrial interests, strongly advocated such membership for Norway; the Agrarians, traditional allies of the Conservatives, rejected such membership as inimical to the national economy, especially agriculture, and in this they were joined by their long-standing left-wing enemies, the Communists. The other political parties of the Norwegian multiparty system experienced serious splits on this issue, as did many mass organisations. The most serious split was found in the trade union council (LO), whose leaders supported Labour's position, while the rank and file of the unions, most of whom were members of the DNA, rejected such membership. The bitter controversy in the unions weakened the hold over the LO by the DNA and opened up the possibility of increased Communist influence in this crucial organisation.

The NKP became one of the most outspoken elements in the anti-EEC coalition and the party leadership was jubilant when an 'advisory referendum' in 1972 rejected membership by a margin of 55 per cent to 45 per cent. For the first time in decades, the Norwegian Communists had demonstrated their ability to make meaningful alliances which could help broaden their appeal.[81]

The 'Common Market case' represented an illustration of the changing political circumstances in Scandinavia which seemingly enhanced the opportunities for the local Communists. During the 1960s and 1970s, much of Western Europe underwent a political and economic crisis, which resulted in considerable fragmentation of the political system in the area and some development towards realignment. Among many individuals and groups, old values were being questioned and occasionally rejected; the resulting political vacuum appeared well suited to those who would like to effect fundamental social change. For the Scandinavian Communists, one of the most important manifestations of this general crisis was the relative decline of the social democratic parties during this period. A generation of rule by the DNA in Norway was broken in 1963, and the political dominance of the Labourites, so much a feature of the post-war era, has been much less prevalent since. In Denmark, the SD (Social Democrats) could only maintain their position through coalitions. The Swedish Labour Party (SAP), while continuing its position as the ruling party, increasingly relied upon support from the VPK, thus significantly enhancing the political position of the Swedish Communists.[82]

Communist policies under these circumstances were unusually flexible, relying upon the ability of the party strategists and tacticians to develop approaches which could suit the prevailing local conditions in the time frame needed. This tactical flexibility was not unique in the history of international Communism; after all, the Comintern had advocated such approaches as part of the policy of 'united fronts' during the period 1921–1927/8 and the 'Labour Party' concept of the late 1920s.[83] The difference was essentially embodied in the fact that the earlier policies were carried out under Soviet auspices, while the new flexibility of the 1960s and 1970s was draped in the spirit of *national* Communism and even rejection of the CPSU as the would-be centre of the movement.

Despite the advantages offered by political events during this period and the development of national Communism in

Scandinavia, the results were disappointing from the Communists' point of view. Except for a period in Sweden, the
local Communist parties failed to enhance their influence in the
parliamentary democracies of the area to any marked degree. In
the trade unions, the social democrats by and large maintained
their control. The control of the peace groups and the Vietnam
movement remained in the hands of social democrats or other
non-Communist elements. The ability of the Norwegian
Communists to capitalise on the EEC issue did not translate
into lasting gains in political influence and power. And the
political polarisation of the Scandinavian countries, which had
opened opportunities for increased Communist leverage on their
immediate right, also brought a bewildering array of other leftist
groups willing, able and anxious to challenge the Communists.
Of the greatest importance in this context were the Danish and
Norwegian Socialist People's parties (SF); these organisations
provided local radicalism with an organisational outlet which
was not tainted by its reputation as a long-standing lackey of
Moscow, recent statements to the contrary notwithstanding.[84]

By the mid-1970s, then, the Scandinavian Communists,
despite their innovative policies, had been outmuscled by the
social democrats and the SF, while at the same time losing
credentials with the extreme left. The 15 years of
'Eurocommunist' policies in Norway and Sweden had not
resulted in dramatic and lasting gains; in Denmark, where the
Communist Party had maintained a more 'orthodox' stance on
many domestic issues, while remaining a rather reliable ally of
the CPSU internationally, some electoral and organisational
successes had been scored. Thus, in the parliamentary elections
in Denmark in 1971, the DKP got 1.4 per cent of the total votes,
but in 1973, this figure had increased to 3.6 per cent. In 1975,
the DKP reached its highest support level in the 1970s; in that
year, the party obtained 4.2 per cent of the total vote. In the elections in 1977, the support for the Danish Communists had fallen
to 3.7 per cent – still a respectable figure by Scandinavian
standards.[85]

In Norway, the NKP has generally fared less well than the
DKP. In 1969, the Communists obtained 1.0 per cent of the
total vote, and in 1977, 0.4 per cent. In 1973, the NKP was
junior partner in the electoral alliance with the SF and assorted
other leftist groups; this alliance, named SV, got 11.2 per cent

of the total that year, but the Communist contribution to this figure was considerably smaller than that of the SF.[86]

In Sweden, the VPK has obtained the following support in recent parliamentary elections: 1970: 4.8 per cent; 1973: 5.3 per cent; 1976: 4.8 per cent.[87] While this proportion is higher than the one found in Denmark, it should be noted that the then SKP was more successful in the 1950s and part of the 1960s, so that the results of the 1970s represent stagnation, even some retreat, whereas the DKP has improved its position in Danish politics, compared to earlier decades.

The improvement in the fortunes of the DKP is likely to be due primarily to the relative economic crisis in Denmark, which produced unprecedented unemployment there, and also to the fact that the Danish social democrats never obtained the dominant position in the left-of-centre arena as did their Norwegian and Swedish counterparts.

As indicated above, the position of the three Scandinavian Communist parties remained marginal in their national politics during the 1960s and 1970s. Under these circumstances, the three parties were confronted with the need to re-assess their policies once again.

10 Iceland: the Success Story Continues

The re-assessment of policy which confronted the Scandinavian Communists in the early and mid-1970s was not necessary in Iceland. As discussed above, the SA-SF had never succumbed to Stalinism even at the height of conformity elsewhere, and the de-Stalinisation process, which had been so painful elsewhere, hadno real counterpart on the island. Instead, the party continued its pragmatic policies, emphasising the need for social and economic reform and betterment in the standard of living, rather than broad visions of revolutionary change. The AB also continued its emphasis on nationalism, and during the 1960s it had plenty of opportunity to show its devotion to the Icelandic national cause, in so far as the country became embroiled in the so-called 'cod war' with the United Kingdom. In this conflict, which was perceived by the Icelanders as an economic problem of the greatest magnitude, the Communists took a hard-line stance and in fact appeared to be even more nationalistic than many of the parties and groups on their right. Such a policy was enormously popular with the Icelandic public, who were thus confirmed in their long-held conviction that the local Communists were active and respectable players in the *national* field of politics, and did not represent foreign powers or parties. This sense of legitimacy in turn helped propel the Icelandic Communists to the pinnacle of power in the period 1971–4, when the party participated in a coalition government.[88]

Another source of Communist influence in Iceland was the pervasive anti-Americanism resulting from the presence of US air crews and other military personnel at Keflavik, a major air base outside the capital of Reykjavik. This factor, together with anti-British feeling engendered by the conflict over fishing rights and territorial waters, produced a favourable climate for anti-Western and anti-NATO views. During the 1960s and 1970s there were periodic negotiations over the status of Keflavik, but the results tended to uphold the *status quo*. The continuing debate on this issue nevertheless produced opportunities for the AB to show its national profile on yet another explosive issue.[89]

When a partial reorganisation took place in the AB in 1968,[90] the result was essentially a continuation of the previous coalition of 'progressive' elements. There were leftist social democrats as well as Communists in this coalition, and even a smattering of left-leaning elements outside the traditional party lines. The dominant position was held by the Communists, who furnished the head of the new party, Ragnar Arnalds. It was nevertheless symptomatic of the broad base of the party (both ideologically and in terms of popular support) that many of the policies conducted by the AB were carried on without any real change. The new AB proved to be every bit as nationalistic and concerned with pragmatic social and economic issues as its predecessor, and ideological rigidity took a back seat in the new coalition as it had in the former party. Once again, such a policy was bound to produce important practical results, as evidenced by AB participation in the coalition government (headed by the Liberals) during the period 1971–4. Even after the AB left the coalition, it has continued as a major force in Icelandic politics.[91]

The successes of the SA–SF, and later the AB, in parliamentary politics was matched by a continuation of Communist control of most of the trade unions. At the same time, the ideological and organisational fragmentation which had so severely reduced the prospects of the DKP, NKP and VPK was of rather small importance in Iceland. During the 1960s there did take place some splits on the left, whereby a small pro-Maoist group emerged (Communist Organisation of Marxists–Leninists). A few other groups also made their entry on the national political scene, some of them with a mixed ideological programme whose appeal was chiefly to students or high-school youth. On the whole, however, the SA–SF and AB succeeded in fending off any major challenges and remained by far the largest and most influential element on the Icelandic left.[92]

By far the most important split in the AB took place in 1967/8, when the group around Hannibal Valdimarsson split out of the coalition to form its own party, the Organisation of Leftists and Liberals (OLL). This considerably weakened the AB for a while, but only temporarily; by the 1970s their Communist-dominated coalition once again figured prominently in Icelandic national elections. Thus, in 1971, the AB obtained 17.1 per cent of the vote, and in 1974 18.3 per cent.[93] During the elections of 25 June 1978 a considerable realignment of Icelandic politics took place; a strong left-wing tendency propelled the AB once more into a coalition government (together with the social democrats and the progressives). The AB obtained 22.9 per cent of the total vote (the social democrats increased their share of the votes from 9.7 per cent in 1974 to 22.0 per cent this year, while the progressives lost many votes and declined to 16.9 per cent from 24.9 per cent in 1974. The largest party remains the Independent Party with 32.7 per cent of the vote, but this was a significant decline compared to 1974, when the party obtained 42.7 per cent of the vote).[94]

The steady march of the AB in electoral popularity and its frequent participation in national coalition governments testify to the viability of the 'national Communist' approach on the island.

One of the primary reasons for the Communists' success in holding their organisation basically intact undoubtedly stemmed from the party's stand on *international* Communism. As discussed above, the SA–SF, and now its successor AB, had always steered clear of ideological entanglements, and this position made it possible to survive the Sino–Soviet dispute without serious repercussions. Instead of taking sides in this dispute, the Icelandic Communists could point out that they had always supported the 'national road' to socialism and Communism, and hence the fact that two parties, the CPSU and the CCP, now struggled over 'models' to be followed had little relevance for Icelandic reality. The SA–SF and AB have emphasised the principle that each party must choose the path to be taken according to local political conditions and opportunities, and this position is certainly supportive of the autonomist stance advocated and practised by the Yugoslavs, Rumanians, Italians, French (since 1974–5) and the Spaniards, to name but a few protagonists of this approach. The Icelandic Communists have occasionally conferred with these parties and have quoted some of the policies of the latter category approvingly. Thus, the AB sent representatives to Bucharest during the crisis over the 'Prague Spring' in 1968, and there have been several subsequent visits to the PCR leadership as well. Contacts with the CPSU, on the other hand, have been minimal, and the SA–SF and AB have repeatedly rejected any notion of a centre of international Communism as absurd.[95]

The consistent AB rejection of any international centre and any one model of socio-economic and political development was most forcefully displayed in the Icelandic attitude towards the Czechoslovak invasion. For days the party castigated the invasion, and the Central Committee even passed a resolution emphasising the need for all Icelandic Communists to condemn such an act and threatening expulsion from the AB for anyone endorsing the 'imperialist activities' of the Soviet Union and her allies. This complete rejection was voiced on other occasions as well. The SA–SF and the AB have consistently refused to endorse any attempts to call international conferences for the purposes of establishing a compulsory policy line; in fact, the Icelanders have refused to participate in most of the parleys which have taken place.[96] In this, as in so many other fields, the Icelandic Communists remain staunchly nationalistic.

11 The Limits of Autonomy: the Scandinavians Reconsider their Position

By early 1970s it had become clear to the DKP, NKP and VPK that even their new and flexible policies had failed to gain much support in their local populations, and it was clear that a reconsideration of policy was necessary. In this endeavour the three parties chose different paths. The DKP, relying upon the continued economic crisis in Denmark (which had brought unemployment to an astonishing 9 per cent) and the continuing fragmentation of the Danish party system, maintained its policies largely intact, i.e. the party continued its policy of limited solidarity with the CPSU and the Soviet Union, while in the domestic sphere it attempted judicious use of united fronts and 'action unity' for the purpose of extending and expanding Communist influence. In Sweden, the VPK leadership under C. J. Hermansson continued its policies of moderation, emphasising co-operation with the social democrats (SAP) domestically while vociferously rejecting Soviet state policies and the position of the CPSU in the international arena.[97]

The most audacious attempts at breaking out of political isolation came from the NKP. The political debate over Norwegian membership of the Common Market had spawned several political groups, many of them against such membership. Involved in such groups were many members of the social democrats (DNA), whose views on this issue stood in sharp contrast to the pro-EEC policies of the party leadership. These elements of temporarily 'homeless' individuals became a major recruiting ground for the Socialist People's Party (SF), the NKP, and also some of the other leftist groups which had sprung upon the Norwegian scene in the 1960s. Out of this confusing welter of groups and individuals there emerged the so-called Socialist Electoral Alliance (SV), comprising the NKP, SF and assorted other groups, who had agreed to pool their resources before the 1973 parliamentary elections.

The SV was very successful in the 1973 elections, obtaining close to 12 per cent of the vote. Almost immediately the party leaders of the NKP and SF began talks designed to formalise the relationship in the SV by means of a merger of the two parties into a unified structure named Socialist Left Party (also SV in Norwegian). The head of the NKP, Reidar Larsen, wholeheartedly supported this approach and campaigned actively for it. In the SF, there was also agreement for such a merger, and this party actually began to dismantle its apparatus in preparation for the change. In the NKP, however, there was much trepidation about such a policy; merger with the SF in the SV would mean the organisational dismantling of the NKP for the first time since its inception in the autumn of 1923, and it appeared likely that the SF would dominate the leadership of the united party. In view of these dire possibilities, the majority of the NKP leadership rejected the 'Larsen line' and ousted the chairman

(November 1975). Larsen's place was taken by Martin Gunnar Knudsen, an old-time *apparatchik* with much more orthodox views on ideology, international solidarity and the Soviet Union. Despite statements emphasising the continuity of policy, the new NKP leadership has been considerably less willing to co-operate with the other elements of the Norwegian left. As a result, the NKP has once again dwindled into insignificance in terms of electoral and mass support. As for Reidar Larsen, the former head of the NKP became a prominent member of the new SV, and was elected to the Norwegian Parliament on the SV ticket.[98]

In the Swedish party, too, the autonomist position of the Hermansson leadership finally reached the limits of tolerable proportions for an important element of the VPK, the group around Hilding Hagberg and the Norrbotten party group. In the spring of 1977, the Hagberg faction split away and re-established itself as the Workers' Communist Party (APK). The main areas and issues which produced this split were familiar ones: Hagberg and his followers charged that the VPK had gone too far in its advocacy of an autonomist position in the international Communist movement, thereby seriously violating international solidarity and helping reactionary forces; furthermore, the VPK's domestic policies were seen as basically lacking in 'class content' and thus smacking of social democracy. Finally, the central leadership was accused of bureaucratism and deficiencies in communicating with the masses.[99]

The split in the Swedish party has reduced the influence of Communist movements in that country, even though the fortunes of such groups have not fallen as low as they did in Norway after the removal of the 'Larsen faction' in the NKP.

The experiences of the Norwegian and Swedish Communist parties suggest several major conclusions about the limits of 'autonomism' and moderation in international and domestic matters. In most West European Communist parties there remains a core of 'hard-liners' whose views will not permit a wholesale challenge to the authority of the Soviet Union as a state and the CPSU as the self-proclaimed leader of the international Communist movement. Whenever such tendencies develop, European Communist parties stand in danger of severe factionalism and possible formal splits. Thus, while relative autonomy from the CPSU and the Soviet Union has become a major fact in the international movement, the *limits* of such a position should also be firmly kept in mind.

A second aspect of the Scandinavian experience with possible lessons for the student of 'Eurocommunism' stems from the Norwegian experiment with organisational dismantling of the Communist *apparat* and the fusion of this *apparat* with other, more powerful, political structures. This issue has become relevant in several countries during the last decade, as Communists have moved to make their programmes more palatable to a wider electorate and broader sectors of the population. Various attempts have been made to enhance the political and organisational flexibility of European Communism in the pursuit of this goal, as witnessed by the PCI's quest for the 'historic compromise', and the PCF's rather abortive electoral alliance with the French socialists. Nowhere did the local Communists go as far as they did in Norway, where the NKP leadership seriously contemplated its own dismantling. Startling as this development was, it also carried with it a predictable rift which in fact demonstrated that the NKP was *not* ready to disappear as a political entity, no matter what the gains of an organisational merger and the electoral and aggregative drawbacks of maintaining a separate entity. The 'core' of the NKP leadership could not stomach such a decision. It also appears unlikely that other European Communist parties will agree to preside over their own organisational demise in the foreseeable future.

If there is still a residue of international solidarity focusing on the Soviet Union and the CPSU, and if the local Communist parties in Western Europe remain dedicated to the maintenance of their organisational entities and a core of ideological beliefs, one may fairly accurately predict the limits of political concessions to be expected from such parties in future situations which may require their participation in coalition governments and other structures associated with pluralistic democracies. While such prospects remain remote in Scandinavia, the behaviour of the DKP, NKP and VPK/APK is nevertheless illustrative of both the dilemma of 'Eurocommunism' and the problems associated with this old, yet recently very relevant, problem. Basically, even Western European Communist parties dedicated to the principles hailed by Carrillo, Berlinguer, Kanapa and Elleinstein can be expected to produce policies which will have a significant impact on the socio-economic systems of their respective states, and the *political* system will likely be transformed to a considerable extent, in conformity with a 'core' of ideological beliefs and programmes. This, then, remains a likely scenario confronting policy-makers in the US and elsewhere, should 'Eurocommunism' succeed in a Western European country.

12 Conclusion

The story of Scandinavian communism (excluding Iceland) is fairly familiar to any student of Western European Communism. During the first few years after the Russian Revolution, socio-economic and political conditions in Europe were relatively favourable for left-wing radicalism. The aftermath of the war brought economic trouble and severe social dislocations. The destruction of old empires, the creation of new states, and, above all, the searching questions about old forms of authority and values – all of these tendencies favoured individuals, groups and movements questioning the existing order and demanding something new in human organisation and political life. Severe economic inequities, which had been further exacerbated by the war, cried out for redress. Into this favourable environment stepped the various Communist parties of Europe. They are riding the crest of revolutionary optimism, which had been strengthened by the successful *coup* in Petrograd, and the initial platforms of these groups found considerable support in wide circles of the European populations. The quest for a new socio-economic and political order seemed appropriate and necessary after the holocaust of world conflagration, and the left-wing forces seemed the ones to complete this quest.

One of the characteristics of early Western European Communism was its emphasis on humanism and the liberation of the human spirit, as well as individual self-fulfilment. Together with this emphasis came the willingness to develop policies which were relevant in the local environment of each party. This 'localism' clashed with the fundamental tenets of centralism and 'hegemonism' displayed by Lenin and his successors in the Comintern. By late 1923, the CPSU had successfully gained unquestioned control over the Comintern and had begun the process of 'Bolshevisation' of Western European parties – essentially a process which ensured the complete subordination of the latter parties to the CPSU, even to the point of direct Soviet intervention in the decision-making processes of these parties and the adoption of Soviet-derived phraseology in the party platforms and slogans. This subjugation of a national profile to Soviet *diktat* had predictable results: Western European Communism in general, and Scandinavian Communism in particular, dwindled into insignificance. It took the exceptional circumstances of another world war and the death of Stalin to bring back some of the flexibility and policy autonomy of the early period after the Russian Revolution.

After 1953, and especially after the outbreak of the Sino–Soviet dispute in 1960, relative autonomy has again been demanded and partly achieved by some of the Scandinavian parties, notably the NKP and VPK. In both cases, the emphasis on 'national roads' and criticism of the CPSU and the Soviet Union resulted in splits in the Norwegian and Swedish parties, whereby more 'orthodox' and pro-Soviet organisations were established. In the Danish case, the DKP never demanded the kind of autonomy which had been achieved by the other two Scandinavian Communist parties, and remained one of the more loyal followers of Moscow in Western Europe. Special socio-economic circumstances in Denmark during the 1960s nevertheless made it possible for the DKP to maintain its position in the Danish electorate, indeed to expand it somewhat.

The emphasis on 'national roads', nationalism and political democracy, which had been evident in the Norwegian and Swedish cases for a period of time prior to the mid-1970s, indicates that 'Eurocommunism', which has become a major focus of interest in the last few years, is in fact a much older phenomenon. It can be argued that 'Eurocommunism' is the *earliest* form of Communist policy, and that the present programme of the PCI, PCE, PCF, VPK and, until 1975, the NKP, in fact hark back to the early 1920s, prior to 'Bolshevisation'. Seen in this perspective, 'Eurocommunism' is not a deviant development; it is rather the intervening decades of CPSU control over the international movement that stand out as extraordinary.

Iceland is a special case in the Nordic context. The Icelandic Communist Party was founded much later than the other parties of the north, and the policies of the SA–SF and AB always emphasised the 'national road' and the need for a broad coalition of the left, while at the same time rejecting an international centre. The Icelandic Communists are therefore the original 'Eurocommunists' – a fact which is illustrated by the spectacular electoral success of the party. The Icelandic case rests, to some extent, upon special circumstances on the island, but it also suggests that there are considerable possibilities for native radicalism on the left in the four Nordic countries. Unfortunately for the three Scandinavian parties, their long history of sectarianism has helped the social democrats and the other socialist parties (SF, SV) of the area to pre-empt the field of leftist popular support. Under these circumstances, the future looks rather bleak for the Danish, Norwegian and Swedish Communists in terms of mass support. For the AB, however, future prospects look reasonably good, as indicated also by the election results of the summer of 1978. Thus Iceland will most likely remain as the most successful example of 'national Communism' in the Nordic countries and, indeed, in all of Western Europe.

Notes

1. An example of this outlook can be found in the *Klassekampen* (*The Class Struggle*), organ of the youth organisation in the Norwegian Labour Party (DNA), e.g. 31 October 1919.
2. I have dealt extensively with this problem in my *The Soviet Communist Party and Scandinavian Communism: the Norwegian Case* (Universitetsforlaget, Oslo, 1973), especially Chs. II, VII.
3. For a discussion of local government and administration under the Tsars, see S. Frederick Starr, *Decentralization and Self-Government in Russia, 1830–1870* (Princton University Press, Princeton, 1972).
4. I have based this summary on a number of works on Scandinavian history, e.g. Sten Carl Oscar Carlsson, *Svensk Historia* (*History of Sweden*) (2 vols., Svenska Bokförlaget, Stockholm, 1964); Stewart Oakley, *A Short History of Denmark* (Praeger Publishers, New York, 1972); Andreas Holmsen, *Norges Historie fra de eldste tider til eneveldets innførelse i 1660* (*History of Norway from the Oldest Times to the Establishment of Absolutism in 1660*) (Universitetsforlaget, Oslo, 1961); and Magnus Jensen, *Norges Historie Under Eneveldet 1660–1814* (*History of Norway under Absolutism 1660–1814*) (Universitetsforlaget, Oslo, 1962).
5. Ibid.
6. An enormous amount of work has been done on Russian history and traditions. See, for example, George Vernadsky (ed.), *A Source Book for Russian History from Early Times to 1919* (3 vols., Yale University Press, New Haven, Conn. 1972), e.g. 'The Popular Response to the Emancipation', pp. 604–5 (from the memoirs of Prince Kropotkin).
7. On the early educational policies of the Scandinavians see, for example, M. Donald Hancock, *Sweden: the Politics of Postindustrial Change* (The Dryden

Press, Hinsdale, Ill., 1972), especially ch. 1; see also Stein Rokkan *et al., Citizens, Elections, Parties* (David McKay, New York, 1970), especially Ch. 3.

8. The DNA position on international supervision and control was fiercely debated in several party congresses. The reports from these congresses show the basic position taken, e.g. in *Arbeiderbladet* (Oslo), 3 November 1923. See also the debates at the plenum of the Executive Committee of the Communist International (ECCI) in 1923, published in *Die Kommunistischen Parteien Skandinaviens und Die Kommunistische Internationale* (Carl Hoym Nachf. Louis Cahnbley, Hamburg, 1923).

9. The principles of organisation and policy were set down at the second Comintern congress; see *Der Zweite Kongress Der Kommunistischen Internationale* (Carl Hoym Nachf. Louis Cahnbley, Hamburg, 1929), especially pp. 443–81.

10. For a discussion of the DNA position, see Knut Langfeldt, *Moskvatesene i norsk politikk* (*The Moscow Theses in Norwegian Politics*) (Universitetsforlaget, Oslo, 1961), pp. 49–59; the Danish Communist Party (DKP) has been discussed by Peter P. Rohde, 'The Communist Party of Denmark' in A. F. Upton, *Communism in Scandinavia and Finland: Politics of Opportunity* (Anchor Books, New York, 1973), pp. 3–35; on Sweden, see Åke Sparring, 'The Communist Party of Sweden', ibid., pp. 61–99.

11. See, for example, 'Iceland' in *Yearbook on International Communist Affairs 1968* (Hoover Institution Press, Stanford, Calif.: 1969), pp. 295–7.

12. *Der Zweite Kongress*, pp. 443–81.

13. Rohde and Sparring in *Communism in Scandinavia and Finland* (on the DKP and SKP); see also my *The Soviet Communist Party and Scandinavian Communism*, especially Ch. II, for the NKP.

14. *Der Zweite Kongress*, pp. 443–81.

15. E.g. Martin Tranmael, 'Die Fragen der Kommunistischen Partei Norwegens', *Die Kommunistische Internationale*, no. 26 (1923), pp. 74–7.

16. Rohde, 'The Communist Party of Denmark' in Upton, *Communism in Scandinavia and Finland* (1973): on Sweden, see Åke Sparring, *Från Höglund Till Hermansson: Om Revisjonismeni Sveriges Kommunistiska Parti* (*From Höglund to Hermansson: About Revisionism in the Communist Party of Sweden*) (Stockholm, 1967).

17. Gilberg, *The Soviet Communist Party*, especially Chs. I, II.

18. The ECCI defended its position in an open letter to the DNA. See 'Die Exekutive der Komintern an den zentralvorstand der Norwegischen Arbeiterpartei', *Inprekorr*, no. 290 (31 October 1922), pp. 1444–6.

19. *Yearbook on International Communist Affairs 1968*, pp. 295–7.

20. Milorad M. Drachkovich, *The Comintern* (F. A. Praeger, New York, 1966).

21. Jane Degras, *The Communist International 1919–1943* (3 vols., Oxford University Press, London, 1956–65), e.g. vol. 2, pp. 432–6 (on trade union policy).

22. Ibid.

23. Ibid.

24. For a discussion of Finnish policy during this period, see Juho Kusti Paasikivi, *Minnen (Memoirs)* (2 vols., Bonmier, Stockholm, 1958). See also George Maude, *The Finnish Dilemma* (Oxford University Press, New York, 1976).

25. This was the case in a purge of 'rightist elements' in the NKP in 1930. For a detailed discussion, see Gilberg, *The Soviet Communist Party*, pp. 71–5.

26. Ibid., pp. 68–80.

27. E.g. Sparring in Upton, *Communism in Scandinavia and Finland*, especially

pp. 68–72.

28. Gilberg, *The Soviet Communist Party*, p. 87.

29. Ibid., p. 94.

30. Franz Borkenau has discussed the failure of the Comintern to compete with the social democrats; see his *European Communism* (Faber and Faber, London, 1953).

31. An example of this kind of reasoning can be found in the decisions of the NKP Central Committee in October 1929, in *Den Nye Kurs. NKPs Centralstyremøtes Beslutninger 26. 27. og 28. Oktober 1929 (The New Course. The Decisions of the NKP Central Committee October 26, 27, and 28, 1929)* (Samtrykk, Oslo, 1929).

32. The war policies of the three parties have been discussed in Rohde. 'The Communist Party of Denmark' and Sparring, 'The Communist Party of Sweden', both in Upton, *Communism in Scandinavia and Finland*, pp. 13–19 and 70–80 respectively. On the NKP, see Gilberg, *The Soviet Communist Party*, Ch. IV.

33. Ibid.

34. The policies of the DKP and the NKP, which now stressed national liberation and the co-operation of all anti-Fascist forces, helped establish legitimacy for the two parties. For a detailed policy statement of the NKP's underground activity, see the letter from Peder Furnbotn to the NKP branches, published in *Vårt partis politikk under krigen (The Policy of Our Party during the War)* (A/S Enersens Trykkeri, Oslo, 1945), pp. 39–45.

35. The order to dissolve the Comintern has been discussed by Adam Ulam in his *Expansion and Coexistence* (Praeger, New York, 1974), pp. 346–7.

36. *Vårt partis politikk under krigen*, pp. 138–62.

37. *Yearbook on International Communist Affairs 1970*, pp. 203–6.

38. The present situation in Iceland (autumn 1978) illustrates this tendency. The AB (a coalition under Communist leadership) is one of three parties presently controlling the government. For a detailed report on the results of the elections in June 1978, see *Thjodviljinn* (Reykjavik), 26 and 27 June 1978.

39. *Yearbook on International Communist Affairs 1970*, pp. 203–6.

40. The programme of the AB was discussed in *Friheten* (Oslo), 27 October–1 November 1969.

41. *Yearbook on International Communist Affairs 1970*, pp. 203–6.

42. Discussed also in Åke Sparring *et al.*, *Kommunismen i norden og krisen i den kommunistiske bevegelse (Communism in the Nordic Countries and the Crisis in the Communist Movement)* (Oslo, 1965).

43. Derived from Upton, *Communism in Scandinavia and Finland*, pp. 19–20, and 80–1 (Denmark and Sweden). For Norway, see Gilberg, *The Soviet Communist Party*, pp. 129–32.

44. The imposition of the 'two-camp theory', of which these programme elements were an integral part, has been discussed by Zbigniew K. Brzezinski, *The Soviet Bloc* (Harvard University Press, Cambridge, Mass., 1967), especially pp. 67–84.

45. Ibid.

46. Ibid.

47. This campaign was especially virulent in Norway. See the reports of the trade union congress (LO) in 1946, in *Kongressen 1946 (The Congress of 1946)* (Oslo, 1946).

48. E.g. *Friheten*, 9 August 1947 (editorial).

49. The CPSU in fact intervened directly in internal party affairs in Scandinavia, e.g. in the NKP purge of 1949–50. For a detailed discussion of the purge, see the statement by the NKP Chairman, Emil Løvlien, at the 1950 Extraordinary Congress, in Norges kommunistiske parti, *Partiets konsolidering og*

Communism in the Nordic Countries 257

oppgjøret med det annet sentrum (The Consolidation of the Party and the Reckoning with the Second Centre) (A/S Norske Forlag Ny Dag, Oslo, 1950).

50. Rohde and Sparring in Upton, *Communism in Scandinavia and Finland*, pp. 21–6 and 84–8 respectively (Denmark and Sweden). For Norway, see Gilberg, *The Soviet Communist Party*, Ch. V. The NKP version of this period can be found in Just Lippe, *Norges Kommunistiske Partis Historie (The History of the Norwegian Communist Party)* (Norges Kannunistiske Parti, Oslo, 1963).

51. See Løvlien, *Partiets konsolidering.*

52. The purge was again discussed in *Friheten*, 29 October 1949, and in *Partiets konsolidering.*

53. See Denmark, Statistiske Department, *Statistisk Årbog 1956 (Statistical Yearbook 1956)*, pp. 239–41; Norway, Central Bureau of Statistics, *Statistical Yearbook 1961*, pp. 318–20; Sweden, Statistiska Centralbyrån, *Statistisk Årsbok för Sverige 1952 (Statistical Yearbook of Sweden 1952)*, pp. 318–20.

54. *Yearbook on International Communist Affairs 1970*, pp. 205–7.

55. Ibid.

56. The draft of the programme can be found in *Friheten*, 21 March 1953.

57. *Yearbook on International Communist Affairs, 1969*, p. 755.

58. Ibid., p. 265.

59. The demands for more information from the CPSU reflected the problems now faced by local Communist leaders, e.g. Reidar R. Larsen in *Friheten*, 22 June 1956:

We must regret that we still have not received complete information from the Soviet CP . . . We are shocked over this lawlessness, and we condemn it, because we fight for security under the law . . . However one looks at the matter, it is still clear that there must have been a period when the collective leadership permitted the cult of the personality to start . . . It is important to have this clarified. It is the case that not only did leading persons selfishly create for themselves authority under which they arbitrarily could act as they pleased, but also that other leading comrades permitted this to happen.

60. For a discussion of the NKP policies towards the Norwegian left in this period, see *Friheten*, 23 March 1957 (editorial).

61. Sveriges Kommunistiska Parti, *Nutid-framtid. Arbertarrörelsens programdebatt. (Present-Future. The Programme Debate in the Labour Movement)* (Stockholm, 1957), especially pp. 132–48.

62. Brzezinski, *The Soviet Bloc*, especially pp. 185–210.

63. See Gilberg, 'Patterns of Nordic Communism', *Problems of Communism* (May–June 1975), pp. 20–35.

64. Ibid.

65. I have derived this material from the relevant Danish press, as follows: *Land og Folk* (DKP); *Fremad* (Danish Communist Youth League); *Kommunistisk Orientering* (KAK); *Kommunist* (KFML), *Ungkommunist* (KUF), and Danish dailies such as *Politiken* (Copenhagen).

66. Derived from *Friheten* (NKP); *Orientering* (SF); *Arbeiderbladet* (DNA); *Klassekampen* (AKP-ML); *Fremad* (KU), and Oslo dailies, especially *Aftenposten.*

67. Ibid.

68. Derived from *Ny Dag* (VPK); *Norrskensflamman* (APK); *Socialistisk Debatt* (APK); *Gnistan* (SKP), and Stockholm dailies such as *Dagens Nyheter* and *Stockholmstidningen.*

69. The first NKP statement on the invasion of Czechoslovakia can be found in *Friheten*, 23–29 August 1968. The VPK reacted in *Ny Dag*, 22–26 August 1968,

and was the first Swedish party to condemn the invasion.

70. Derived from an examination of the DKP, NKP and VPK dailies and the main organ of the PCR, *Scinteia*. See also my paper, 'The PCR and West European Communist Parties during the Last Decade: Autonomy and "National Roads" in Practice', presented at the 1978 Annual Conference of the International Studies Association, Washington, D.C., 22–25 February 1978 (to be published in a book edited by Walter Bacon, Pergamon Press, 1979).

71. Ibid.

72. Ibid.

73. The most scathing denunciation of 'state Communism' was voiced by Santiago Carrillo of the Spanish party (PCE) in his famous book *'Eurocommunism' and the State* (Lawrence Hill, Westport, Conn., 1978).

74. Gilberg, 'Patterns of Nordic Communism', for Denmark, Norway and Iceland. The Swedish position is derived from *Ny Dag*. See also interview with Hermansson in *Dagen Nyheter* (Stockholm), 1 April 1977.

75. Ibid.

76. Gilberg, 'Patterns of Nordic Communism', especially pp. 28–30.

77. E.g. *Friheten*, 21–26 August 1972, in which Reidar Larsen also criticised domestic policies in the Soviet Union.

78. 'Patterns of Nordic Communism', pp. 23–7.

79. This became one of the major campaign platforms for NKP Chairman Reidar Larsen in the electoral debates on Norwegian television in the summer and autumn of 1973.

80. E.g. Hermansson of the VPK in *Socialistisk Debatt* (*Socialist Debate*) (Stockholm), no. 5 (1977).

81. This alliance survived partly intact until the 1973 elections, in which the Socialist Electoral Alliance (SV) obtained 16 of 150 seats in the Parliament (Storting). See *Arbeiderbladet*, 12 and 13 September 1973 for complete results of the election.

82. The position of the VPK in Swedish politics has been discussed in *Yearbook on International Communist Affairs 1973*, pp. 223–5. The VPK's position on domestic issues was spelled out in great detail by Hermansson in *Ny Dag*, 4–8 February 1972.

83. For a discussion of this concept, see Gilberg, *The Soviet Communist Party*, pp. 65–7.

84. The successes of the SV in Norway in 1973 showed the extent to which such radicalism on the left could capitalise on selected issues such as the EEC debate.

85. Derived from the statistical yearbooks of Denmark, selected years, as follows: Denmark, Statistiske Departement, *Statistisk Aŕbog 1978*, pp. 340–2.

86. Derived from the statistical yearbooks of Norway as follows: Norway, Central Bureau of Statistics, *Statistical Yearbook 1977*, pp. 375–8.

87. Derived from the statistical yearbooks of Sweden, as follows: Sweden, Statistiska Centralbyrån, *Statistisk Årsbok för Sverige 1977*, pp. 491–2.

88. Gilberg, 'Patterns of Nordic Communism', pp. 32–5.

89. Ibid.

90. See *Yearbook on International Communist Affairs 1969*, pp. 429–33.

91. The AB is now back in a coalition government with the social democrats and the progressives. For election results, see *Thjodviljinn*, 26 and 27 June 1978.

92. Gilberg, 'Patterns of Nordic Communism', pp. 32–5.

93. *Yearbook of Nordic Statistics* (The Nordic Council, Stockholm, 1974), pp. 256–7.

94. *Thjodviljinn*, 26 and 27 June 1978.

95. Gilberg, 'Patterns of Nordic Communism', pp. 32–5.
96. Ibid.
97. See, for example, Hermansson in *Ny Dag*, 4–8 February 1972.
98. Per Egil Hegge, '"Disunited" Front in Norway,' *Problems of Communism* (May–June 1976), pp. 49–59.
99. See Rolf Hagel, Chairman of the APK, in *Norrskensflamman*, 30 March 1977.

8

AUSTRIA: FROM ORTHODOXY TO
'NORMALISATION'

Karl Stadler

To study the history and the role of the Communist Party of
Austria (KPÖ) in the context of Eurocommunism may at first
sight appear unjustified, for this is the party which has survived
intact every one of the crises that the world Communist
movement experienced since 1945: the Titoist heresy, the
Hungarian Revolution, the Chinese defection and the Prague
Spring. It has lost several generations of leading cadres in the
process, and most of its members and voters; but this does not
appear to diminish its loyalty to the CPSU. If one cared to
prophesy, one might reckon with the probability that just as an
Austrian delegate was the first, in March 1919, to propose the
founding of the Communist International, so the KPÖ will be the
last of the parties outside the 'Socialist Camp' to leave the Soviet
embrace.

But what makes Austria remarkable among the post-1945
nations of Europe is that she was the only one under (partial)
Soviet occupation to be evacuated after the 1955 state treaty with
her social structure intact, her political system of a Western
mould, and her Communist Party of no weight or influence. The
explanation for this lies in the very origin of the new state in
1918 when it resisted the temptation to follow the example of
Soviet Russia, thus avoiding the disasters of Hungary and
Bavaria, and embarked instead on the course of a Western-style
parliamentary democracy.

Even though the twin pressures of Italian Fascism and German
National Socialism induced Austrian right-wing groups to set up
their own Austro-Fascist version of the corporate state in 1934,
Austria was always considered part of the Western political
system, a fact which the Soviet Union recognised in its political
strategy during the second World War. The division of Eastern
Europe into separate spheres of influence which the Allies agreed
upon at the Yalta Conference in 1945 left Austria clearly outside
the Soviet sphere. Whether the Russian foothold in eastern
Austria as part of the quadripartite occupation of the country left

open an option for the subsequent dismemberment of Austria as happened in the parallel case of Germany must remain idle speculation.

Austrians are fond of ascribing the survival of their national unity to the diplomatic skill of their post-1945 statesmen; to this must undoubtedly be added the fact that Austria was of less importance than Germany in the post-war power game; that the Russians adhered strictly to the letter of their international commitments; and finally that they used Austria to demonstrate the new orientation in their foreign policy after the death of Stalin. But the Austrian story might also have taken a different turn: if the Western powers had made a false move (such as setting up a rival Austrian government, possibly in Salzburg in the US zone, in opposition to the Renner government in Vienna, as the Austrian pretender Otto Habsburg proposed), or if internal developments in Austria (such as a strong pro-Russian sentiment in the Soviet zone leading to the break-up of the all-party coalition government and the inclusion of eastern Austria in the Soviets' Eastern European domain) had played into the hands of the Russians. Fortunately for Austria, this did not happen.

We may not always learn enough from history to avoid making the same mistake twice, but in the case of Austria the lesson of 1934 and its fateful consequences in 1938 was not lost on the two great political camps, conservatives and socialists, many of whose leaders had endured a similar fate under Nazi rule. This new-found national unity proved stronger than right-wing separatist tendencies; it also worked against the Communist Party, which identified itself too closely with the Soviet interest; and it survived the break-up, in 1966, of the great coalition and the periods of one-party government, of the conservatives between 1966 and 1970 and of the socialists since 1970.

If these were the historic conditions that militated against the KPÖ after 1945, what of the subjective factors?

1 The First Republic

The insignificance of the Austrian Communist Party throughout its sixty years' existence – with the possible exception of a few turbulent months in 1919 and the period of the anti-Fascist underground struggle from 1934 to 1945 – is often explained by reference to the fact that the Austrian socialists were themselves so far to the left that there was no room for another radical Marxist party. There is certainly some truth in this assertion. 'Austro-Marxism' was a school of socialist theory and practice which combined the brilliant ideologue Otto Bauer with the learned reformist Karl Renner, the hard-hitting parliamentarian oppositionists with the sober municipal administrators of 'Red Vienna', the great philosophers and scholars with the creators of the first model of the modern welfare state. The Social Democratic Workers' Party of Austria (SDAP) was to the 'left' of most labour and socialist parties in its Marxist analysis of society and its affirmation of the class struggle including (theoretically) the temporary dictatorship of the proletariat to ward off a Fascist attack on democracy (Linz Programme, 1926). But it was no more 'left' than the British Labour Party, the SPD or the Scandinavians when it came to conducting practical politics in a hostile capitalist environment – it only sounded so; and later critics referred to the Austro–Marxists as 'sheep in wolves' clothing', 'Girondists masquerading as Jacobins'.

However, it was probably more than their ideological position or their radical language that made socialists immune to attacks from the left. There was first the charismatic role of Victor Adler, the man who had united the warring factions of moderates and radicals at the party conference at Hainfeld in 1888–9. He bequeathed to the party a healthy dislike of factionalism and put unity above all else – even above principles, as his critics would say. After his death in 1918 his mantle fell on his son Friedrich Adler, hero of the radicalised masses for the assassination of the Prime Minister in 1916, and on others of the wartime left, notably Otto Bauer. While the right wing with Karl Renner governed the country, the left wing took over the party organisation whose position to the left of the Labour and Socialist International even led to a short-lived grouping with like-minded parties in the 'International $2\frac{1}{2}$'.

It is tempting to speculate on the course Austrian history might have taken if Friedrich Adler had accepted the invitation to lead the newly founded Communist Party and had taken a large number of followers with him. As it was, without him the KPÖ started life without a single well known leader or official. Instead it was led by a curious mixture of radical working men, political adventurers, uprooted intellectuals often of Eastern European or Jewish origin, and a number of former prisoners of war who had participated in the Russian Revolution.[1] What mass basis it had was among the unemployed and the returned soldiers, whereas the workers' councils and the urban populations generally remained in the socialist camp.

Third, there was the demarcation line between European labour and Bolshevism clearly drawn by Otto Bauer, which succeeded in plausibly combining an expression of solidarity, even admiration, for the Russian Revolution with the utter rejection of Communism as totally unsuitable to Western European conditions.[2] This seemed the more convincing to the working class, since the period 1918 to 1920 was the time when many of the traditional political and social demands of Austrian labour were at last realised by the young Republic, especially in the field of social legislation: what need was there for a Communist party and bloody revolution?

It is not quite so obvious why working-class loyalty and support for the SDAP remained unimpaired in later years when the police could shoot 89 workers in the streets of Vienna (1927), when the constitution had to be amended under right-wing pressure (1929), when the Heimwehr movement proclaimed a Fascist state as its aim (1930), and when Chancellor Dollfuss suspended Parliament and began to govern by emergency decrees (1933). Even when the workers at last rose up in defence of the Republic, in February 1934, it was done against the will and the instructions of the party executive. In all those years the SDAP, in spite of its cautious and defensive policy, lost little of its mass support to the Communists – partly because of its clever tactics of allowing a radical opposition within its own ranks and partly because of the utter unattractiveness of the KPÖ. Its modest chance, ineptly used, only came in the Austro–Fascist period of 1934 to 1938 with the destruction of the democratic system and the workers' organisations.[3]

On the face of it, Communist policy and warnings seemed at last to be vindicated by events: the social democratic reliance on the parliamentary road to socialism proved an illusion, the ruling classes when faced with a socialist majority resorted to Fascist methods, and abetted by the imperialist Western powers the Fascist bloc was preparing an attack on the only workers' state, the Soviet Union. Although the Austrian working class – unlike the German – had at least put up a token resistance, without a strong Communist Party it was bound to fail, and it had failed;

the moral seemed obvious.

For a time the early underground groupings that attempted to rebuild a socialist party out of the ruins of a once mighty movement were clearly on the defensive, ideologically as well as organisationally, for the KPÖ had been banned the year before and was ready with an underground party organisation to receive into its ranks disappointed socialists, create a new trade union structure, and open negotiations with the socialists for a united front from a position of strength it had never known before. But the parity with the underground 'Revolutionary Socialists' which the KPÖ now enjoyed by no means indicated the conversion of the majority of the 600,000 former social democrats to Communism. In the first instance, as in all other resistance movements that were to arise in Europe in the following years, only the bravest and most determined join an underground movement and risk their freedom, their jobs, and possibly their lives. The great majority may still sympathise with the activists, support them in political demonstrations or in industrial action, donate to their secret funds and read their leaflets and newspapers, but they cannot be enlisted in a network of illegal party organisations. Thus the claim that during the Fascist period the KPÖ had become 'the other great workers' party' is justified only in respect of the active members of the left-wing underground; the great mass of socialist party members and voters bided their time and remained pretty well what they had always been, as the election results of 1945 were to prove.

The Communist ascendancy was also short-lived: even radical left-wing socialists found it increasingly difficult to co-operate with a highly centralised party that received its marching orders from abroad and was clearly an agency of the Soviet leadership even when, under Georgi Dimitroff, the Comintern had temporarily changed its course and proclaimed the policy of popular fronts against Fascism. In addition to this, the series of Moscow trials, which the Communists defended vociferously, revived all the socialist suspicions which the common struggle had temporarily allayed. And the one positive contribution to a united Austrian front against Nazism, Alfred Klahr's thesis on the development of the Austrian nation, was overlaid with unprincipled concessions to reactionary traditionalist sentiment.

Similar concessions marked the whole of the people's front campaign internationally. The more murderous the Stalinist terror became inside the Soviet Union, the more conciliatory to bourgeois interests, real or imaginary, the Communist parties appeared. It did not pass unnoticed in the socialist underground that the red flag was replaced by the tricolour in the demonstrations of the French Communists, who now preferred to call themselves 'Communist Frenchmen'; that the CPGB advocated a 'people's front' extending from Harry Pollitt to Winston Churchill; and that in war-torn Spain the Communist Party used the struggle against Fascism for a war of extermination against the left of the POUM and the anarchists. Events in Spain were a particularly sensitive issue in the Austrian underground which provided a strong contingent of the International Brigades, and aid to Spain was one of the few issues on which socialist-Communist co-operation initially functioned well

But the real parting of the ways came in August 1939 with the Hitler–Stalin Pact. From one day to the next the party line changed, and Communists were expected to accept the new course as unquestioningly as they had accepted the Dimitroff line of the Seventh World Congress. The remarkable thing was that the great majority did, after much initial confusion and heart-searching, as we know from the records of the Gestapo and the infamous 'people's courts' of the Nazis. Such loyalty to the Soviet Union and its interests did not, however, extend to the socialists, especially since all critics of the pact and sympathisers with the Western powers were branded in the underground Communist press as agents of Western imperialism. The German attack on the Soviet Union in June 1941 ended this sorry chapter in working-class history, but the Communist *volte-face* was not forgotten when the time came to express political preferences in a general election.[4]

2 The End of the War

What new strength and influence Communist parties possessed in 1944/5 all over the world was the result of the high prestige they had acquired in the anti-Fascist struggle. It is probably true to say that in most countries Communists were the bravest and the best organised of the resistance movements: no sacrifice seemed too great to assist the Soviet state in its heroic defence against the German invaders. That in this laudable endeavour caution was often thrown to the winds, and that the heavy price paid in human lives did not always match the actual achievements in no way detracts from the Communist contribution to the Allied cause. This was probably the greatest single political factor favouring the KPÖ after it emerged from the underground in 1945.

But there were other, practical, factors as well. That eastern Austria, and especially Vienna, was liberated by the Red Army, and that it took several months before Western forces moved into Vienna, gave the KPÖ the initial advantage of being the only party trusted and supported by the victors. Additional points in its favour were the possession of a military unit, the Austrian batallion of the Yugoslav partisan army, which supplied reliable members of the reorganised police force in Vienna; a central leadership which had prepared itself for its tasks in its Moscow exile; and party cadres steeled by the experience of underground work in Austria and abroad and in Nazi concentration camps, and by military service in one or the other resistance movement. Not surprisingly, Communist hopes ran very high at that time.

But some of these factors, instead of assisting the KPÖ, did considerable damage to its prospects. The presence of the Red Army was not an unmixed blessing, because for many months the conduct of troops who had experienced war at its worst left much to be desired, and the policy of arbitrary arrests and confiscation, followed by the take-over of all 'German' property and a hard occupation regime made the Communist Party which had to justify these policies appear as the 'Russian Party'. The advantages it had over other parties, especially its control over security and education through the two Communist members of the government, added to the general mistrust. As in other Eastern European countries, the return of the 'Bolshevik core' of the leadership from Moscow[5] did not increase its popularity; the socialists benefiting from the traditional loyalty of the working class reformed their party as a union of social democrats and revolutionary socialists and proclaimed that 'the class struggle was henceforth to be conducted within the government', while the People's Party, successor to the Christian Socials of Dollfuss and Schuschnigg and of other non-socialist groups, suddenly (and temporarily!) discovered an affinity to the British Labour Party. After twelve years of unrest, Fascism and war the people wanted moderate policies from people whom they knew and trusted.

What it really amounted to was that the new line of the KPÖ, patriotic and moderate, was simply not taken at its face value, but seen as another Communist tactic, like so many others before. This was due in part to memories of pre-war and wartime shifts and changes, in part also to first-hand impressions of Communism at work which large members of soldiers had gathered during the campaigns on Soviet soil. The uncritical and enthusiastic admiration for all things Russian boomeranged on Communist parties after 1945, and their protestations that they, too, were national parties were not believed.

The patriotic line of the KPÖ which was made possible by the seventh World Congress of the Comintern and was officially adopted in 1936–7 was further elaborated during the period of Nazi occupation and war in underground literature and broadcasts from Moscow.[6] The perspective was of a government of national unity representing the different social classes and political groupings (with the exception of the Nazis), the political parties to join for national purposes in a 'national front', supported by all-party trade unions, women's, youth and students' organisations. There were to be no revolutionary social changes, and the country was to return to the constitution of the First Republic. For the working classes the party envisaged not a united workers' party, which the socialists would have refused anyway, but merely a united front and a policy of co-operation.

Needless to say, the other two parties were unwilling to go beyond a government of national unity with the Communists, which was a necessary step at a time when the Red Army was in sole occupation of Vienna and the KPÖ moreover took a leading and wholly admirable part in the reconstruction of public life, of the administration and the economy. Its dilemma was that to make its line credible it had to abstain from an independent line in the government and could offer no plausible alternatives to majority decisions. The isolation of the party once it had withdrawn from government in 1947 stemmed from this prolonged insistence on a national unity of which it formed no real part; it became once more, as Josef Toch rightly calls it, an enclave in the political landscape of Austria.[7]

3 The Second Republic of Austria

The history of the KPÖ since the establishment of the Second Republic can best be summarised under two headings. There was, first, the role it played in national affairs, and, second, its own internal development; neither is exactly a success story.

When Karl Renner was allowed by the Soviet authorities to form a provisional Austrian government in April 1947, the Communists were treated as if they represented a considerable part of the electorate: Johann Koplenig, a diehard Stalinist and pre-war party leader, became Vice-Chancellor, Franz Honner, another old Communist and trade unionist, Minister of the Interior, and Ernst Fischer, a former social democrat writer and journalist, was made Minister of Education and Propaganda. It has never been established what the Communists' estimate of their strength was, but it could not have been far below 20 to 25 per cent, or they would not have agreed to the holding of parliamentary elections in November 1945, within nine months after the end of the war. This, in retrospect, may have been a tactical blunder, for the results, a mere 5 per cent of the total vote, immediately deprived them of the position of equal partnership with the other two parties and reduced them to one government post – the politically innocuous Ministry of Power.

John Erhardt, US Political Adviser in Austria, reported to Washington that Ernst Fischer had named four reasons for this disastrous result: the strength of traditional party allegiances, the desire for a return to normalcy, women's family solidarity with Nazi relatives, and the Russian occupation. Fischer's expectation that the KPÖ would leave the government altogether and that its role would be that of an 'anti-Fascist gadfly in Parliament'[8] was not realised until two years later when, in November 1947, the remaining Communist Minister resigned in protest against a currency reform law. The real reason may, however, well have been that after he had agreed with the whole government to accept Marshall Aid, the Soviet Union had denounced this as incompatible with the sovereign independence of states, and his resignation was the only way left open to him and his party.

In the meantime the KPÖ had lost face on two other burning political issues, both to do with the wretched problem of German assets in Austria to which the Soviets – like the other Allied Powers – were entitled by the Potsdam agreement. In view of the fact that all Austrian state and much private property (mostly Jewish) had passed into German hands after March 1938, it was extremely difficult to define German assets, and unlike the Western powers the Soviets took a hard line on this. In order to save as much as possible of its national assets, the Renner government passed a nationalisation law in the summer of 1945 which the Russians vetoed; after the second control agreement, however, an identical law was passed, against Communist opposition, in July 1946; it has made Austria the non-socialist country with the largest state-owned economy.

The Russians ignored the law in their occupation zone and set up the so-called USIA administration of about 300 enterprises, with approximately 60,000 employees, a Russian economic enclave in Austria. On both these issues, nationalisation and German assets, the KPÖ took a stand which supported the Russian claims and therefore contributed to its reputation as the 'Russian Party'.

There was one other occasion when Communists might have decisively influenced the course of Austrian politics. This came in September/October 1950, when working-class discontent with the fourth wage-price agreement resulted in a nation-wide protest on the part of wage-earners which the Communists attempted to exploit for their own purposes. This wave of strikes and demonstrations, subsequently referred to as the 'October Putsch', might well have caused a serious political crisis if the KPÖ had not bungled it. It was certainly not a *putsch*, and the Soviet authorities kept at a safe distance, but it was probably the last chance the KPÖ had to increase its influence, especially among the trade unions.

When at last the State Treaty was signed and brought Austria her full freedom after ten years of four-power occupation, only conservatives and socialists were given any credit for it: the KPÖ, which had never attempted to resolve a deadlock or offer suggestions that differed from the Soviet line, shared the blame for the long delay which was presented as being exclusively due to Soviet obstruction.

Anton Pelinka, a perceptive analyst of the Austrian political scene, offers the following seven reasons for the lack of Communist success in Austria:

(1) the KPÖ was unable to overcome its position as an outsider in the political spectrum;

(2) the early establishment of the Renner government fixed the pattern for a Western-style parliamentary system;

(3) the outcome of the November 1945 elections was the

most important single decision against Communism in Austria;

(4) lacking popular support, the only other chance for the KPÖ would have been a 'German solution' with the aid of the Soviet authorities. As the Soviet attitude towards the currency reform and the events of October 1950 showed, this was not their intention;

(5) the reputation of the KPÖ as the 'Russian Party' further militated against its chances. The ten years' presence of the Red Army in Austria brought more disadvantages to the party than it helped;

(6) in consequence it was considered an extra-territorial enclave by the two principal political camps;

(7) the conflict with the Communists as a 'hostile' and 'alien' element helped the non-Communist parties towards a policy of consensus and integration in the early period of the Second Republic.[9]

4 Elections since 1945

The steady decline of the KPÖ is best illustrated by the number of votes cast for it in successive national and local elections. In the eleven parliamentary elections held so far, the Communist share of the total vote dropped from 5.4 per cent to 0.96 per cent, though in absolute figures there was a slight increase in 1949 (the first elections held under normal conditions and after the return of POWs) and in 1953 at a time of great economic hardships. The disguises adopted at three elections, when the Communists entered the lists under different names (1949: Left Bloc; 1953: Austrian People's Opposition; 1956: Communists and Left Socialists) do not seem to have brought the desired results.

There is no accounting for the loss of nearly two-thirds of the party's voting potential between 1962 and 1970. The tactically disastrous decision in the 1966 elections to abstain (except in Vienna) seems to have accelerated the process of disenchantment (while doing great harm to the Socialists, who were criticised by their opponents for accepting Communist support). But it would appear that that part of the left-wing floating vote which was persuaded in 1966 that a Conservative victory had to be avoided at all costs did not subsequently revert to voting Communist. The decline in party membership – at present around 20,000 – went parallel with the electoral decline.

For obvious reasons the stipulation of the 1929 constitution

Table 8.1: Parliamentary Elections 1945–1974: the Communist Vote

	Votes	Percentage	Seats obtained
1945	174,257	5.4	4
1949	213,066	5.1	5
1953	228,159	5.3	4
1956	192,438	4.4	3
1959	142,478	3.3	0
1962	135,520	3.0	0
1966 (Vienna only)	18,636	0.4	0
1970	44,750	0.9	0
1971	61,762	1.3	0
1975	55,032	1.2	0
1979	45,270	0.96	0

that the Federal President be elected by popular vote was first observed in May 1951, after the death of Karl Renner. This was the one and only time the KPÖ decided on a candidate of its own, an unknown militant, who secured 219,969 votes against 1,682,768 for Theodor Körner, the successful socialist candidate, again a mere 5.1 per cent of the total vote.

Austria's economic structure is reflected in the election results for the nine provincial diets or *Landtage*: there was never any Communist representation in Vorarlberg, Tirol, Salzburg and Upper Austria; Burgenland lost its solitary member in 1956, Lower Austria its three members in 1959. Vienna, which had once had seven members, lost its last two in 1969. Carinthia, which had started with three and dropped to one, and Styria, which had gone from two to one, lost their last Communists in 1970. In the last-mentioned five *Lands* the Communist share of the vote today ranges from 0.36 per cent (Burgenland) to 1.27 per cent (Vienna). In the whole of Austria, among thousands of local councillors, there are 105 Communists: 61 in Lower Austria, 22 in Styria, 10 in Carinthia, 8 in Upper Austria and 2 each in Burgenland and Salzburg.

As is to be expected, Communist percentages are somewhat higher in elections to purely working-class bodies, such as Chambers of Labour and works councils in individual enterprises. Chambers of Labour are (almost uniquely Austrian) institutions representing all wage- and salary earners and acting in an advisory capacity on labour, economic and social legislation. In the last elections of Chamber councillors (*Kammerräte*) in 1974, the 1.9 million electors returned 531 socialists, 239 Christian trade unionists, 29 liberals, 10 Communists and one dissident Communist, a total of 810 representatives. Again, the KPÖ was only represented in Vienna and Styria (with 3 seats each), Lower Austria (2), Upper Austria and Carinthia (1 each), but in the elections of June 1979 they lost six of their 10 seats. As for works councils, in Austria's great national steel works, the VOEST-Alpine in Linz, for instance, the Communist share among manual workers is just over 6 per cent, and 2.3 per cent among white-collar workers. But even the most conscientious and courageous engagement of party members in the workshop or on union committees does not always yield political results: in this respect Austria is no different from many other industrial nations.

5 The International Scene

If the presence of Soviet troops and Soviet economic enclaves in Austria militated against the chances of the KPÖ, developments inside the adjoining 'people's democracies', notably in Czechoslovakia and Hungary, did even greater damage: the piecemeal destruction of democratic parties and parliamentary institutions, followed by the monstrous trials of Rajk, Slansky and others, was read as a warning by Austrians of where partnership with a Communist Party might lead. Strangely enough, none of these events affected the KPÖ internally, and the moral of Tito's defection was not understood; on the contrary, it inspired a violently anti-Titoist play, *The Great Betrayal*, by Ernst Fischer, later hero of the Communist dissidents. The dependence on the Soviet party was so complete that the first stirrings of conscience only came with Khrushchev's speech at the Twentieth Congress of the CPSU in 1956, but practical consequences for the Austrian party were not discussed until nine years later.

This speech, at first denounced as 'a fabrication of the US secret service', by criticising the terrorist rule of Stalin, offered Communist parties outside the Soviet Union a chance to break with the unwholesome past, but, significantly, this was not seized by Koplenig and Fürnberg (the *éminence grise* of the KPÖ), and it took events much nearer home before the Austrian party started to move.

The upheavals of late autumn 1956 in Poland and Hungary were at first officially explained as being due to 'mistakes' of the leadership, but when the Hungarian Revolution was crushed by the Red Army, the repercussions in neighbouring Austria were significant: while the KPÖ readily accepted the Soviet version of a counter-revolutionary attempt instigated by Western imperialism, approximately one-third of the membership left the party. An important section of critical activists, however, remained to continue the struggle for reform from within. These 'revisionists', the Eurocommunist element in the party, left ten years later after the Czech crisis; an earlier attempt to secure the adoption by the KPÖ of a Eurocommunist position, and the temporary confusion into which the party machine was thrown by events in Prague culminating in the condemnation of the invasion by the party's Central Committee, seemed to augur well for them.[10] But by March 1971 the party was safely back in the orthodox fold, at a cost of a further loss of membership, including most of the more experienced members of the Central Committee, editors of the party press, and intellectuals.

The present position of the KPÖ is the very reverse of Eurocommunism, if this term implies the emancipation from the CPSU and the recognition of pluralism in the world Communist movement.[11] Instead, the Austrian party has moved back to a Moscow-centred position which, by accepting the hegemony of the CPSU, has ruined its chances of operating successfully, or even plausibly, in the Austrian political system. It still keeps up the pretence that there is no serious rift in international Communism (apart from the Chinese CP), deals with Eurocommunist arguments, if it cannot ignore them, more in sorrow than in anger, but reserves its enthusiastic support for the orthodox parties.

It is inevitable that a small party like the KPÖ should depend on 'fraternal support' from the 'Socialist Camp', in particular the USSR and the German Democratic Republic. This support is bound to take two forms: financial, for the annual income of 5 million Austrian schillings which the party collected in dues and gifts over the last three years is utterly inadequate for maintaining its large organising staff; the estimated real income – six to seven times as much – is probably derived from contributions of a large number of trading companies located in Vienna for doing business with the Soviet bloc countries.

The ideological support – or supervision – is conducted largely via East Germany's ruling party, the SED. It must be assumed that, as in the days of the old Comintern, there is a direct link with the Soviet party and government operating through diplomatic channels, frequent personal contacts in both countries, and attendance at the periodic Communist conferences. But for current ideological and organisational problems the party that lent itself to the role of Big Brother has always been the ruling party of the only German-speaking Communist state, the German Democratic Republic. In this country, Austrian Communists find publishers for their work, obtain academic titles and posts, and occupy important positions in the economic and cultural life; a useful substitute for the innumerable contacts that used to exist all over Eastern Europe before the expulsion of the German minorities.

Relations between the SED and the KPÖ have never been very cordial, but never better than now after the 'normalisation' of the KPÖ. Kurt Seliger, the Austrian party's press representative in East Berlin up to 1969, has described the relationship in a well documented article in *Deutschland Archiv*.[12] As early as 1953 the SED found occasion to criticise Ernst Fischer, then member of the Austrian Party's Politbureau, for his non-Marxist reading of German history – in connection with an opera on Dr Faustus! – and his deviation from 'socialist realism'. Whereas at this stage Fischer was criticised for his literary writings only and was still considered a leading 'theoretician of Marxism', by the mid-sixties he had become a revisionist, member of a 'right-opportunist' faction in the KPÖ, and linked with the revisionists of the CSSR and the GDR's own Robert Havemann. Seliger's account of how the SED reacted to the spread of 'revisionism' among the leading cadres of the KPÖ and to the early condemnation of the invasion of the CSSR by the Central Committee is an illuminating study of 'inter-party relationships' in the Communist world.

What of the prospects for the future? Short of a devastating economic crisis, one cannot make out an event or a combination of circumstances that would endow the KPÖ with the credibility and prestige which a political party requires. On the other hand, as there is no effective opposition to the socialist party or to the all-party trade union federation, a reformed, 'revisionist' Communist Party might well meet a need. But there is no sign of such a development in the KPÖ as at present constituted, and the Austrian elections of 1979, parliamentary and regional, demonstrated its essential weakness once again.

Notes

1. Hans Hautmann, *Die verlorene Räterepublik* (Vienna, 1971).
2. Otto Bauer, *Bolschewismus oder Sozialdemokratie* (1920); *Der neue Kurs in Sowjetrussland* (1921).
3. Franz West, *Die Linke im Ständestaat Österreich. Revolutionäre Sozialisten und Kommunisten 1934—1938* (Vienna, 1978).
4. K. Stadler, *Österreich 1938–1945 im Spiegel der NS-Akten* (Vienna, 1966), p. 206.
5. Theodor Prager, *Zwischen London und Moskau. Bekenntnisse eines Revisionisten* (Vienna, 1975), p. 157.
6. Fritz Keller, 'KPÖ und nationale Frage', *Österreichische Zeitschrift für Politikwissenschaft*, no. 2 (1977), p. 183.
7. Josef Toch, 'Enklave KPÖ' in J. Hannak (ed.), *Bestandaufnahme Österreich 1945–1963* (Vienna, 1963).
8. Foreign Relations of the United States, *Diplomatic Papers 1945*, vol. III (Washington, D.C., 1968), p. 664.
9. Anton Pelinka, 'Auseinandersetzung mit dem Kommunismus' in Weinzierl and Skalnik (eds.), *Österreich, Die Zweite Republik*, vol. I (1969).
10. Leopold Spira, 'Der 20. Parteitag der KPdSU und die Auswirkungen auf die KPÖ' in *Geschichte der österreichischen Arbeiterbewegung* (Vienna, 1978), p. 103.
11. Heinz Gärtner, 'Eine sowjetorientierte KP – Die Kommunistische Partei Österreichs – ein Vergleich', *Österreichische Zeitschrift für Politikwissenschaft*, no. 1 (1978), p. 43.
12. Kurt Seliger, 'SED: Gute Beziehungen zur normalisierten KPÖ', *Deutschland Archiv* (August 1976).

APPENDIX: The Electoral Strength of Communism in Western Europe

Country	Percentage Vote	Up/Down	Year	Comment
Austria	0.96	down	1979	
Belgium	3.25	up	1978	
Cyprus		up	1976	9 seats out of 35. Second largest party.
Denmark	3.9	down	1977	
Finland	17.9	down	1979	In alliance.
France	20.6	down	1978	
Greece	9.36	up	1977	This was for orthodox KKE; the Eurocommunist KKE-interior gained 2.7 per cent.
Iceland	22.9	up	1978	Second largest of 4 big parties.
Italy	30.4	down	1979	First loss since 1948.
Luxemburg	10.4	down	1974	
Netherlands	1.7	down	1977	Down from 4.5 per cent.
Portugal	14.6	up	1976	Anti-Eurocommunism.
Spain	10.0	up	1979	
Sweden	5.6	up	1979	
Switzerland	2.2	down	1975	
UK	0.05	down	1979	
West Germany	0.3	same	1976	Slightly up in actual votes.

NOTES ON CONTRIBUTORS

Dr David Childs, Reader in Politics, University of Nottingham, author of *Marx and the Marxists, East Germany, Germany Since 1918* and other studies.

Dr Martin Clark, Lecturer in Politics, University of Edinburgh, author of *Antonio Gramsci and the Revolution that Failed* and various other studies, mainly on Italian politics and history.

Philip Elliott is a research fellow at the Centre for Mass Communication Research, University of Leicester. His published works include *The Making of a Television Series, The Sociology of the Professions* and *The Reporting of Northern Ireland*.

Professor Trond Gilberg is Professor of Political Science, Pennsylvania State University, and author of *The Soviet Communist Party and Scandinavian Communism: the Norwegian Case*.

Dr David Hine, Lecturer in Politics, University of Newcastle upon Tyne. His DPhil thesis was written at Nuffield College, Oxford, on the Italian Socialist Party and the centre-left coalition. He has written a number of articles on Italian politics.

Dr Peter Morris, Lecturer in Politics at University of Nottingham, where his main teaching and research interests are in the government and politics of modern France.

Eusebio Mujal-Leon is a doctoral candidate in politics at Massachusetts Institute of Technology and has published a number of analyses of the Iberian left. Chapter 3 first appeared in *Problems of Communism* (July–August 1978).

Dr Philip Schlesinger, Senior Lecturer in Sociology at Thames Polytechnic, author of *Putting 'Reality' Together: BBC News* and of various academic articles on journalism, counter-insurgency thought and ideological production. He is currently collaborating with Philip Elliott on a study of the debate on Eurocommunism.

Dr Derek Spring, Senior Lecturer in Russian and East European History at the University of Nottingham, author of articles on late Tsarist foreign and colonial policy, and currently working on a book, *Russian Foreign Policy, 1870–1917*. He is also the author of the film 'The Winter War and its European Context', produced for the Inter-University History Film Consortium.

Seija Spring is a graduate of the universities of Helsinki and Nottingham. She has also studied for a year at the University of Leningrad and is the author of a thesis on Soviet electoral law and practice.

Professor Karl Stadler, University of Linz in Austria, is author of *The Birth of the Austrian Republic, Austria*, and many other works in German and English.

INDEX

Aalto, A. A. 188, 196
Aaltonen 180
Aaronovitch, Sam 30–1
Ackermann, Anton 17, 18
Across the Board 41, 56
Adler, Friedrich 262; Victor 262
Afanas'yev, V. 97–8
Africa, Soviet policy in 134, 154,
    155, 156
Agnelli, Giovanni 136
Aitio 196
Albania 15, 26, 27, 235
Alenius, Ele 178, 182, 191, 192–4,
    196, 200
Algeria 159
Allende, Salvador 28, 68
alliance strategy 57, 58; Finnish 170,
    172, 175–8, 181, 183; French
    149, 155, 157, 158–62, 165–8,
    169, 251; Icelandic 220, 226,
    246; Italian 122, 124, 125, 140;
    Scandinavian 235, 243, 244, 249,
    251, 253; *see also* coalitions;
    fronts
Althusser, Louis 58, 164, 166
Amendola, Giorgio 62–3
American Communist Political
    Association 14, 17
American League against War and
    Fascism 11
Andreotti, Giulio 124, 140
Antich, Puig 77
Areilza, José Maria 83
Arias Navarro, Carlos 77, 83, 86
Arnalds, Ragnar 246
Aron, Raymond 48, 49, 50, 58
Asia, South East 152, 241
Atlantic Alliance 67, 137–8, 147–8,
    153, 154, 155, 160; *see also*
    NATO
Atlantic Quarterly 56
Austria 14, 58, Chap. 8 *passim*; KPÖ
    Chap. 8 *passim*, and Soviet
    Union 260, 261, 264, 265,
    266–7, 269–70, 272–3, electoral
    support 268, 270–2, 276,
    membership 270, 273
autogestion 131, 166

autonomy 61, 147, 150, 156, 206,
    210, 229, 235–6, 248–52, 253;
    see also polycentrism; roads to
    socialism
Azcárate, Manuel 40, 62, 139

Bahro, Rudolf 33
Balibar, E. 58
Barbieri, Frane 40–1, 58
Bauer, Otto 262, 263
Baulin, J. 153
Belgium 14, 276
Bennelli, Cardinal 127
Berlinguer, Enrico 28, 55, 59–60,
    62, 98, 123, 124, 126, 127, 132,
    133, 135–40 *passim*, 149, 154,
    239, 251
Bettiza, Enzo 40
Bidault, Georges 151
Björklund, Ilkka-Christian 200
Blum, Léon 158
Borbón Parma, Carlos Hugo de 80
Boyer, Albert 136
Brabo, Pilar 88
Brandt, Willy 28
Brezhnev, Leonid 98, 154; –
    doctrine 184
Britain 10, 12–13, 214, 215, 245–6,
    276; CPGB 12–13, 16, 17,
    19–22, 150, 236, 265, and Soviet
    Union 21, 27, 31–2, electoral
    support 12–13, 19, 31, 276,
    membership 23, 32; Labour
    Party 7, 12, 13, 16, 17, 20, 67,
    117, 262, 266
British Road to Socialism 19
British-Soviet Friendship Society 21
Browder, Earl 14, 17
Brzesinski, Zbigniew 43
Bukharin, N. I. 163, 209
Bulganin, N. A. 24
Bulgaria 17, 18

cadres 8, 21, 95, 105, 116, 162, 216,
    225, 260, 266, 274
Camacho, Marcelino 83, 89, 92, 93
capitalism 8, 38, 45, 57, 61, 66, 68,
    132, 140, 162, 179, 187, 190

279

Carli. Guido 42, 45–6. 136
Carlos, Prince Juan 79, 82, 86
Carrero Blanco, Admiral Luis
    76–7, 79, 80
Carrillo, Santiago 8, 16, 29–31, 40,
    45, 55, 59–60, 61, 62, 75, 80,
    82, 84, 90, 92, 96–103, 106, 135,
    138, 139, 149, 151, 239, 251
Carter, President 133, 137
Castro, President 25, 27
Catellano, Pablo 78
Catholic Church 120, 123, 215–18,
    130, 207
Ceausescu, President 155
centralism, democratic 20, 31, 46,
    48, 50, 58, 102, 115, 132, 134,
    164, 186, 190, 202, 210
Childs, David 7–36, 277
Chile 28, 68, 92, 123
China 19, 25, 27, 137, 154, 156,
    230–1, 237, 260; CCP 234,
    235–6, 247; *see also* Sino-Soviet
    dispute
Chirac, Jacques 43
Chou En-lai 230
Christianity 78, 126, 206, 207
Churchill, Winston 11, 12, 14, 15,
    40, 265
Clark, Martin 32, 112–46, 277
Claudín, Fernando 31, 58, 60, 62
coalitions 14, 15, 16; Austrian 261;
    Finnish 175, 182, 195–6;
    Icelandic 220, 226–7, 246–7,
    253; Italian 33, 122;
    Scandinavian 216, 220, 221, 223,
    226, 242, 246–7, 251; Spanish
    85, 92, 106
Cold War 37, 38, 40, 57, 151, 158,
    175, 182
Colonna, Flavio 131
Comecon 236
Cominform 17, 18, 222, 223
Cominterm 9, 11, 15, 16, 129, 151,
    208, 210–14, 217, 219, 243, 252,
    264, 267, 274; Seventh Congress
    10, 265, 267
Comisiones Obreras (CCOO) *see*
    trades unions, Spanish
Comment 29
Commentary 47–8, 51, 53, 54, 55,
    66–7
Common Wealth Party 12, 13
Communist Parties *see under
    individual countries*; Conferences
    (1957) 25, (Moscow 1960) 25,

(Berlin 1976) 59, 60, 147–8,
    156, 237, (pan-European) 39
Cornforth, Maurice 65
Corriere della Sera 40
Council on Foreign Relations (CFR)
    43, 99
Cuba 26, 134, 155, 156
Cunhal, Alvaro 147, 161
Cyprus 27, 276
Czechoslovakia 18, 27, 31, 68, 75,
    136, 154, 156, 184, 186, 236,
    237, 248, 260, 272, 273, 274

Daily Telegraph, The 53
Daily Worker, The 22
Dalma, Alfons 39
Darke, Bob 20
Del Noce, Augusto 39
democracy 7, 10, 18, 19, 27, 33, 41,
    44, 46, 50, 58, 60–1, 65, 66,
    131–2, 140, 147–8, 157–70, 172,
    175–9, 185, 186, 202, 206–8,
    218, 240, 253, 260; *see also*
    centralism, democratic
Denmark 14, 23, Chap. 7 *passim*,
    DKP, and Soviet Union 214–16,
    223–5, 228–35, 237–8, 249, 253,
    electoral support 221, 225,
    244–5, 276, fragmentation
    232–5, 238, ideology 240–1,
    national coalition 216–18, 221,
    241, 243; SF 230, 244
détente 38, 39, 45, 68, 136, 137,
    139, 156
deviations 14, 15, 187, 213, 216,
    219, 220, 226, 227, 229, 235,
    238, 253; *see also* revisionism
Devlin, Kevin 45
Dictatorship of the Proletariat 33,
    146
Dimitrov, Georgi 10, 11, 17, 264,
    265
Dollfuss, Chancellor 263
Domhoff 43
Donat-Cattin, Carlo 125
Dubcek, Alexander 27, 68, 136, 154
Duclos, Jacques 17, 18
Dutt, R. P. 22

Earle, John 45–6
*Economic Problems of Socialism in
    USSR* 22
Economist, The 53, 55
education 208
Einheit 17

elites 11, Chap. 2 *passim*, 77, 164, 221, 232–3
Elleinstein, Jean 149, 163, 164, 165, 169, 239, 251
Elliott, P. 7, 37–73, 277
Encounter 40, 48, 49, 50, 53, 54
Engels, F. 8, 57, 186
Erhardt, John 268
essentialism 42, 49–52, 57, 67
Eurocommunism and the State 29, 45, 59, 96, 99
Europe, Eastern 9, 14, 16, 18–19, 28, 32, 33, 45, 50, 52, 64, 68, 126, 128, 134, 136, 139, 150, 163, 212, 222, 224, 228, 235, 236, 239, 260, 274; *see also individual countries*
European Community (EEC) 41, 46, 63, 80, 137, 148, 154, 155, 160, 242–3, 244, 249
Euskadi ta Askatasnu (ETA) 76
Evening Standard 67

Fabre, J. 58
factionalism 23, 115, 183–203, 213, 214, 223, 227, 233–5, 238, 247, 250, 262
Fajon, E. 164
Fascism 9, 10, 11, 21, 47, 121, 131, 141, 174, 179, 214, 260, 263, 264, 265
Faure, Edgar 149
Finland 14, 33, 136, Chap. 6 *passim*, 214, 215, 241; SKP Chap. 6 *passim*, alliance policy 172, 174, 175, 177–8, 180–1, 189, 191–201, and Soviet Union 173–4, 177, 182, 184, 194, 202, electoral support 172, 173, 174, 176, 180–1, 189, 201, 276, factionalism 183–203, membership 172, 174, 177, 192, 195, participation in government 172, 174, 175, 177, 180–3, 189–91, 196, 197, 207
Fischer, Ernst 27, 268, 272, 274
Fiterman, Charles 149
Fizbin, H. 169
Foreign Affairs 42, 43, 45, 46, 48, 167
Foreign Policy 41, 42, 43
Foreign Policy, Society for (Bonn) 43
Forlani 124
Fraga Iribarne, Manuel 83, 87, 91

France 8, 11, 14, 15, 17, 29, 33, Chap. 5 *passim*, 214, 215; nuclear deterrent 153, 157, 164; PCF 15, 17, 38, 44, 53, 58, 59, 60, 62, 64, 97, 138, Chap. 5 *passim*, 248, 265, alliance strategy 149, 153, 155, 157–61, 165–8, and Soviet Union 10, 147, 149, 150–7, 158, 163, 169, 170, 212, 248, and West 147–8, 152–3, 154, 155, 160, Common Programme 64, 149, 151, 160–1, 165–7, electoral support 148, 158–9, 167, 168, 169, 276, ideology 161–3, membership 148, 159, 164–5, 169, 22nd Congress 31, 58, 149–50; PS 149, 160–1, 166–8
Franco, General 74–5, 77, 79–80, 83, 84, 86, 90, 93, 95; Francoism 62, 76, 81; Nicolas 80
French, Sid 32
Fried, Arthur 151
Friheten 232
fronts, national 267; popular 10, 16, 150–1, 158, 174, 176, 192, 214, 264; united 213, 214, 222, 241, 243, 249, 264
Fürnberg 272
Furnbotn, Peter 225

Gagarin, Yuri 24
Gallacher, William 12, 22
Garaudy, Roger 27, 165
Garcia, Cipriano 83
Garcia, Enrique 97
Gati, Charles 42
Gaulle, President de 151, 152, 153, 158–9
Geertz, C. 64
Georgetown University 50, 51
German Democratic Republic 28, 273, 274; SED 18, 28, 64, 274
Germany 14, 27, 28, 136, 154, 211, 214, 215, 216, 221, 261, 276; assets in Austria 266, 268–9; SPD 7, 117, 158, 262
Gierek, E. 126
Gilberg, Trond 23, 205–57, 277
Giménez, Joaquín Ruiz 78, 85
Ginsburg, Alexander 29
Giornale Nuovo, Il 40
Giovanni, Biagio de 131
Giscard d'Estaing, President 28, 153, 154, 167

Glucksmann, André 55
Godson, Roy 50, 51
Goldsborough, James O. 42, 44, 61
Gollan, John 19, 31
Gomulka, W. 17, 28
González, Felipe 77, 78, 91, 105
Gramsci, Antonio 57, 113, 127,
    128–32, 140, 148; – Institutes
    115
Greece 12, 15, 27, 28
Grimau, Julian 87
Guardian, The 54

Habsburg, Otto 261
Hagberg, Hilding 232, 250
Halberstam, David 43
Hammar, Bo 237
Haseler, Stephen 50, 51, 67
Havemann, Robert 33, 274
Hayek, F. 67
Heffer, Eric 54
Helsinki Conference on Security and
    Cooperation 28
Heritage Foundation 51
Hermansson, C. J. 230, 232, 249,
    250
Hine, David 32, 112–46, 277
Hitler, Adolf 18, 21, 150–1; – Stalin
    Pact 9, 11, 151, 214, 265
Hobsbawm, Eric 63
Holland 11–12; CP 12, 236
Holland, Stewart 55
Honner, Franz 268
human rights 28, 133, 200, 240
Humanité, L' 148, 163, 167, 168

Ibárrurri, Dolores 90, 100
Iceland 14, 33, 208, 210, 213,
    218–21, 226–8, 245–8, 254;
    SA-SF/AB 220, 226, 246–8, 254
    and Soviet Union 227, 248,
    electoral support 220, 247, 276,
    fragmentation 247
ideology 8, Chap. 2 *passim*, 115,
    120–34, 140, 183–8, 190–6,
    198–200, 210–12, 213, 226, 238,
    239–41, 274
imperialism 8, 134, 135, 215, 223,
    236, 242, 265
inflation 84, 105
Ingrao, Pietro 133
Institutes: American Enterprise – for
    Public Policy Research 56;
    Bundes – für Ostwissenschaftliche
    und Internationale Studien

(Cologne) 45; Hoover – on War,
    Revolution and Peace 56;
    International – for Strategic Studies
    56; – of Contemporary History 47;
    Royal – of International Affairs
    (RIIA) 43
International, Communist 134,
    209–13, 247–8, 250–1, 260;
    Second 7, 38, 66, 210; Socialist
    78, 138, 262; Third 8, 38, 213;
    '2½' 262
Israel 27, 152
Italy 11, 14, 15, 17, 33, 46, 68,
    Chap. 4 *passim*; PCI 15, 31, 33,
    38, 42, 46, 53, 56, 62–3, 64, 68,
    Chap. 4 *passim*, 151, 156, 161–2,
    212, 236, 248, alliance strategy
    122–8, 130, and Soviet Union
    27, 97, 132, 134–6, 138–9, 151,
    152, 239, and trade unions 116,
    133, and West 137–8, 154,
    electoral support 119–20, 125,
    276, 'historic compromise' 28,
    33, 106, 123–8, 130, 134, 139,
    251, ideology 121–35, 140,
    membership 23, 113, 114,
    115–16, 125

Japan 63, 136
Jespersen, Knud 232, 238
Jews, in Soviet Union 27, 33
Jiménez de Parga, Manuel 95
Johnson, Paul 67
Juan de Borbón, Don 79
Juan Carlos I, King 76, 79, 82, 83,
    85, 86, 88

Kainulainen 186, 201
Kamenev, L.B. 209
Kanapa, Jean 43, 46, 63–4, 149,
    167, 239, 251
Kansan Uutiset 176, 177, 178, 184,
    192, 193, 194, 200
Karjalainen 189
Kautsky, Karl 8, 57
Keflavik base 246
Kekkonen, President 175, 181, 182,
    195, 196
Khrushchev, N. S. 23, 25, 26, 152,
    177, 228, 231, 232, 272
Kissinger, Henry 52, 55, 56, 68, 137
Kivistö 196
Klahr, Alfred 264
Knudsen, Martin Gunnar 250
Koestler, Arthur 8

Koivisto 182
Koivunen, Matti 182
Kolakowski, Leszet 50
Koplenig, Johann 268, 272
Körner, Theodor 271
Kostov, Traicho 18
Kriegel, Annie 50, 55, 150
Kronstadt Mutiny 9
Kuusinen, Hertta 176, 178
Kuusinen, Otto Ville 173

La Malfa, Ugo 42, 134, 140
Labour, Chambers of 271–2
Labour Monthly 22
Labour Party *see* Britain
Lama, Luciano 125
Lange, Peter 42
Laqueur, Walter 47–8, 51, 53, 55
Larsen, Aksel 228, 229, 230, 232, 238
Larson, Reidar 232, 237, 249–50
Laurent, Paul 165
Ledeen, Michael 51–2, 55
Left Book Club (Britain) 11
Lehto, Oivo 195
Lenin, V. I. 7–8, 24, 30, 31, 57, 127, 135, 186, 205, 209, 211, 212, 213, 252; Leninism 17, 49, 96, 99–103, 131, 132, 159, 162, 180, 181, 227
Leroy, R. 164, 169
Leskinen 182
Levi, Arrigo 39, 40, 42, 58
Lieber, Robert 42, 44
Lippmann, Walter 40
Líster, Enrique 97
Llopis, Rodolfo 77, 78
Longo, Luigi 134, 138
Lopez, Antonio Garcia 78
Lövlien, Emil 225
Löwenthal, Richard 50
Luther, Martin 207; Lutheranism 207, 211
Luxembourg 14, 27
Luxemburg, Rosa 8, 57

McInnes, Neil 46–7, 48, 50
McLennan, Gordon 31
Macridis, Roy 156, 170
Mao Tse-tung 22; Maoism 229, 234–5, 240, 247
Marchais, George 60, 62, 63, 149–50, 154, 155, 156, 160, 161, 163, 164, 165, 167, 168, 169

Marchetti, Xavier 52
Marín, Francisco Romero 82
Marx, Karl 8, 16, 27, 57, 65, 186, 205, 209; Marxism 7–8, 24, 31, 33, 37, 48, 50, 57, 61–2, 76, 126, 127, 148, 190, 205, 211, 226, 229, 262; – Leninism 33, 79, 181, 186, 190–1, 199, 233–4, 247
Medici, Giuseppe 136
Mendès-France, Pierre 158
Merediz, José Ramón Herrero 101
Middle East 27, 154
Miettunen 196
Mitterand, Francois 52, 153, 159, 167, 168
models 16, 19, 26, 63, 132, 147, 150, 200, 212, 220; Soviet 24–5, 27, 31, 38, 75, 132, 135, 147, 162–3, 170, 191, 222, 229, 236, 247–8; Yugoslav 130–1, 227; *see also* roads to socialism
Mollet, Guy 158
Molotov, V. M. 151
Monde, Le 164
Montaldo, Jean 154–5
Montero, Simón Sánchez 101
Morning Star 60
Moro, Aldo 120, 124
Morris, Peter 147–71, 277
Moynihan, Daniel P. 52
Mujal-Leon, Eusebio 74–111, 277
Mújica, Enrique 78
Mundo Obrero 81, 86
Mussolini, Benito 21, 47

Napolitano, Giorgio 43, 46, 62, 63, 137
National Strategy Information Center 51
nationalisation 90, 160, 166, 175, 269
nationalism 7, 190, 217–18; French 63, 150, 153, 155, 159; Icelandic 208, 218–21, 245–6, 248, 253–4; Norwegian 208, 218, 242–4, 253; Spanish regional 88, 101, 106; Swedish 218, 253; *see also* autonomy; roads to socialism
NATO 45, 46, 63, 67, 137–8, 140, 148, 152, 153, 154, 183, 193, 241–2, 246
Nazis 10, 11, 12, 14, 216, 217, 221, 260, 264, 265
neutrality 205, 216, 217, 242

New Left Review 23
New Times 61, 62, 96, 138
Newsweek 39, 42, 49, 55, 86
Nichols, Peter 42
Nixon, President 29
non-alignment 140
Nörlund, Ib 232
Norway 14, Chap. 7 *passim*; NKP
    alliance (SV) 249–50, 251, and
    EEC 242–4; and Soviet Union
    214–16, 222–5, 228–37, 238,
    239, 241, 250, electoral support
    221, 226, 244, 249, 276,
    fragmentation 232–5, ideology
    240–1, national coalition 216–18,
    221–3, 241

Orlov, Yuri 29
Owen, David 50, 51, 52–3, 54

Paasikivi, President 175
Paasio, Rafael 181, 182
Pajetta, Giancarlo 26, 126, 136, 137
Pallach, Josep 88
Pauker, Anna 26
Pekkala, Mauno 174, 195
Pelinka, Anton 269
Pennanen, Jarno 176
Pertsov, V. 97
Pessi, Ville 177, 178, 179, 180
Peter, King 15
Piratin, Phil 13
Plekhanov, G.V. 8
Plissonnier, Gaston 155, 156
pluralism 115, 127, 129–34 *passim*,
    138, 140, 147, 160, 161–2, 211,
    212, 218, 240, 251, 273
Poher 153
Poland 17, 25, 27, 28, 136, 139,
    151, 215, 230, 273
Policy Review 51, 54
Pollitt, Harry 22, 265
polycentrism 25, 134–9, 230, 235–6
Pompidou, President 153
Ponomorev 155
Popov 43, 58
Popper, Karl 65
Portugal 27, 28, 29, 33, 68, 74, 79,
    81, 82, 161
Problems of Communism 43, 44, 53
Proudhon, Pierre-Joseph 131
purges 16, 27, 214, 216, 222, 224–5,
    227, 228, 232
Pyatkus, Viktoras 29

Radek, K. 209
Radice, Lucio Lombardo 49, 62
Radio Free Europe 45, 49
Rajk, L. 18, 272
Redondo, Nicolas 94
reform 7, 15, 23, 245, 276; Finnish
    175, 177–80, 187, 198; Italian
    'structural' 118–19, 121, 123;
    Spanish 76, 83–4, 87, 89, 90, 93
religion 207, 211; *see also* Catholic
    Church
Renner, Karl 261, 262, 268–9, 271
Reuther, Walter 14
Revel, Jean-Francois 43, 48–9, 66–7
revisionism 42, 57, 58, 187, 190,
    194, 273, 275; *see also* deviations
revolution 7, 38, 79, 121, 180, 181,
    199, 209, 211, 212, 214, 231,
    234, 240, 245, 263
Richardson, Elliot 43
Ridruejo, Dionisio 78
Rinascita 116, 126
roads to socialism 16, 17, 18, 28, 38,
    59–60, 136, 173, 199, 227, 235,
    238, 239, 263; British 19;
    Finnish 174, 178–9, 183, 186,
    192–3; Italian 121, 130, 132,
    135; Scandinavian 229, 238–40,
    247–8, 253; Yugoslav 15, 227,
    248; *see also* autonomy; models
Robles, José Maria Gil 78
Robrieux, Philippe 152
Romeo, Rosario 51
Roosevelt, President F. D. 14, 152
Rothstein, Andrew 27
Rumania 26, 27, 136, 155, 156,
    157, 235, 237, 248; PCR 26,
    236, 237–8, 248
Ryömä, Mauri 176

Saarinen, Aarne 180, 188, 189,
    190–1, 193, 194–9, 201, 202,
    203
Saarto, Veikko 189, 196
Salomaa, Erkki 178, 180, 183, 185,
    188
Salve, Francisco Garcia 83
Sartorius, Nicolás 83
Sartre, J. P. 147
Sassoon, D. 55
Schlesinger, P. 7, 37–73, 277–8
Schmidt, Helmut 139
Schumpeter, Joseph 66
Schuschnigg, Kurt von 266
Segre, Sergio 43, 46, 137

Seliger, Kurt 174
Setälä, Rauno 180, 181
Sette, Pietro 136
Shanks, Michael 25
Signorile, Claudio 135
Silberman, Laurence 42
Sinisalo, Taisto 181, 188, 190–1,
  196, 197, 198, 199, 201, 202
Sino-Soviet dispute 25, 26, 33, 79,
  231, 233, 235–6, 237, 247, 253
Slansky, Rudolf 18, 272
Soboul, Albert 165
Solzhenitsyn, Alexander 25, 29
Sonnenfeldt, Helmut 52
Sorsa 196, 198, 200
Soviet Union 11, 23–7, 30, 32,
  96–8, 132, 134–6, 138–9, 147,
  149, 150–8, 163, 169, 173–4,
  175, 177, 178, 182, 184, 186,
  193, 199, 202, 205–12, 214–15,
  216–17, 221, 236, 241, 260–1,
  263, 265, 267, 268–9; CPSU,
  and other parties 7, 27, 29–32,
  see also individual parties,
  challenges to 29–30, Chap. 2
  passim, 96–8, 147, 228–9, 236,
  238–9, 250, *see also* Sino-Soviet
  dispute, hegemony 8–11, 14,
  23–6, 38, 139, 150, 170, 210–16,
  222–5, 227, 228–30, 231, 232,
  236, 238, 241, 249, 250, 252–3,
  264–5, 269, 272–4, 20th
  Congress 23–6, 152, 176, 228,
  232, 272; model 24–7, 31, 38,
  75, 132, 135, 147, 162–3, 170,
  191, 222, 229, 236, 247–8; *see
  also* Cominform; Cominterm
Spain 10, 16, 28, 29, 33, Chap. 3
  passim, 265; PCE 16, 31, 38, 53,
  59, Chap. 3 *passim*, 154, 212,
  236, 248, and Leninism 75,
  99–103, and Soviet Union 62,
  74, 75, 96–8, 135, 139, 239, *see
  also* Carrillo, and unions
  (CCOO) 75, 82, 89, 93, 94–6,
  103, CD 85, coalition policy 79,
  80, 81, 84, 85, 92, 107, electoral
  support 16, 74, 75–6, 91, 104,
  106, JD 80, 81, 84, 85,
  membership 99, 100, Pacto de la
  Monclao 92–4, 105, 106; PSOE
  76, 77–8, 79, 80, 84, 91, 92, 93,
  94, 104, 105, 106, 107
Spinelli, Altiero 49
Spring, D. W. 172–204, 278; –,

Seija 172–204, 278
Stadler, Karl 260–75, 278
Stalin, Joseph 8, 12, 14, 15, 18, 19,
  21–3, 26, 27, 33, 150, 151, 152,
  158, 163, 173, 175, 176, 179,
  214, 217, 222, 224, 227, 228,
  229, 231, 232, 261, 272;
  de-Stalinisation 48, 152, 229,
  232–3, 238, 245; Stalinism 38,
  45, 47, 221–4, 227, 228, 232,
  238,245
Stehle 43
Steinkuhler, Manfred 40–1
Streiff, Gérard 63
strikes 12, 28, 81, 84–5, 125, 189,
  269
Suárez, Adolfo 74, 76, 86–7, 91, 92,
  95, 104, 106, 107
Suonpää, Leo 182
Suslov, Mikhail 136
Sweden 12, 78, Chap. 7 *passim*;
  SKP, and Soviet Union 214–16,
  222–4, 228–37, 238, 239, 249,
  electoral support 221–3, 226,
  245, 276, fragmentation 232–5,
  250, ideology 240–1, national
  coalition 216–18, 221, 241
Switzerland 12

Tamames, Ramón 40, 86
Tanner, V. 172, 181, 182
Tarradellas, Josep 88
Tereshkova, Valentina 24
Thatcher, Margaret 54, 67
theories, containment 41–7, 49, 54,
  55, 57; totalitarianism 47–8, 52,
  66–7
Thorez, Maurice 17, 151–3, 154,
  158
Tiedonantaja 184, 188, 191, 194,
  199, 200
Tiedote 183
Tierno Galván, Enrique 78
Tiersky, Ronald 44, 45, 58, 150,
  157–8, 161
Tiesko, Anna-Liisa 189
Tilanne 176
Time 55
Times, The 45, 54, 151
Timmermann, Heinz 43, 45
Tito, President 8–9, 18, 23, 33, 130,
  137, 231, 272; Titoism 222, 224,
  225, 227, 231, 235, 260
Toch, Joseph 267
Togliatti, Palmiro 17, 25–6, 112,

135, 152, 230
trade unions 7, 12, 13, 14; Austrian
    264, 267, 269; Finnish 172, 173,
    179, 189, 192, 195, 199; French
    (CGT) 148, 166; Icelandic 220,
    246; Italian (CGIL) 116, 125,
    133; Scandinavian 205, 215, 221,
    223, 242, 244; Spanish (CCOO)
    75, 80, 82–3, 84–5, 89, 93–6,
    102–3, (OS) 89, 93–6, (UGT)
    86, 93–6, 105
Tuominen, Erkki 189
Työkansan Sanomat 176

Ulbricht, Walter 28
unemployment 34, 84, 105, 140,
    195, 196, 245, 248
Unitá, L' 116, 134
United Nations 174
United States 10, 41, 96, 97, 98, 99,
    134, 137, 152, 153, 155, 223,
    241–2, 246, 252; CPUSA 11,
    13–14, 17
Urban, George 49, 50, 52

Valdimarsson, Hannibal 247
Vance, Cyrus 42
Vatican 126–8
Vermeersch, Jeanette 152, 156, 163
Vietnam 27, 68, 154, 156, 241
Vogt, Jörgen 232

Vološinov 65

Waldeck–Rochet, E. 152, 154, 159
Wallace, Henry 13
wars: First World 7, 8, 205, 211,
    215, 252; Second World 11, 16,
    74, 94, 167, 200, 213, 215, 216,
    217, 218, 221, 241, 253, 260;
    Six Day 152; Vietnam 241
Warsaw Pact 27, 45, 75, 136, 155,
    184, 235
Washington Papers 48, 51
Washington Review 51, 52, 54
Wilson, Harold 54
Wojtyla, Cardinal 128
women's organisations: Austrian
    267; Finnish 175; Italian 113,
    117; Spanish 84, 104
World Today, The 43, 45

youth organisations 175, 205, 233–5,
    267
Yugoslavia 14, 15, 18, 24, 26, 27,
    41, 136, 139, 157, 222, 236,
    248; model 130–1, 227

Zaccagnini 124
Zagladin 139, 155
Zaire 154
Zamyatin 136
Zinoviev, G.E. 209